# Mereology

Also available from Bloomsbury

*The Bloomsbury Companion to Metaphysics*, edited by Neil A. Manson
and Robert W. Barnard
*A Critical Introduction to Properties*, Sophie R. Allen
*Metaphysics*, Jonathan Tallant
*Ontology and Metaontology: A Contemporary Guide*, Francesco Berto
and Matteo Plebani

# Mereology

## A Philosophical Introduction

Giorgio Lando

BLOOMSBURY ACADEMIC
LONDON · NEW YORK · OXFORD · NEW DELHI · SYDNEY

BLOOMSBURY ACADEMIC
Bloomsbury Publishing Plc
50 Bedford Square, London, WC1B 3DP, UK
1385 Broadway, New York, NY 10018, USA

BLOOMSBURY, BLOOMSBURY ACADEMIC and the
Diana logo are trademarks of Bloomsbury Publishing Plc

First published 2017
Paperback edition first published 2018

A catalogue record for this book is available from the British Library.

Library of Congress Cataloging-in-Publication Data
Names: Lando, Giorgio, author.
Title: Mereology : a philosophical introduction / Giorgio Lando.
Description: New York : Bloomsbury Academic, 2017. | Includes bibliographical
references and index.
Identifiers: LCCN 2016058157| ISBN 9781472583666 (hb) | ISBN 9781472583680 (epdf)
Subjects: LCSH: Whole and parts (Philosophy)
Classification: LCC BD396 .L36 2017 | DDC 111/.82–dc23
LC record available at https://lccn.loc.gov/2016058157

ISBN: HB: 978-1-4725-8366-6
PB: 978-1-3500-9473-4
ePDF: 978-1-4725-8368-0
ePub: 978-1-4725-8367-3

Typeset by Integra Software Services Pvt. Ltd.

To find out more about our authors and books visit
www.bloomsbury.com and sign up for our newsletters.

# Contents

# Acknowledgments

I have presented early versions of some chapters of this book at various conferences and workshops in Geneva, Zagreb, Exeter, Madrid, and Milan. I would like to thank all the people who organized and/or attended these events, and in particular Aaron Cotnoir, Alessandro Giordani, Arianna Betti, Ciro De Florio, Claudio Calosi, Daniel Korman, Giuliano Torrengo, Kevin Mulligan, Kit Fine, Massimiliano Carrara, and Peter Simons. A draft of the book has also been used as a reference text for two graduate seminars on mereology at the Scuola Normale Superiore in Pisa (Italy) in 2015 and 2016. I would like to thank the entire audience of these seminars for their patience, and in particular Andrea Strollo, Lorenzo Azzano, and Martina Botti for raising insightful questions, and for shaking their heads to express disagreement. I would also like to thank Massimo Mugnai for organizing lots of interesting and motivating seminars and research events at the Scuola Normale Superiore in those same years, and for making me aware that Leibniz's mereology is so interesting and stunningly similar to the doctrine which is analyzed and defended in this book. Andrea Borghini, Martina Botti, and Massimiliano Carrara have shared with me some very significant aspects of my research work over the last years, and I would like to offer them a particularly warm thanks. Claudio Calosi, Massimiliano Carrara, Giulia Felappi, Simone Gozzano, and Andrea Strollo have read and commented the entire manuscript, and contributed to amending a lot of mistakes. Fabio Carestiato did not read the manuscript but encouraged me to write it. Sergio Knipe has been a sensible and meticulous proofreader. Carmel Isaac and all the staff at Integra Software Services Pvt. Ltd. have followed the entire production process of the book with remarkable care.

Finally, Diego Romei has proven a constant source of inspiration, warmth, and love during these years, and the book is dedicated to him.

# Introduction: What is Mereology?

## 0.1 A general, yet narrow, theory of parthood and composition

My hands are parts of my body, countries are parts of continents, words can be seen as parts of sentences. Another relation is strictly connected to parthood: the relation that connects many things to a single thing that includes whatever is in the many things and nothing extraneous to them; this many-one relation can be dubbed *composition*. Four legs and a top compose the table in front of me, the Netherlands, Belgium, and Luxembourg compose Benelux. Mereology is about these relations: parthood and composition.

The purpose of this book is to present, motivate, and defend a peculiar philosophical thesis about parthood and composition. This thesis has been influential—or even dominant—for much of the twentieth century, and has been endorsed by pivotal figures such as Goodman, Quine, and Lewis. However, no entire book has ever been devoted to its defense, and the thesis is nowadays rejected by many scholars.

The thesis is that there is a single, general, exhaustive theory of parthood and composition. This theory, usually called Classical Extensional Mereology, can be easily summed up. It claims that:

(a) parthood is transitive (if a first thing is part of a second thing, and this second thing is part of a third thing, then the first thing is part of the third as well);
(b) given some things, there is at most one thing composed by them;
(c) given some things, no matter how heterogeneous and disparate they are, there is at least one thing composed by them.

The adoption of the thesis that there is a unique, general, and exhaustive theory of parthood and composition is strictly connected to a rather narrow understanding of the explanatory scope of mereology as a philosophical discipline. This narrow understanding will be adopted in this book, but is not always adopted when parthood and composition are discussed in philosophy. In some cases, the interest in the relations of parthood and composition is deeply entangled with problems that, according to the narrow understanding of mereology as a discipline which I am going to adopt, belong to other areas of metaphysics.

Consider, as a first example, *the essential/accidental distinction*. Is there a difference between a functional and pivotal part of my body, such as my brain or heart, and more peripheral parts, such as the nail on the last toe of my right foot? Are some parts of a whole such that their annihilation would annihilate the whole too? Another example: the *supervenience or emergence* of the properties of complex entities over the properties and relation of their parts. Do the properties and interrelation of the molecules composing my body *determine* the properties of my body?

According to the narrow understanding of mereology as a discipline I am going to adopt, essentiality, dependence, and supervenience lie beyond the explanatory scope of *mereology*. Mereology is *only* about *the formal features of the relation of parthood, and about identity and existence conditions for wholes*.

At a first glance, this restriction of the explanatory scope of *mereology* might seem unmotivated. Why should mereology be *only* about the formal features of parthood, and about existence and identity conditions for wholes? Is mereology not simply the theory of parthood, as the etymology of the word "mereology" (from the Greek *méros*, part) reveals? Then, why should the explanatory scope of mereology be narrowed down to such a degree? After all, the essential/accidental and dependent/independent divides *can* be applied to parts and wholes, and the philosophical debates about supervenience and emergence in many cases concern the macroscopic level of wholes on the one hand, and the level of their basic pieces or parts on the other.

This line of thought is not very compelling in itself. The mere fact that *parts are pervasive* does not prove that mereology should be integrated with *any* metaphysical theory. Consider the analogous cases of identity and existence. At least according to some influential philosophical stances, *everything* exists and is self-identical, so that there is a trivial sense in which existence and identity are related to *any other* philosophical topic. Obviously, whatever exists and whatever is self-identical instantiates properties, which can be accidental or essential; and the existence of some things can be thought to *depend* on the existence of other things. But this is not a good reason to embroil the theory of existence and the theory of identity with so many other—plausibly related, but still distinct—metaphysical problems.

In order to show that mereology should deal with essentialism, supervenience etc., it would be necessary to show that there is a substantial connection between what concerns parthood and composition and these other topics: that it is not possible to study parthood and composition in general, by themselves, without setting them in relation to other areas of metaphysics.

One purpose of this book is to show that this is not the case; that the philosophical thesis I wish to analyze and defend is right in restricting its attention to the formal features of parthood, and to identity and existence conditions for wholes. This does not mean that these are the only questions worth studying; but that the restriction applied isolates a legitimate, interesting and reasonably self-constrained philosophical topic.

## 0.2 Mereology as a discipline, mereology as a theory, mereology as a philosophical thesis

Some confusion about the explanatory scope of mereology can be attributed to the fact that, in the contemporary philosophical literature, the term "mereology" is used in different ways. We have already presented mereology from different perspectives in the previous section: it is a discipline that can be understood narrowly or more widely; it is also a theory, according to which parthood is transitive and, given some things, there is a single thing composed by them; and it is also the philosophical thesis (the thesis defended in this book) that this theory is the single, general theory of parthood and composition.

It is useful to explicitly distinguish these different perspectives. Throughout the book, at least when an equivocation could arise, we will distinguish between *mereology*$_{dis}$ (mereology as a discipline), *mereology*$_{theo}$ (mereology as a theory), and *mereology*$_{phi}$ (mereology as a philosophical thesis). Obviously, none of the three is *the only right way* to use the word "mereology." It is also important to connect these three understandings of mereology to some alternative, more usual labels. Moreover, some finer distinctions can and should be drawn within the three understandings of mereology.

*Mereology*$_{dis}$ (mereology as a discipline) is simply the study of the relation of parthood and of strictly related topics. This study can be general, or focused on specific domains of parts and wholes (parts and wholes in language, in living organisms, in social entities, in mathematics, and so on). Also, when it is conceived in general—as is more common among philosophers—this study can vary greatly in terms of topics and conclusions. When mereology$_{dis}$ is general and not focused on specific domains, we will also use the expression "philosophical mereology" for it.

*Mereology*$_{theo}$ (mereology as a theory) is a theory that characterizes parthood and other connected relations (such as composition) in a certain way. This characterization is provided by some axioms, formulated within a given logical framework. These axioms imply some theorems: these theorems are the content of a certain mereology$_{theo}$. We can also identify a certain mereology$_{theo}$ with a class of theorems, provable within a certain axiomatic system.

Within this understanding of mereology, sometimes a specific theory is indicated as the mereology$_{theo}$ *par excellence*: this theory is the so-called *Classical Extensional Mereology*, and has been formulated—in different forms, with different purposes, and in different contexts—by logicians and philosophers such as Leśniewski, Tarski, and Goodman. The claims that parthood is transitive and that, given some things, there is at most and at least one (that is to say, exactly one) thing composed by them are axioms or theorems (depending on the specific axiomatization) of Classical Extensional Mereology, the mereology$_{theo}$ *par excellence*.

Classical Extensional Mereology does not say of itself that it is the unique, general, and exhaustive theory of parthood and composition. Its theorems do not establish what is in the domain of their quantifiers. As a matter of fact, Classical Extensional Mereology has been thought by its creators to concern, in some cases, specific domains (such as geometry, in Tarski's case), and in other cases reality as a whole (as in Goodman's case), but the intended application or interpretation of mereology$_{theo}$ does not belong to mereology$_{theo}$ itself.

It is *mereology*$_{phi}$ that has this role: mereology$_{phi}$ (mereology as a philosophical thesis) is the philosophical thesis or contention that Classical Extensional Mereology (the mereology$_{theo}$ *par excellence*) *is* the general and exhaustive theory of parthood and composition[1]. It is the philosophical thesis that, in a *large and significant* domain of things, parthood *is* transitive, and that, given some things, *there is* one and only one thing composed of them. In the most radical (perhaps too radical, as we will see) version of mereology$_{phi}$, this large and significant domain is actually the unrestricted domain: the level of generality and exhaustiveness of the theory is taken to be maximum.

Mereology$_{phi}$ has also been dubbed *mereological monism* by Kit Fine[2] (who *is not* a mereological monist himself, and uses the expression polemically), and we will switch between the expressions "mereology$_{phi}$" and "mereological monism" as mere stylistic variants. Mereological monism is mereological, insofar as it is a thesis about parthood and composition (that is, because it belongs to mereology$_{dis}$

as a subject). And it is a kind of monism, insofar as it is the thesis that there is a *single, correct* theory of parthood and composition, which characterizes parthood and composition in a specific way.

This book is a presentation and defense of mereology$_{phi}$, also known as mereological monism. In order to present mereological monism, we need to present the mereology$_{theo}$ that, according to mereological monism, is the unique, general, exhaustive theory of parthood and composition, namely Classical Extensional Mereology, the mereology$_{theo}$ *par excellence*. Everything we are interested in discussing belongs to mereology$_{dis}$, according to the narrow understanding of it as a discipline that only concerns the formal features of parthood and identity and existence conditions for wholes.

Thus, mereology$_{phi}$, mereology$_{theo}$, and mereology$_{dis}$ all have a role in the book. But since its main purpose is to present and defend mereology$_{phi}$, many aspects of mereology$_{theo}$ and mereology$_{dis}$ are left aside. As regards mereology$_{dis}$, any problem that does *not* concern either the formal features of parthood or identity and existence conditions for wholes (and, thus, belongs only to a wider understanding of mereology$_{dis}$) will be discussed only when the risk arises of some interference between such problems and the proper, narrow subject matter of mereology$_{dis}$.

As far as mereology$_{theo}$ is concerned, in most cases we will focus on a single axiomatization of Classical Extensional Mereology. Nonclassical mereologies will be discussed only as terms of comparison: in some cases, we will show that the way in which Classical Extensional Mereology characterizes parthood and composition is preferable to the way in which the latter are characterized by nonclassical mereologies. But we will also contend that there is nothing technically wrong with nonclassical mereologies. The reasons to adopt mereological monism, and hence favor Classical Extensional Mereology over nonclassical alternatives, are not of a technical nature; they are *philosophical* reasons.

## 0.3 Mereological monism and David Lewis: The reasons for this book

The informed reader at this point may have gotten the impression that there is nothing really new in the philosophical thesis defended in this book: mereological monism looks extremely similar to the conception of mereology staunchly proposed by David Lewis, arguably the most influential analytic philosopher of the last forty years, and before him by Goodman and others.

Indeed, in analyzing and defending the various aspects of mereological monism throughout the book, we will make frequent references to Lewis's and Goodman's formulations and arguments and, in most cases, we will endorse them.

In spite of the closeness between Lewis's viewpoint on parts and composition and my own, there are two broad reasons why I hope that my exposition and defense will not prove a useless repetition of what has already been stated by Lewis.

The *first* is that nobody—not even Lewis himself—has explicitly investigated in a book-length study (or any study of equivalent depth) the reasons for mereological monism from a sympathetic viewpoint. Most of the current literature on mereology$_{dis}$ *opposes* mereological monism, and takes Lewis's declarations on parts and composition as its main critical target. But Lewis's most systematic and extensive treatment of mereological monism consists of only sixteen (dense, beautiful, and rewarding) pages in his last book, *Parts of Classes*, whose main topic *is not* mereology but set theory.[3] Mereology is introduced in *Parts of Classes* with the specific purpose of analyzing set theory, in the hope of making some of its philosophical mysteries less mysterious and more treatable.

A quick look at the rest of the contemporary literature on mereology$_{dis}$ might leave the casual reader perplexed as to *why* many authoritative analytic philosophers of the twentieth century endorsed mereology$_{phi}$, since mereology$_{phi}$ is now treated as a deeply wrong thesis, which has been largely refuted by lots of counterexamples. The most extensive book on mereology$_{dis}$ is Peter Simons's *Parts*[4]: an invaluable source of information about the history of mereology in the twentieth century, this work draws useful comparisons between various ways of axiomatizing Classical Extensional Mereology, as well as some nonclassical mereologies. However, Simons's book is also dominated by the reiterated claim that Classical Extensional Mereology serves no real purpose in metaphysics, and that its alleged deficiencies derive precisely from attributing too *narrow* an explanatory scope to mereology$_{dis}$. According to Simons, the theory of parthood and composition *should* be integrated with an adequate treatment of *other* metaphysical issues, mostly involving temporal change and modality.

The extremely accurate and extensive entry on mereology in the *Stanford Encyclopedia of Philosophy* by Achille Varzi[5] (who, through some of his research papers, has greatly contributed to defend mereological monism and whose works will often be quoted in this book) is an extremely valuable resource, in particular about the inferential relations between various mereological principles. But—mainly due to its nature of reference text, and to the related need to countenance a variety of viewpoints about mereology$_{dis}$ and mereology$_{theo}$—Varzi's entry does not really disclose or analyze the reasons for mereological monism.

Many other books discussing philosophical topics closely associated with the notions of parthood and composition (such as Koslicki's *The Structure of Objects* and Sattig's *The Double Lives of Objects*[6]) usually include a relatively succinct exposition of Classical Extensional Mereology, and then proceed to rapidly show why it would be too strong as a theory of parthood, or too poor as a theory of constitution. In order to find a sympathetic exposition of Classical Extensional Mereology, the reader is forced to go back to Eberle's 1970 *Nominalistic Systems*,[7] which was a great study in its day, but was made largely obsolete by the later literature.

The present book does not aim to compete with Simons's and Varzi's works on their own terrain: both are much more complete as introductions to mereology$_{theo}$, and Simons's book is also a great introduction to mereology$_{dis}$, more broadly conceived—even if it is inevitably a bit dated, after thirty years of intense metaphysical research on the topic. However, if you wish to understand *why* it is at least reasonable and defensible to hold the metaphysical doctrines—for example—that no two wholes have the same parts, and that, given some things—no matter how sparse—there is something they compose, then you are looking for a sympathetic introduction to mereology$_{phi}$, or mereological monism, and this book aims to satisfy your need.

The *second* reason why I hope that my work is not a mere, and simply more prolix, repetition of what Lewis thought about parthood and composition is that I *disagree* with *some* of Lewis's views on parthood and composition, although I agree with the majority of them. To be more precise, I believe that while his synthetic defenses of the principles of Classical Extensional Mereology remain compelling and mostly undefeated to this day, some of his accompanying stances actually stand at the basis of the discredit into which mereological monism has fallen.

I will indicate in advance, in the following four Sections (0.4–0.7), my main disagreements with Lewis—the four aspects with respect to which the kind of mereological monism defended in this book *differs* from Lewis's mereological monism. All the claims made below will be further discussed and refined throughout the book. My disagreement with Lewis inevitably depends on a certain interpretation of what he thought about mereology, and these interpretations too will be expounded later on in the book.

# 0.4 Mereology is not logic

First, *there is no interesting sense in which mereology is a logical doctrine.* We will discuss (in Chapter 3) one sense in which Classical Extensional Mereology (mereology$_{theo}$) can be considered *formal*, but it is a sense of formality whereby formality only coincides with generality and topic-neutrality, and is a feature that can be instantiated *to different degrees.* By contrast, the formality of Classical Extensional Mereology does not consist in the fact that it is possible to assess its principles independently of the interpretation of its predicates, such as P (*parthood*). This is a significant difference between mereology and logic.

In general, the comparison between mereology and logic seems to me rather misleading. Obviously, mereology$_{theo}$ can be axiomatized in a certain logic (in Part Three—and in particular in Chapter 10—we will discuss which logical framework is most suitable for this purpose). However, this does not make mereology$_{theo}$ a logical theory in any interesting sense: mereology$_{theo}$ can be expressed and axiomatized in a logical framework, but it is not logic in the sense in which this logical framework is logic (in the sense—say—in which first-order logic is logic).

While mereology$_{theo}$ is logic only in the uninteresting sense that it can be expressed and axiomatized in a certain logic, mereology$_{phi}$ is not logic at all. Mereology$_{phi}$ is a metaphysical doctrine, deeply connected to a specific kind of *nominalism* that we will try to define in detail. Mereology$_{phi}$ can be defended through a combination of a priori arguments in favor of the general truth of Classical Extensional Mereology, and of strategies to explain away alleged counterexamples to its principles. Neither a priori arguments nor the ways of disposing of counterexamples can fully prescind from quite general metaphysical, nominalistically inclined motivations. This procedure would be utterly unacceptable if mereology$_{phi}$ were a logical doctrine.

The claim that mereology is not logic will be discussed in Chapters 3 and 10.

# 0.5 Mereology is imperfectly understood, problematic, and dubious

Second, *mereology is not—in any of the ways of construing it—"perfectly understood, unproblematic, and certain,"* as Lewis instead emphatically declared it to be.[8] Lewis's contention is deeply connected to his tendency to see mereology as a kind of logic: Lewis tends to consider mereology a sort of neutral tool (on a par with logic[9]), to be applied to more controversial philosophical doctrines (such as modal realism, or the doctrine of natural properties), without being in itself the subject of interesting controversies. This is perhaps the reason why he did not feel the need to spend more than sixteen consecutive pages on mereology in all of his philosophical writings.

At a first glance, the three adjectives ("perfectly understood, unproblematic, and certain") could be taken as an innocuous, subjective and emphatic declaration of mereological monism. When I am really convinced of the doctrine *d*, I can express my belief by saying that I feel to have "perfectly understood" *d*, and that *d* seems to me to be so "certain" that its alleged problems are not such to my mind ("unproblematic").

Plausibly enough, however, Lewis—with the above words and his repeated claims that "non-mereological composition" would be an almost contradictory expression—was not simply emphasizing his own adherence to mereological monism, but was claiming that mereological monism *should not* be a topic of philosophical controversy. And this is wrong. There are lots of things that need to be explained, and lots of distinctions that need to be drawn, in order to make mereological monism—in many respects, a *counterintuitive* doctrine—convincing.

As already noted, the acceptance of mereological monism is deeply bound up with the adoption of broad nominalistic presuppositions that are not everyone's cup of tea. Thus, an in-depth analysis and balanced assessment of mereological monism is needed (the main purpose of this book is to provide this assessment), and there is no sensible way in which any serious mereological monist can *avoid* this requirement.

## 0.6 Mereology and abstract entities

Third, *the application of mereological monism to abstract entities raises special concerns*. Lewis (in his book on mereology and set theory, *Parts of Classes*), and other philosophers such as Goodman before him, identified abstract entities as a major field of application for mereology. However, as we will see (in particular in our discussion of Extensionalism in Part Two), it is much easier to defend the principles of Classical Extensional Mereology in the domain of concrete, spatiotemporal entities. By contrast, when abstract entities are at stake, it sometimes seems extremely easy to violate various mereological principles: it is enough to *stipulate* that some abstract entities violate them. Given that mereology *is not* logic, these stipulations can be developed into solid, consistent, and even useful theories.

Mereological monism is not a constraint on what can be *stipulated*, but a controversial, contentful, interesting, and philosophically motivated metaphysical hypothesis about what is out there. Thus, it is possible to make stipulations that run afoul of mereological principles. However, this has not prevented mereological monists from attempting to reconcile recalcitrant abstract entities with their doctrines. After all, once the stipulations are made, they can in many cases be interpreted in several ways. And many mereological monists (such as Goodman and Lewis) have gone to great lengths to show that some abstract entities that would seem to violate mereological principles—most notably, sets—*can* be made to respect them.

Given the prominence of this topic in Goodman's and Lewis's works, the erroneous impression arises that a (or even *the*) primary challenge for mereology$_{phi}$ is to cope with abstract entities, and with sets in particular. But I hope to show in this book that this is wrong: abstract entities are both the most difficult and the least important field of application of mereological monism, and there is nothing surprising in the fact that counterexamples to mereological principles can be found among abstract entities. Concrete entities are the decisive field of application for mereological monism.

In a sense, this means that I concede that mereological monism *is not absolutely general and absolutely topic-neutral*: the categorical divide between abstract and concrete entities makes a lot of difference for mereological monism. My defense of mereological monism is focused on concrete entities, and I will show how and why the prospects of mereological monism about abstract entities are much less rosy.

This is a restriction for mereological monism, but not a fatal one. Since it *is not* logic, mereology can be general, formal, or topic-neutral to a very high degree (as is definitely the case if it holds for the entire domain of concrete entities), without being *absolutely* general, formal, or topic-neutral.

It is possible to insist that, if there are exceptions to mereological monism (such as those in the realm of abstract entities), then mereological monism is refuted. Indeed, Classical Extensional Mereology would fail to be the *absolutely* general and *perfectly* exhaustive theory of parthood and composition, no matter how limited or self-constrained the counterexamples are; insofar as other theories are needed to cope with the counterexamples, a single theory is not enough. At most, a sort of *quasi-monism* could be defended, according to which Classical Extensional Mereology tells the truth about a very wide range of entities.

However, throughout the book, the claim that Classical Extensional Mereology is the general and exhaustive theory of parthood and composition is not understood to imply absoluteness and perfection: generality, formality, and exhaustiveness—in the sense in which these concepts are here understood—come in degrees, and the general thesis of the book is that Classical Extensional Mereology is a *highly* general theory of parthood and composition.[10] Analogously, mereological monism is understood as the thesis that there is *only one highly general* theory of parthood and composition. Given these stipulations about terms such as "general" and "monism," the difficulties of mereological monism in the realm of abstract entities do not refute it.

This difference with Lewis will be discussed in particular in Chapter 8, but it is also anticipated (through an analysis of Lewis's view) in Chapter 5, and later applied to other topics in Chapters 12 and 13.

## 0.7 Mereological monism versus composition as identity

Fourth, *the so-called thesis of Composition as Identity is not an integral part of mereological monism*, and will not be defended in this book. According to Lewis, "composition […] is like identity."[11] As we have seen, according to mereological monism, given some things, there is a unique thing that they compose. By linking composition and identity, Lewis sets forth a further, distinct thesis, according to which the many-one relation between the parts and the unique thing they compose is analogous to identity. The intimacy of this many-one relation is often underlined by other identity-like expressions, such as "the whole is nothing over and above its parts" and "the whole and the parts are the same portion of reality." Other philosophers, in more recent times,[12] have radicalized Lewis's stance, and claimed that composition works exactly like identity, in the sense that it is governed by the same principles that govern identity.

The thesis of Composition as Identity raises lots of problems, which are being discussed in an increasing literature.[13] The most serious problem is that a whole and its parts are so different (so radically *discernible*) that there is no interesting content in the analogy between composition and identity. As we will see, composition has—according to mereological monism—some formal features (such as reflexivity) that suggest a superficial analogy with identity. But Leibniz's Law (the principle of the Indiscernibility of Identicals) is a pivotal aspect of identity. And the sustained efforts, in the literature on Composition as Identity, to extend it to composition *fail*, while the contention (which Lewis himself makes) that composition is analogous to identity, *in spite of the fact* that Leibniz's Law fails for composition, is simply *empty*: there is no residual interesting analogy to be drawn with identity, once you exclude Leibniz's Law from the domain of shared features.

It is not the main purpose of this book to refute the Composition as Identity thesis, but I aim to show that it is possible to present and defend mereological monism without endorsing Composition as Identity at all, and without using its typical, obscure, tendentiously circular jargon according to which a whole is "nothing over and above its parts," or "a whole and its parts are the same portion of reality." Composition as Identity is not a constitutive thesis of mereological monism, and I aim to show this by presenting mereological monism without any reference to such doctrine. To my mind, Composition as Identity is quite the opposite of a constitutive aspect of mereological monism: it is a severely unclear, implausible thesis that risks giving mereological monism a bad name by mere association.

Thus, the main role of Composition as Identity in the core of this book is to be absent: mereological monism is best defended without any reference to Composition as Identity. Composition as Identity is explicitly discussed only in the Appendix, where I show that the primary defect of Composition as Identity is to be in contrast with the narrow understanding of mereology$_{dis}$, which is adopted in this book. Insofar as Leibniz's Law is a constitutive principle of identity, to claim that a whole is identical to its parts *is* to claim either that they share all or some of their properties or that something similar is the case (e.g., that the features of a whole determine the features of its parts, and vice versa). This consequence has nothing to do with the formal features of parthood, and with the identity and existence conditions for wholes, which mereology$_{dis}$ is about.

Through Leibniz's Law and the need to endow composition with a feature at least analogous to indiscernibility, mereology ends up being embroiled in problems about properties and supervenience. Our theory of parthood and composition—no matter how general and exhaustive it may be—should not imply controversial theses on these important, difficult, and quite separate areas of metaphysical research.

## 0.8 The plan of the book

I could sum up the differences between my own mereological monism and Lewis's doctrine as follows: according to this book, mereology is not logic, but a problematic metaphysical doctrine; it fails to work for many abstract entities; and we should not say that a whole is identical to its parts. Still, mereological monism is a defensible and promising metaphysical doctrine about concrete entities. This—I contend—is the interesting core of mereological monism.

These foretastes of the main theses of the book might seem to the casual reader to be rather abstract and intimidating. Hopefully, the rest of the book will show that mereological monism is quite a simple doctrine, which can be illustrated and defended even for the benefit of nonspecialist readers without excessive efforts, by relying in particular on examples from so-called ordinary objects and from other relatively familiar domains, such as language (in which letters, words, expressions, and sentences are very commonly thought to be part—or to be composed—of one another).

The book is divided into three parts and an Appendix. Each of the three parts is further articulated into chapters.

Part One explains what mereology$_{\text{phi}}$ is about, and attributes some basic features to the parthood relation. These basic features and some potential counterexamples to them are illustrated with a constant attention to methodology, in order to make the reader progressively familiar with the kinds of theses, arguments, and methods that are at stake in this sector of metaphysics.

Part Two is about Uniqueness of Composition, that is, the principle that the same things do not compose more than one thing, and Extensionalism, the related principle that complex entities are identical if and only if they have the same proper parts (what "proper part" means will be explained in due course). I will distinguish between these and other principles, and discuss the connection between them and a certain kind of nominalism. Then, some alleged counterexamples to Extensionalism in the domain of concrete entities will be discussed and shown to be convincingly reconcilable with Extensionalism. Finally, I will explain why Extensionalism is a much more credible doctrine for concrete entities than it is for abstract ones.

Part Three is about Unrestricted Composition, that is, the principle that, given some things (no matter how heterogeneous and disparate they are), there is at least one thing they compose. The existing arguments in favor of this thesis are analyzed and shown to be compelling. The common idea that there is something outrageously counterintuitive in unrestricted composition is also analyzed.

Finally, in the Appendix, I show that—as already anticipated in the previous section—the so-called thesis of Composition as Identity, far from belonging to mereological monism, runs counter to the need to separate the explanatory scope of mereological monism from other areas of metaphysics.

The abstracts of Parts One, Two, and Three provide further details about the contents of each chapter, and can be used as a guide to navigate the entire book.

# Part One

# The Methodology of Mereological Monism

## Abstract

This part of the book presents mereology as the formal study of the relation of parthood and of some cognate relations and operations. Chapter 1 shows that mereology selects and systematizes some prototypical instances of parthood from the spatial domain. The resulting characterization of parthood is then taken as a criterion for distinguishing in other domains literal parthood from merely metaphorical occurrences of "part" (and similar terms), as well as from other relations. Moreover, it is shown that the formal characterization of parthood is constrained by some intuitive expectations about what parthood is. Chapter 2 discusses the role of mereology in other philosophical debates, and in particular shows how mereology can help to refute certain philosophical theories, or to restrict the range of admissible solutions for a philosophical problem. Chapter 3 distinguishes several ways of construing formality, and discusses the links between mereology and the so-called formal ontology. According to some interpretations of formality, mereology is formal; according to others, it is not. The kind of formality enjoyed by mereology also explains the tight links between parthood, existence, and identity. Finally, in Chapter 4, the methodology of mereology sketched in the previous chapters is applied to a discussion of the transitivity, reflexivity, and antisymmetry of parthood. It is also shown how the methodology of mereological monism differs from that of mereological pluralism.

# Natural Language, Literal Parthood, and Philosophical Mereology

## 1.1 Mereology and the lexical meaning of "part"

My bed is part of the furniture in my room. My youth is part of my life. And gin is part of gin-tonic. Is there a single sense in which these disparate things are part of one another? This question could be generalized, and framed as a question about lexical meaning: is the term "part" univocal in English, or does it have different meanings in different contexts? If it is construed as a question about lexical meaning, the question is likely to elicit an immediate *negative* answer.

In this book, however, I am going to apply the concept of part to lots of things, and to argue in favor of the thesis that, at the end of the day, there is a single, exhaustive theory of parthood. The concept of part I will analyze is rather refined and specific, and is not meant to correspond strictly to the meaning of "part" in English. But it is still sufficiently entrenched within the standard meaning of "part" that it is not by sheer chance that we can still employ this term to designate what the book is about, instead of having to coin an exclusively philosophical word for it.

Moreover, in the course of the analysis, I will discuss alternative, *pluralist* approaches, according to which there is *not* a single, exhaustive theory of parthood, but there are many. However, in most cases, these pluralist approaches to parthood are not motivated by the need for the philosophical analysis to provide a perfect and exhaustive account of the lexical meaning of "part" (or of the equivalent terms in other languages). In other words—no matter if you are a mereological monist or not—the immediate negative answer to the question about the univocity or non-univocity of "part" in English is of limited importance for mereology$_{dis}$.

However, it is interesting to analyze, in this initial chapter, the immediate propensity to deny the univocity of "part" in English. This is needed in order to prevent *simplistic*, broadly relativist objections to all the various claims we are going to discuss about the theory of parthood: the kind of objections that, given any claim whatsoever about parthood, simply contend that "it depends," or ask for the confirmation of a complete survey on the usage of "part"—or of other terms within the same semantic area, such as "piece," "portion," "bit," or even "component" and "constituent."

Mereology$_{dis}$ is not about this kind of survey, and does not presuppose it. A usage of "part" or "bit" that does not respect the principle of a theory of parthood does not refute, by itself, that theory of parthood or its ambitions to be general and exhaustive. Nonetheless, considerations about natural language do play a role in mereology, because—again—it is not by sheer chance that we use the term "part" in the philosophical theory of parthood. As in the case of many other philosophical investigations, the philosophical theory in question is about something that also has a role outside of philosophy. Parts are everywhere. An atom of oxygen is said to be part of a molecule of water, my left elbow is said to be part of my left arm, and the word "Christmas" is said to be part of the sentence "I wish you a merry Christmas." In a love affair between Jane and Harold, it may happen that Jane says to Harold: "I am part of you, and you are part of me." Mereology is conceived as the theory of parts—also and mainly parts outside of philosophy.

This does not mean that mereology should take into account every single occurrence of "part" and cognate expressions in English and other languages (as we will see, Jane's declaration to Harold should not worry us too much); but we should make sure that overrefinement does not turn our theory into the theory of something else altogether.

## 1.2 "Part" and cognate terms: Three distinctions

Let us consider the following English sentences (some of them have been already mentioned), in which either the term "part" or semantically cognate terms (namely "piece" and "component") are employed in various syntactic positions:

(a) The Kemalists are part of the parliament.
(b) The leg is part of the table.
(c) I want to eat a piece of that cake.
(d) Luxembourg is part of the European Union.
(e) Many components of my car are expensive to replace.

(f)  The word "Christmas" is part of the sentence "I wish you a merry Christmas."
(g)  I am part of you, and you are part of me.

I am going to draw three rough but important distinctions between these sentences, in order to help clarify the relation between mereology and the lexical meaning of English terms such as "part." The three distinctions concern *spatial location*, *selectivity*, and *formality*.

In considering these three distinctions, it is important to keep in mind that *we are not inferring mereological principles from a quick, vague, and potentially arbitrary lexical analysis*. By contrast, we aim to show that philosophical mereology (mereology$_{dis}$) is not completely detached from the ordinary usages of "part" and of some cognate words. It is possible to select (on purpose and a posteriori) some occurrences of these terms and analyze them in order to give a preliminary idea of what philosophical mereology is about.

A *first* distinction concerns the relation between parthood and *spatial location*. In some cases (namely (b), (c), and (e)), it seems clear that space is involved:

(b)  The leg is part of the table.
(c)  I want to eat a piece of that cake.
(e)  Many components of my car are expensive to replace.

The question here is not just that the things which are said to be part one of another have a location in space. After all, for example, also the Kemalists in (a) and the lovers in (g) have a spatial location. But in (b), (c), and (e) there is something more: it seems that a kind of spatial parthood is involved.

At a rough, provisional approximation, we could say that in these cases there is a sort of correspondence between the instance of parthood about which the sentences are and another instance of parthood that subsists between the corresponding regions of space. Given a thing *x*, let us call *region (x)* the region of space occupied by *x*. It seems, then, that my heart is part of my body if and only if *region (heart)* is part of *region (body)*. This seems to be a constitutive feature of cases such as (b), (c), and (e). In other cases, a similar principle of harmony[1] between entities and the regions of space they occupy does not hold at all.

The Kemalist members of parliament (to which the referential expression "The Kemalists" in (a) refers to) are people occupying collectively a sparse and disconnected region of space. But it is not clear in what sense this sparse region of space is part of a region of space occupied by the parliament.

As far as (f) ("The word 'Christmas' is part of the sentence 'I wish you a merry Christmas'") is concerned, sentences and words are often understood as abstract types having many concrete tokens. It is highly controversial whether such abstract linguistic types have any spatial location at all and, if they do, where they are located. In any case, the (eventual) inclusion of the region of space (eventually) occupied by the word in the region of space (eventually) occupied by the sentence is not constitutive of the parthood relation expressed in (f): this parthood relation can subsist independent of any controversial claim about linguistic types and their spatial locations.

In (g) ("I am part of you, and you are part of me."), it seems that, whatever the claim actually means, there is no consequence for the spatial location of the lovers: there is no expectation that the region of space occupied by the former lover is part of the region occupied by the latter lover, or vice versa.

In the case of (d) ("Luxembourg is part of the European Union."), it is not clear whether space plays a role, due to the fact that the referential expressions ("Luxembourg" and "The European Union") are ambiguous. They could be interpreted as referring to physical geography, in which case the region occupied by Luxembourg would be part of the wider region occupied by the European Union; moreover, this mirroring between the entities at stake and the regions of space they occupy would play a constitutive role in the parthood claim. But the referential expressions "Luxembourg" and "The European Union" could also refer to institutions (a state and an international organization, respectively), and it is not clear whether institutions are in space at all.

A *second* distinction concerns *selectivity*. It seems that in some cases $x$ qualifies as a part of $y$ on the necessary condition that $x$ has clear, sharp boundaries within $y$, and/or has a specific function in the workings of $y$. In other cases, there is no such requirement.

The term "component" employed in (e) ("Many components of my car are expensive to replace.") is selective. The oil filter of the car has clear, visible boundaries, as well as a distinctive function; it qualifies as a component of the car. By contrast, the right half of the oil filter has neither a clear, visible boundary nor a distinctive function; thus, we would not classify it among the components of a car. The fact that it is not viable to replace it and that it has probably no defined price (so that it does not make much sense to ask if it is expensive or cheap to replace the right half of the oil filter) has no bearing on the truth-conditions of (e): we simply do not include the right half of the oil filter among the things (e) is about. In (a) ("The Kemalists are part of the parliament."), also "parts" is used in a selective way: no half-Kemalist, for example, would be said to be part of the parliament in the same sense; the same holds for recombinations of left legs of Kemalists.

In (c) ("I want to eat a piece of that cake."), by contrast, the expression "a piece" is typically nonselective: any portion of the cake counts as a piece. If I were given a minuscule crumb of cake, my desire for a piece of cake would probably remain unsatisfied, because what I actually wanted was a reasonably big piece. But this seems to depend on pragmatic elements concerning desire for food and its satisfaction. My protest against the offer of a minuscule crumb of cake would rest not on the fact that the crumb is not a piece, but on the fact that my desire has been interpreted *too literally*: the crumb is indeed a piece of the cake, but I wanted a reasonably big piece of it, not an arbitrarily small one.

In (b) ("The leg is part of the table."), "part" is not selective either: it seems that half legs are as much part of the table as whole legs. If I add the indeterminate article "a" to "part" or replace "part" with "component," then the degree of selectivity seems to increase. Only the top, each of the legs, and other significantly selected parts of a table can be sensibly said to be "a part" of it.

A *third* and last distinction concerns the *formal features* of parthood as a *relation*. Parthood is a *binary* relation: it is not a property had by a single thing. When I make a parthood claim, I indicate an $x$ that is the part (the first *relatum*) and a $y$ that is the whole (the second *relatum*). Relations, in general, are characterized by certain formal features. We will make frequent references to some of these formal features, so it is useful to introduce some of them from the beginning.

A relation $R$ is *reflexive* if and only if, for every $x$, $x$ is in the relation $R$ with $x$ (that is, with itself). $R$ is *symmetric* if and only if, for every $x$ and every $y$, if $x$ is in the relation $R$ with $y$, then $y$ is in the relation $R$ with $x$. $R$ is *antisymmetric* if and only if, for every $x$ and every $y$, if $x$ is in the relation $R$ with $y$ and $y$ is in the relation $R$ with $x$, then $x$ and $y$ are identical (thus, $x$ and $y$ are actually only one thing). Finally, $R$ is *transitive* if and only if, for every $x$, every $y$ and every $z$, if $x$ is in the relation $R$ with $y$ and $y$ is in the relation $R$ with $z$, then $x$ is in the relation $R$ with $z$.

Let us focus on transitivity and antisymmetry, and go back to our samples (a)–(g) of the usage of English terms in the lexical area of "part." From most of the sentences, nothing about the formal features of the parthood relation involved can be immediately grasped. However, upon closer investigation we meet some interesting exceptions. As regards transitivity, it may be observed that it seems to interact with *selectivity*. When terms such as "component" (in e) and "parts" (in a) are used selectively, transitivity seems to be at risk.

In (a) ("The Kemalists are part of the parliament."), consider the kidneys of a Kemalist MP: they are parts of the MP. The MP, as her colleagues, is part of the parliament. However, it seems that the kidneys are not part of the parliament. In (e) ("Many components of my car are expensive to replace."), consider the float chamber of a carburetor (the part of the carburetor where the fuel enters and is provisionally stored). It is a component of the carburetor, and the carburetor is a component of the car. But is the float chamber a component of the car? If we were asked to give a list of the components of the car, we would list the carburetor for sure, and, once we have listed it, we would not feel the need to list also the subparts, since that portion of the car has been already *covered* by the carburetor. Thus, transitivity can be at least doubted.

By contrast, the nonselective cases seem to favor transitivity. In (c) ("I want to eat a piece of that cake."), a piece of a piece of a cake counts as a piece of the cake, no matter how small and unsatisfying it is. And what is part of part of the table counts as part of the table as well.

Antisymmetry is prima facie difficult to apply to parthood claims (a)–(f), but if we consider them more carefully, we find that antisymmetry would hold in a sort of limiting case, on which we do not often reflect. Antisymmetry concerns what happens when two things $x$ and $y$ are reciprocally part one of the other: in this case, if parthood is an antisymmetric relation, then $x$ and $y$ are identical.

In cases (a)–(f), no instance of reciprocal parthood emerges directly. Non-reciprocity seems to be expected pragmatically. Consider (b) ("The leg is part of the table."): if we claim that the leg is part of the table, this is because the table and the leg are different—albeit intimately connected—things. Suppose that a table is so broken or worn out that only one of its legs remains. In this scenario I would not claim that the leg is part of the table: it would be a misleading way of speaking. This is connected with another expectation: that the leg does not *exhaust* the table; in other words, that the table has other parts (such as its top). If there were no other parts, then I would not claim that the leg is part of the table. This claim might not be judged false, perhaps, but it would certainly be regarded as *improper,* and somewhat misleading.

The kind of antisymmetry that is presupposed by claims such as (a)–(f) relegates cases of reciprocal parthood to deviant exceptions in which it would be strange to make a parthood claim. In these deviant cases, the presupposition is that there is identity between the *relata* of the parthood relation. On the basis of case (c) ("I want to eat a piece of that cake."), suppose that I am given a piece of a cake such that the cake itself is part of the piece. This is a deviant situation, and the only way to make sense of it is to imagine that I have been given the entire cake. In this limiting case, the piece of the cake is actually identical to the cake, in accordance with antisymmetry.

Antisymmetry tends to be presupposed in all those cases where the connection with spatial location is at play and the above sketched harmony holds. (c) is one of these cases.

In general, suppose that the harmony holds, so that $x$ is part of $y$, and $y$ is part of $x$; then, *region(x)* is part of *region(y)*, and *region(y)* is part of *region(x)*. Thus, reciprocity also concerns the parthood relation between regions of space. Now, focus on the parthood between regions of space: if a region of space is part of another, this means that the latter comprises all the former, possibly in addition to something else. But if two regions are part of one another, then neither of them can comprise *something else*. The hypothesis of two regions of space that are part of one another, but are different nonetheless, does not make sense.

By contrast, (g) ("I am part of you, and you are part of me.") does not presuppose antisymmetry. (g) *is* a claim of reciprocal parthood, and *is not* expected to imply the identity of its *relata*. Jane (the person who utters (g)) could complete her declaration to Harold as in (h) or as in (i), without incurring a contradiction in either case:

(h)  I am part of you, you are part of me, and we are one and the same person.
(i)  I am part of you, you are part of me, but we are different people.

Thus, if we were to take (i) seriously, we would have to conclude the two lovers can be part of one another, without thereby being identical. But should we?

## 1.3 Literal parthood versus metaphorical parthood

Should we take (g), as well as its completions (h) and (i), seriously? More generally, what is the bearing of the considerations and distinctions arising from the analysis of claims of parthood in natural language on that branch of metaphysics that studies the relation of parthood? We have anticipated that, on the one hand, the purpose of philosophical mereology is not to study the lexical semantics of "part" and cognate words in one or more natural languages, but also that, on the other hand, there is not sheer homonymy between parts in philosophical mereology and parts outside of it. How are we to reconcile these two claims?

Let us propose a provisional characterization of what philosophical mereology (or mereology$_{dis}$, according to the disambiguation of "mereology" proposed in the Introduction, Section 0.2) does. This characterization will be further refined throughout this book.

Mereology$_{dis}$ *selects* certain usages of the notion of part in philosophical and nonphilosophical contexts that are perceived to be more *literal* than others. The reason to select literal occurrences is the expectation that they are conceived as a description of parthood relations in reality, and not as a metaphor of some other feature of the world (such as the relation of love between Jane and Harold). These literal usages are not only to be found in a specific natural language such as English, or in other natural languages. They also occur in those sciences that are expressed in a formal language. This selection isolates the subject matter of mereology$_{dis}$: the realm within which confirmations and counterexamples to its principles should be sought.

Obviously, the fact that some parthood claims are meant *literally* does not imply that they are *true*: a parthood claim (as a claim on many other subjects) can be literal and false at the same time. But the purpose of mereology *is not* to identify true parthood claims. And it is clearly not up to metaphysicians— or philosophers in general—to identify the parts of molecules, biological organisms, or cars. Mereology$_{dis}$ is only expected to identify the formal features, such as the transitivity and antisymmetry mentioned earlier, of a relation of parthood—and of some other important relations and operations to be introduced later on—that can be seriously and literally applied to the world.

These formal features will not determine what is part of a car or of a molecule of water. At most, they will warrant the legitimacy of some inferences. For example, the thesis that parthood is transitive legitimates the following inference from two parthood claims to another parthood claim:

> Sicily is part of Greece
> Greece is part of Asia
> *therefore*
> Sicily is part of Asia

but does not tell us whether its premises are true (in this case we know that they are false, but not because of our competence in mereology$_{dis}$).

Thus, mereology privileges literal claims of parthood over metaphorical claims. But it can be far from easy to draw a sharp distinction between literal and metaphorical claims, in general. We might feel that there is something which is not purely descriptive and literal in (g), and that (b) and (c) are more concrete and down-to-earth examples. However, in many other cases, the brute appeal to the distinction between literal and metaphorical risks being a source of methodological arbitrariness.[2]

Suppose that I am in the process of building a theory of parthood. Am I free to reject any counterexample (any failure of transitivity, such as those ensuing from the analysis of (a) and (e) discussed earlier) as metaphorical? Or to accept any confirmation as literal? Admittedly, some contextual elements could somewhat constrain this freedom: we may have general reasons to think that, in the context of love talk, metaphors are more abundant than in other fields. This might suggest that we keep (g), (h), and (i) out of the domain of eligible counterexamples or confirmations for the principles of philosophical mereology.

But some cases are more controversial, and pose a real risk of arbitrariness. Consider (a) and (f) in particular. As regards (a), are Kemalists *literally* parts of the parliament? Is the parliament (an institution, a social entity) something that has parts? Or is "parts" here a metaphor for a more articulate and substantial social relation, involving the right to enter a certain building and participate in certain discussions and decisions? Could the formal features of this substantial social relation be different from those of literal parthood?

In the case of (f), are abstract entities (such as types of sentences and words) *literally involved* in parthood relations? Perhaps our tendency to apply terms such as "part" to linguistic types is somewhat improper: a sort of metonymy to express that some concrete tokens of these types (some concrete "Christmas" inscriptions) are part of one another.[3]

## 1.4 Spatial parthood, paradigmatic parthood

Questions about the literal or metaphorical character of claims can be really difficult to resolve. But we can look back at two of the distinctions we drew earlier while discussing claims (a)–(g), in order to find some clues. First of all, space: spatial parthood often has the role of paradigmatic literal parthood. The circumstance that the harmony mentioned earlier holds is an indication that we purport to describe reality. When parthood is systematically paired with spatial containment (as the principle of harmony signals), there are good reasons to think that it is a case of literal parthood.

We should not mistake this *heuristic* test for a necessary and sufficient condition for being a case of literal parthood, which mereology aims to *select* and *systematize*. It is not a *sufficient* condition because metaphors are often elaborate, and may involve space itself: in these cases, we could try to further analyze our claims about the relations between regions of space, and look at their context or articulation. More importantly, it is not a necessary condition.

Spatial parts are a *paradigm* for mereology, but they are not its exclusive subject matter. Why, for example, should the temporal sense in which my youth is part of my life be excluded from the domain of mereology? It seems that the kind of involved containment is no less literal than in the spatial cases: one could even envisage a sort of harmony with the relations between time intervals. What would be metaphorical in it?

Similarly, on what basis should we assume that abstract entities—which are often thought to lack a spatial location by definition—are prevented *qua* abstract from playing the role of parts or wholes? Is there not a prima facie clear sense of containment whereby which the set of even numbers is in the set natural numbers? Even in the case of linguistic types, why should the above metonymical interpretation be the right one? It seems that letter types are in word types, and that word types are in sentence types; and the burden of proof would appear to fall upon those who argue that this containment is nonliteral.

We will come back to our examples later. In order to understand in what sense spatial parts are a paradigm for mereology, but are not its exclusive subject matter, we may turn to another of the distinctions drawn above (the third). *Formal* features of parthood (such as transitivity and antisymmetry) are very important in mereology. Spatial parthood is a paradigm. As such, it can help us to identify the formal features of parthood in general. As we will see over the course of the book, the formal features of parthood are also connected to the formal features of other relations and operations concerning parts and wholes (such as *overlap* and *fusion*).

Suppose that the analysis of spatial, paradigmatic instances of parthood relations is enough to obtain a relatively precise formal characterization of parthood as a relation. If so, we could have an important guideline in identifying other instances of genuine, literal parthood. Genuine, literal parthood would no longer be distinguished by the literalness or seriousness with which some claims are meant to concern reality: it would simply be the relation that works exactly like the paradigmatic cases. A sentence such as (g) would still be excluded from the scope of mereology, but not for the highly specific and rather elusive reason that love talk is often metaphorical, but because it violates antisymmetry, which—as we have seen—is a patent feature of paradigmatic spatial parthood.

Some doubts could be legitimately raised about this methodology. For example, one could observe that the method is not a perfectly reliable one for distinguishing between literal and metaphorical uses of "part" and related terms: after all, a metaphor could be so rigorous as to be formally indistinguishable from its literal counterpart. The only difference between metaphorical and literal uses of "part" might be that metaphors are meant precisely as metaphors.

My reply to this objection is that the purpose of the method is not to distinguish between literal and metaphorical occurrences of "part": its purpose is to *replace* this kind of distinction, which is shaky and difficult to draw. The main advantage of the method is that it identifies the subject matter of mereology in a *principled* and *projectable* way: principled, because the formal study of relations is a well-developed theory, of which the above definitions of reflexivity, symmetry, and so on, are only elementary samples; projectable, because once the formal profile of parthood is defined on the basis of paradigmatic cases, new candidate instances of parthood can be evaluated. In particular, candidate instances can be discarded if they exhibit different formal features (as happens with the non-antisymmetric relation in (g)).

It is important to remark that this methodology for mereology$_{dis}$ does not lead unavoidably to the adoption of mereological monism or mereology$_{phi}$, that is, the thesis according to which a single theory exhaustively characterizes parthood and other cognate relations and operations. I will endorse and defend mereological monism in this book, but as a substantial metaphysical thesis, and not as a mere consequence of the provisional characterization of mereology$_{dis}$ just outlined. The characterization of mereology$_{dis}$ does not settle whether an investigation of paradigmatic, spatial instances of parthood reveals the existence of a single relation of parthood or of multiple relations of parthood, each with its specific formal features; nor does it suggest how many theories should study these relations.

## 1.5 Formal features and intuitive constraints

At this point, a different doubt could be raised. Once the formal features of parthood and other connected relations and operations are established on the basis of an analysis of paradigmatic cases of spatial parthood, we are allowed to discard other candidate instances if they work in a different way (i.e., they have different formal features). In other words, it is *necessary* for a relation to possess those formal features in order for it to qualify as a genuine parthood relation. But it is less clear whether the condition is also *sufficient*. Is it enough to share with paradigmatic, spatial parthood formal features such as antisymmetry (antisymmetry is here merely a basic example of a formal feature of paradigmatic parthood) in order to qualify as genuine parthood?

Suppose that the relation between any grandmother and her favorite grandchild turns out to work, from a formal point of view, exactly like spatial, paradigmatic parthood. This is not a very realistic example (the relation at stake seems to be neither transitive nor antisymmetrical), but it is still useful to consider it: would the sharing of formal features be enough to classify as genuine parthood a relation that *clearly* does not amount to that at all?

This seems to be an instance of a more general problem: are formal features enough to isolate a subject matter? In the specific case of parthood, the answer seems to be: no, they are not enough. There are also *intuitive constraints* on what counts as parthood. Formal features allow for a discrimination within an already limited domain of relations that have something to do with *containment* and *being in*. No kind of containment or being in connects grandmothers and their favorite grandchildren. Thus, the formal features of the relation between each grandmother and her favorite grandchild do not matter from the viewpoint of mereology: no matter how this relation works, it is not a case of parthood.

I am not going to say anything more specific on these intuitive constraints. It is enough to note that the problem of a prior delimitation of a subject matter arises for any nonlogical relation. Nobody believes that formal features are sufficient to identify the relation of similarity, or of brotherhood, or of parallelism. In all these cases, as well as in the case of parthood, no serious, specific doubt arises about the prior, intuitive delimitation of the subject matter: only lines and curves can be parallel, only animals can be brothers, only when some properties are shared can there be similarity; and only when some kind of containment or being in is involved can there be parthood.

Basically, all the relations involved in sentences (a)–(g) in Section 1.1 respect the intuitive constraints, including the love talk in (g): no matter how metaphorical and formally deviant, the love talk in (g) concerns a kind of mutual containment. Claim (g) belongs to the intuitively constrained domain of relations involving a kind of containment and being in. The formal constraints, inspired by prototypical, spatial cases of literal parthood, allow us to discriminate genuine relations of parthood *within* this intuitively constrained domain. These formal constraints will exclude (g) (due to the fact that (g) blatantly violates antisymmetry), in spite of the fact that (g) involves some kind of containment or being in.

No serious debate on mereology hinges on the intuitive constraint, because in each case it is clear what respects the constraint, and what does not. It can be difficult to characterize the intuitive constraint in an informative and noncircular way, and the nature of intuition is obviously a huge philosophical problem. However, this should not worry us. The formal features of parthood and of other cognate relations and operations are what philosophical mereology is about. These formal features are necessary conditions for being a genuine parthood relation. They are not sufficient conditions, because the domain of eligible relations is constrained by an intuitive condition. But no serious doubt arises on this intuitive condition. We can therefore legitimately focus on the formal features of parthood and of other cognate relations and operations.

## 1.6 Mereology is about nonselective parthood

The second distinction we have drawn in Section 1.2 is also important for determining the scope of mereology. Mereology is about *nonselective parthood*; selective notions of parthood (often expressed by cognate terms such as "component" in (e)) are not its subject matter. This is a stipulation, yet not an unmotivated one.

First of all, the stipulation corresponds to the way in which mereology has been understood by most philosophers whose works we will be discussing in this book. Moreover, the stipulation is actually germane to the methodology of mereology$_{dis}$ we sketched earlier. We have claimed that mereology$_{dis}$ considers paradigmatic instances of parthood and systematizes their formal features; afterwards, the ensuing formal characterization also becomes a guideline for identifying other, less paradigmatic, genuine instances of parthood.

A formal, general characterization is hopeless in the case of selective parthood or componency. In the case of (e), selective componency needs to discriminate, within a car, between the oil filter and the right half of the oil filter: only the oil filter qualifies as a selected component of a car, for only the oil filter is clearly delimited, and has a specific function in the workings of the car. But there is nothing *formal* in this discrimination (we will consider what kind of *formality* is at stake here in Chapter 3): in order to draw this discrimination, we need quite specific information about how a car works.

This kind of information is not easily projectable onto other fields: the criterion for being clearly delimited and having a specific function within a car are arguably different from the criterion for being clearly delimited and having a specific function in a microphysical system, or in a living organism.

The reason why philosophical mereology focuses on nonselective parthood— and not on selective parthood—is that selective parthood is specific to various fields, and depends on highly local features of things (such as cars), about which philosophy has nothing to say.

Nonetheless, it is worth remarking that the analysis of nonselective parthood could be relevant to the investigation of a more subject-specific and selective kind of parthood. Privileged parts and components are nonetheless parts in the nonselective sense. There is a sense in which *both* the oil filter and the right half of the oil filter are parts of the car, and mereology is about *that* sense of "part." It is up to domain-specific theories of components to discriminate between them.

We can now summarize the characterization of philosophical mereology (mereology$_{dis}$) discussed in this chapter. Philosophical mereology is about the formal features of parthood and some cognate relations and operations. It assumes some paradigmatic, literal, spatial instances of parthood, and projects their features in order to identify other genuine instances of parthood. Moreover, it focuses on nonselective parthood, since selective parthood is too domain-specific to be a plausible subject for metaphysics. Our upcoming presentation and defense of mereological monism (mereology$_{phi}$) will presuppose this characterization of mereology$_{dis}$.

# Mereological Monism: A Desirable Philosophical Thesis

## 2.1 How to maximize the discriminating power

Mereology$_{dis}$ is expected to select and systematize paradigmatic cases of parthood. These cases will display some formal features. Once they have been systematized, we obtain a criterion to discriminate literal cases of parthood. I have claimed in Chapter 1, Section 1.4 that this approach does not make mereological monism trivial: the result of the selection and systematization might be that—*contra* mereological monism—there are several kinds of parthood relations, each with different formal features.

Nonetheless, this methodology contributes to making mereological monism a *desirable* philosophical thesis. If true, mereological monism would maximize the discriminating power of our methodology; a single theory would univocally characterize a single relation of parthood (as well as the other cognate relations we are going to introduce). We would have a simple and secure basis for concluding that a certain relation is not parthood.

By contrast, pluralism might prove to be an indefinite source of revisionism: given a potential case of non-parthood, the alternative of keeping it as a new variety of parthood would never be ruled out once and for all. Given a new case, we would always be in a sort of dilemma. Is this a case of non-parthood, or a formally different variety of parthood? It could prove difficult to choose one of the horns of this dilemma in a principled way.

As a matter of fact, mereological monism—which is rarely defended nowadays—was for a long time the dominant view. If we restrict our attention to the last thirty years, its most ardent and explicit advocate was Lewis. Lewis used mereological monism as a powerful discriminating tool. In particular, he conceived mereological monism as a way of *refuting* some philosophical claims: if a certain theory claims that $x$ is part of $y$, but some formal principle governing parthood is therein violated, then this is enough to conclude that there is something false in that theory.

In his 1991 book *Parts of Classes*[1] (which, while being mainly a book about sets, includes a sort of manifesto of mereological monism that we will often be referring to), Lewis argues against the claim that the elements of a set are parts of it,[2] on the basis of the fact that set-theoretic membership works differently from parthood from a formal point of view. He writes:

> Membership could not be (a special case of) the part-whole relation because of a difference in formal character. (Lewis 1991, p. 5)

The formal difference to which Lewis refers concerns transitivity. Let us see how Lewis's reasoning can be made explicit. According to mereological monism (mereology$_{phi}$, the philosophical thesis Lewis endorses), Classical Extensional Mereology (CEM henceforth), a theory (a mereology$_{theo}$) elaborated in the first half of the twentieth century by logicians such as Leśniewski and Tarski and philosophers such as Goodman, is the general and exhaustive theory of parthood. According to this theory, the relation of parthood is transitive.

In our analysis of some occurrences of "part" and related terms in Chapter 1, we have observed that *nonselective* parthood (the variety of parthood such that every bit or piece—no matter how arbitrarily subdivided and devoid of a specific function—qualifies as part) seems to be transitive. And we have also observed that *de facto* (but for some good reasons, Chapter 1, Section 1.6) mereology focuses on nonselective parthood. Thus, as far as transitivity is concerned, the contention that CEM is the general, exhaustive theory of parthood confirms this impression.

Lewis uses transitivity to discriminate between genuine parthood (the relation which mereology$_{dis}$ is about, and which is exhaustively characterized by CEM according to mereology$_{phi}$) and set-theoretic membership.

Consider $T$, the set of all tabby cats. All the members of $T$ are cats. Consider also $B$, the set of the sets each of which includes all the cats of a certain breed. All the members of $B$ are sets of cats. Since tabby cats are a breed of cats, $T$ is an element of $B$. Finally, consider Smudge, a tabby cat. If set-theoretic membership qualified as a parthood relation, we could take two of its instances and apply transitivity to them: Smudge is an element of $T$, and $T$ is an element of $B$; by transitivity, it would follow that Smudge is an element of $B$. But Smudge *is not* an element of $B$: Smudge is a cat, and no element of $B$ is a cat (the elements of B are sets of cats). Transitivity fails, and membership ends up being formally different from genuine parthood.

## 2.2 Mereological monism as a refutation tool: An example

In order to better appreciate the epistemological advantage of mereological monism over mereological pluralism, let us focus on a slightly more elaborate example of its application to a philosophical debate, as a potential refutation tool. According to a noble tradition in philosophy—endorsed for example by many British empiricists, as well as many contemporary trope theorists[3]—properties are parts of the individuals instantiating them. Suppose that, in the context of such a philosophical stance, the following claim is taken as an adequate characterization of instantiation itself:

> *Instantiation:* An individual *t* instantiates a property *P* if and only if *P* is part of *t*.

Given a property and an individual, the subsistence of a relation of parthood between them would be, according to *Instantiation*, a necessary and sufficient condition for the subsistence of a relation of instantiation between them.

Now, consider a blue pen (it is full of blue ink and writes in blue) that happens to have a red cap. The cap is red. In other words, the cap instantiates redness. According to *Instantiation*, it follows that redness is part of the cap. But then there is also a prototypical, spatial instance of parthood at hand: the cap is part of the pen. By transitivity, if redness is part of the cap, and the cap is part of the pen, then redness is also part of the pen. According to *Instantiation*, parthood between a property and an individual is also a sufficient condition for instantiation. As a consequence, the pen instantiates redness. In other words, the pen is red. But the pen *is not* red (it is not full of red ink, it does not write in red).

Thus, we have an argument with a seemingly unacceptable conclusion.

1. The cap is red. (premiss)
2. Redness is part of the cap. (from 1, by the left-to-right direction of *Instantiation*)
3. The cap is part of the pen. (premiss)
4. Redness is part of the pen. (from 2 and 3, by transitivity)
5. The pen is red. (conclusion, from 4, by the right-to-left direction of *Instantiation*)

The premisses (1 and 3) are not controversial theses, but harmless local hypotheses. It would not make philosophical sense to reject them. Thus, we have three broad options:

(a)  to reject transitivity;

(b)  to reject *Instantiation;*

(c)  to accept conclusion 5 (by interpreting it in a way that makes it, *contra* appearances, acceptable).

At this point of the philosophical dialectics, mereological monism intervenes and tells us that (a) is not a viable option. Transitivity is dictated by the general, exhaustive theory of parthood (CEM). The selection and systematization of prototypical instances of parthood indicates transitivity as a feature of parthood. Thus, transitivity enjoys a privileged kind of solidity, and should prevail over *Instantiation* (thereby leading us to choose (b)), and over any doubtful interpretation of 5 (thereby leading us to choose (c)).

Of course, a mereological pluralist—as well as a mereological monist according to whom transitivity is not a feature of parthood—will disagree about the solidity of transitivity. But the example shows quite clearly the inferential advantage enjoyed by standard mereological monists over their opponents. When they are confronted with the above argument, the advantage is that mereological monists can toss (a) aside, thus restricting the domain of possible choices.

Option (b) is, in a sense, the most desirable outcome for the backers of mereological monism. If we opt for (b), mereological monism would lead us to refute a philosophical contention, namely a certain analysis of instantiation. Option (b) can be developed in various ways. For example, *Instantiation* could be weakened: parthood could be seen as a necessary but not sufficient condition for instantiation, and only the left-to-right direction of *Instantiation* would hold. This would be enough to block the inference from 4 to 5 in the argument. It is not a small concession though: parthood would cease to provide an adequate characterization of instantiation.

However, it is interesting to consider option (c) as well, in order to show that mereological monism is not *all-powerful.* In many cases, when mereological monism threatens to refute a contention, other surrounding claims can actually be adjusted, in order to avoid the refutation. Mereological monism still has the dialectical power to enforce these adjustments (when they are viable, and the theory at stake is not simply refuted); and these adjustments at times (as in the present case) reveal something about the ties between parthood and other basic philosophical concepts.

The simplest way to adjust 5 and make it palatable (thereby embracing (c) and not having to reject any premise or principle used in the argument) is to admit that, after all, there is a sense in which the pen is red, insofar as it has a red part (namely, the cap).

This adjustment has a cost, because it forces us to repress our propensity to deny 5. This propensity is connected to our propensity to claim that the pen is blue, in the light of a seemingly plausible general principle about pens, according to which pens inherit their color from that of the ink inside them (that ink that is injected onto the paper when the pen is used); and to infer that it is not red from the fact that it is blue, in the light of the principle that nothing can be of two incompatible colors at the same time.

One could even claim that this adjustment amounts to renouncing the mereological characterization of instantiation, and as a result is not much different from (b): (5) is reinterpreted to mean that the pen is in part red, thus what parthood between a property and an individual warrants is that the individual instantiates the property *at least in part*. But the initial purpose of the theory was to characterize instantiation *simpliciter*, and not partial instantiation.

At this stage, the dialectics of the argument could continue in various directions. As far as we are concerned, we have given an example of how mereological monism can act as a refutation tool in a philosophical debate, and in what limited sense this makes mereological monism an epistemically desirable thesis.

## 2.3 Classical Extensional Mereology: From above and from below

Of course, the epistemic desirability of mereological monism does not *imply* that mereological monism is true. In order to evaluate mereological monism, we need to investigate its contents. Since mereological monism is the philosophical thesis according to which CEM is the general exhaustive theory of parthood and some other cognate relations and operations, to investigate the contents of mereological monism (mereology$_{phi}$) is to investigate the contents of CEM (mereology$_{theo}$).

CEM can be presented—and indeed *is* presented in the literature—*from above* or *from below*. A presentation from above typically consists of a compact list of axioms, which can be accepted or rejected as a single package. A presentation from below typically consists of a longer list of axioms of increasing force. It is possible to reject some of the stronger axioms in a presentation from below, while accepting the weaker ones. But in both cases, there are several alternative axiomatizations. In this book CEM is presented from above, with a focus on a single axiomatization. Let us see what the distinction between presentations from above and presentations from below consists in, and why a presentation from above is preferable for our purposes.

In the presentation from above adopted in this book, CEM consists of three simple and inferentially strong principles: Transitivity; Uniqueness of Composition; Unrestricted Composition. The formulations of Uniqueness of Composition and Unrestricted Composition require some care (in particular in order to express the operation of composition, as we will see), and come in several variants. But in general the presentations of CEM from above have an *easily graspable* and *patently controversial* philosophical content.

In other words, the principles of CEM, when it is presented from above, are a *perspicuous* object of philosophical controversy. For analogous reasons, when applied to philosophical theories as in our previous example involving transitivity and instantiation, the principles of CEM in the presentations from above tend to make it quite evident whether the theory at stake is compatible with the contention that CEM is the general exhaustive theory of parthood (that is, with mereological monism), or not.

The main drawback of the presentations from above is that they are not very *modular*: if you doubt one or more of their principles, it is not easy to detach them from the others, because what remains risks being an unstable and not very interesting compound. The presentations from below are preferable *from an analytic viewpoint*: they present CEM as a series of principles of increasing force, and, if you doubt some principles, it is easier to limit your adoption of CEM to a certain point of the series. On the other hand, as we will see in relation to presentations from below in Part Two (in particular in Chapter 9), some of the levels at which you can stop do not offer clear reasons to stop there.

When you do not stop at a certain level (that is, when you do not reject some of the principles), the presentations of CEM from above and from below identify exactly the same class of theorems: if a theory is seen as a class of theorems, CEM is a *single* theory, which can be axiomatized in several ways. Presentations from above and presentations from below, by contrast, play different roles in the dialectics between mereological monism and its opponents.

The task for any champion of mereological monism (and one of my main aims in this book) is to defend CEM in its presentation from above, by arguing in favor of the three perspicuous and strong principles, as well as by explaining away or debunking alleged counterexamples to them. By contrast, the opponents of mereological monism should first of all show that one or more of the three principles are wrong. After that, they can weaken, revise, enrich CEM, or integrate it with other theories of parthood. For the purpose of weakening and revising CEM, a modular version from below could prove to be more convenient.

These different roles correspond to the preferences displayed in the literature. Lewis and other philosophical upholders of mereological monism, such as Goodman,[4] tend to present CEM from above. Scholars that actually wish to criticize its pretension to be a fully adequate and exhaustive theory of parthood— such as Peter Simons—or wish to identify a less controversial core within it tend to present it from below.[5]

This book belongs to the former tradition. Therefore, in presenting and defending mereological monism, and in evaluating its claim of being a powerful philosophical tool (and in particular a refutation tool, as we have seen in Section 2.2), we will adopt a presentation of CEM from above. Thus, we will analyze Transitivity, Uniqueness of Composition, and Unrestricted Composition, and discuss potential counterexamples to them, along with arguments for and against.

# Is Mereology Formal?

## 3.1 Three senses of formality

According to mereological monism, CEM is the single, exhaustive theory of parthood and cognate relations and operations. In CEM, there is substantially only a single relation of parthood.[1] The idea is that one and the same relation of parthood applies across the board, no matter what entities are involved and how they are mutually related. This single relation would be *topic-neutral*: it does not matter to which category parts and wholes belong (i.e., whether they are abstract or concrete entities, universals or particulars, artifacts or living organisms).

*Topic-neutrality* is one of the ways in which the claim that mereology is formal can be understood.[2] When it is understood in such terms, I believe that it is a true claim: mereology is formal. But it is important to make it as clear as possible what this means, and to differentiate it from other ways of construing *formality*, according to which it is false and misleading to claim that mereology is formal.

The debate about the concept of *formality* is very complex, in particular in the philosophy of logic, and this is not the place to retrace it.[3] It is enough to say that logic is often said to be formal, and a kind of *ontology* (namely formal ontology) is often compared to the formality of logic. The label *formal ontology* comes from Husserl, who in his *Logical Investigations* also set forth a philosophical theory of parthood, and classified the theory of parthood as an instance of formal ontology. More recently, the concept of formal ontology has been taken up again and used to refer to those parts of philosophical ontology that do not concern specific categories (properties, sets, numbers, artifacts, etc.) but can be applied across the board. In this characterization of formal ontology, the investigation of parthood and other mereological relations is often understood to belong to formal ontology. Another candidate subject matter for formal ontology is identity, but it is a controversial candidate, because identity is often thought to be a *logical* notion. Other frequent examples are ontological dependence (that is, the modal or explanatory connection between the existence of a certain entity and the existence of another one), and—more recently—grounding (the kind of metaphysical explanation that would be expressed by philosophical locutions such as *in virtue of*).

The comparison with logic is often thought to be clarifying. According to Barry Smith, for example, formal ontology would be for the world what formal logic is for theories about the world.[4] However, the comparison with logic leaves the concept of formality largely underdetermined, and only some ways of construing it make sense for mereology.

Let us distinguish three senses of formality. Formality in the first sense consists in a kind of indifference to the semantic interpretation of the vocabulary. Formality in the second sense consists in topic-neutrality. Formality in the third sense consists in restraining from determining the extension of a certain relation, that is, what is actually connected by that relation. My thesis is that mereology$_{theo}$ enjoys primarily formality in the second sense at a high degree, and also enjoys formality in the third sense.

By contrast, it does not enjoy formality in the first sense. Formality, when it is understood in this first sense, concerns primarily *inferences* in a certain field: if the validity of inferences in a certain field can be assessed without considering a certain interpretation of the vocabulary, then that field can be said to be formal in this sense. The idea is that it does not matter how the involved sentences (and their subsentential constituents) are interpreted (this would correspond to the content of the sentences involved): what matters is only the form of the sentences involved.

For example, in propositional logic, the inference from a conjunction to one of its conjuncts is valid quite independently of the semantic interpretation of the nonlogical vocabulary. From "Pegasus is a bear and Trump is a hero" it follows that "Trump is a hero," as much as from "Oedipus is the son of Jocasta and Jocasta is the lover of Oedipus" it follows that "Jocasta is the lover of Oedipus." It does not matter how the conjuncts and the terms within them are interpreted (nor does it matter if they are true or false).

Analogously, in the theory of identity, from "Cicero is Tully" and "Tully is the greatest Roman orator," it follows that "Cicero is the greatest Roman orator," as much as from "Pisa is Berlin" and "Berlin is the smallest village in Iceland" it follows that "Pisa is the smallest village in Iceland." It does not matter how the terms are interpreted (nor does it matter if the sentences are true or false). The theory of identity—according to which identity is transitive—justifies the inferences, quite independently of any interpretation.

In this sense, mereology *is not* formal. The predicate for parthood (as well as the other predicates defined on the basis of it, and which will be introduced later on) is interpreted in a certain way. This is connected to our remark in Chapter 1, Section 1.5 that the *formal features* that mereological monism attributes to parthood are not sufficient conditions for a parthood relation: there are some intuitive constraints about the domain of eligible relations. While these constraints—as we have seen—are never the subject of interesting controversies, they prevent mereology from being formal in this first sense.

An additional and connected reason why mereology does not enjoy this kind of formality is that this kind of formality *cannot be instantiated in degrees*. Either the validity of some inferences depends purely on the form of the premises, or not; either it matters how the sentences and the terms in them are interpreted, or not. By contrast, the kind of formality to which mereology can aspire *comes in degrees*. Its topic-neutrality is not bound to be *absolute*. Perhaps the principles of CEM characterize exhaustively parthood and other cognate entities for *all artifacts*, but not for living organisms, perhaps for all concrete entities, but not for abstract entities. In Parts Two and Three of this book we suggest that this latter restriction (i.e., the exclusion of abstract entities) is actually plausible, or at least that abstract entities are a much more difficult domain of application for mereological monism than concrete ones.

This restriction does not nullify the formality of mereological monism: it is still a highly general metaphysical doctrine. It is still *largely topic-neutral*: the domain of concrete things is highly heterogeneous. Still, it is not possible to make sense of this kind of formality, if formality is understood in this first sense.

The second way of construing formality takes it merely as a *kind of generality*. In this sense, topic-neutrality does not consist in the fact that the semantic interpretation of predicates, constants, or sentences does not matter; rather, it simply consists in the high level of generality of the principles of mereology: these principles are simply *true* of a lot of things. We can include lots of heterogeneous, disparate things in the domain of their quantifiers. It is precisely in this sense that mereology *can* be said to be formal: it is expected to be *general* and *topic-neutral* at a very high degree.[5]

Finally, there is a third kind of formality, and in this sense too mereology is formal. This sense does not concern only mereology$_{phi}$, but also philosophical mereology (mereology$_{dis}$) in general. It is a sense of formality that can be accepted also by mereological pluralists, in spite of the fact that, according to them, it is false that there is a single, *highly general* theory of parthood and cognate relations and operations. For a mereological pluralist, mereology$_{theo}$ *is not* highly general and topic-neutral; by contrast, according to mereological monism, it is. But still, there is a sense in which mereology$_{dis}$ is formal, quite independently of any disagreement about mereological principles and their generality. Philosophical mereology should not be expected to determine what is part of what: what parts a car, or a person, or a water molecule have. Philosophical mereology does not aim to define the *extension* of the parthood predicate. It concerns only questions such as: is parthood transitive or not? Given some things, is there a single thing composed by them?

When confronted with these questions, mereological monists and mereological pluralists will give different answers, and will disagree on the degree of generality to be expected from the answers. Nonetheless, they will agree that philosophy is not about establishing if specific instances of parthood hold or not. In this sense, mereology$_{dis}$ does not concern the content (the extension) of the parthood relation, but the way in which parthood works.

Thus, we have distinguished three senses of formality. In a *first sense*, formality is a feature of some inferences, whose validity can be established quite independently of the semantic interpretation of the premises. In this first sense, mereology is not formal. In a *second sense*, formality is a feature of theories, and simply consists in generality: in holding true of a lot of disparate things. In this second sense, according to mereological monism (the philosophical thesis that this book aims to present and defend), mereology has a high degree of formality. In a *third sense*, formality is still a feature of theories, and consists in their abstaining from the pretension to determine what falls within the extension i.e., the content of some predicates and what does not. In this third sense, virtually every scholar of philosophical mereology agrees that philosophical mereology is formal.

## 3.2 How to show that mereology is formal

Let us focus on the second sense of formality, according to which formality is generality, and comes in degree. Mereological monism claims that CEM is a highly formal theory. But how is it possible to *argue* in favor of this claim? What kinds of reasons can be adduced in support of this claim? Mainly reasons of two kinds.

First, *positive arguments* in support of the principles of CEM. In most cases, these arguments are not purely deductive: they can be characterized as *inferences to the best explanation*. As is commonly the case with inferences to the best explanation, the premises of these arguments (the *explananda*) should be shown to be real evidence, worth of an explanation. Besides, it must be shown that the principle or principles of mereology at stake are really the best *explanans* at our disposal. They should be compared with other explanations, and shown to be preferable, for example, because they are simpler or because they are supported by some independent evidence. Inferences to the best explanation are known to be *fallible* inferences, and to raise lots of difficult methodological problems.

As in these other disciplines, deduction too may play a role within the inferences to the best explanations: in order to find their best explanation, it is important to scrutinize what the premises entail; and in order to establish if a certain explanation is the best (for example, because it is simpler), it is pivotal to know what it entails. In the case of mereology for example, mereology$_{\text{theo}}$ is not confined to its axioms, but extends to whatever is derivable within it, and any theorem of CEM has a role in the inferences to the best explanation in support of CEM.

In other cases, *alleged counterexamples* to the principles of CEM are shown to be *ineffective*. In pursuing this latter defensive strategy, it is important to *weigh* potential counterexamples, consistently with the methodology set forth in Chapter 1. Some potential counterexamples concern paradigmatic, literal, space involving cases that mereology aims to systematize and project, in order to obtain a reliable guideline for identifying other genuine instances of parthood. When potential counterexamples concern these cases, the only option for mereological monists is to show that they are not real counterexamples: either they are actually compatible with CEM or they do not obtain.

By contrast, when mereological principles are *projected* onto non-prototypical relations, the mereological monist can either show that they are not real counterexamples or claim that they are not real cases of parthood. In the second case, the mereological monist is actually applying her methodology: she is using CEM's principles to distinguish parthood from non-parthood; and in particular, she is establishing that a certain relation *is not* an instance of parthood, *just because* it fails to obey CEM's principles.

The first kind of strategy (the one that involves arguments in support of the CEM principles) is *positive*: if successful, it shows (albeit in the fallible way that is typical of inferences to the best explanation) that the principles of mereology are preferable to other competing principles about parthood and other cognate relations. By contrast, the second kind of strategy is *defensive*: it shows that it is possible to resist the attempts made by the adversaries of mereological monism to refute it (and in particular to refute the claim that CEM is formal or general).

We have seen in the previous section that formality, in the sense at stake (that is, if it is simply equated to generality), can come in degrees. This means that, in some cases, the mereological monist can also *surrender*; she can concede that some counterexamples are indeed counterexamples, and genuine instances of parthood. In these cases, the degree of generality of mereological monism decreases: the entities at stake in the counterexample are conceded to be an exception to mereological monism. Still, if these counterexamples concern only some well-delimited categories of entities, mereological monism can continue to enjoy a relatively high degree of formality or generality.

## 3.3 Formality, existence, identity

It is important to remark that the kind of formality or generality which—according to mereological monism—parthood enjoys makes it akin to existence and identity. Also in the case of existence and identity there is a sort of standard philosophical stance—sometimes dubbed *Quinean orthodoxy*, insofar as Quine was its most ardent proponent—according to which existence and identity are univocal, in the sense that there is only one way to exist that applies to any kind of entity.

Thus, Quinean orthodoxy also counts as a kind of *monism* about existence and identity. Actually, later we will see that mereology has a close link to existence and identity; and that probably the most substantial (and contentious) philosophical content of mereological monism consists in the identity and existence conditions it attributes to complex entities; and that these conditions are as formal—that is, as highly general—as mereology's characterization of parthood. Thus, mereology is a formal theory that is largely about identity and existence.

What about the arguments in favor of these various kinds of monism? The arguments usually provided in favor of Quinean orthodoxy by philosophers such as Peter Van Inwagen[6] concern, for example, the possibility of explaining any apparent difference between various ways of existing and being identical as differences between the heterogeneous things that exist and are involved in identity relations. These arguments may also point to the links between existence and identity and numerical predications, and exploit the apparent univocity of numerical predications as an argument in favor of the univocity of existence and identity.

These arguments cannot be directly exported to mereological monism, and prima facie look very different from the kinds of arguments for mereological monism outlined in the previous section (inferences to the best explanation, strategies to show that the alleged counterexamples are not such). Nonetheless, the typical arguments in favor of Quinean orthodoxy about existence and identity play a role in the defense of mereological monism: namely, when the mereological pluralist claims that there are various relations of parthood, her monist opponent tends to reply that what vary are the natures of wholes and parts, and that parthood—inasmuch as it is highly formal or general—is expected to apply uniformly to heterogeneous entities of several categories: there is no need to make *parthood itself* non-univocal (just as there is no need to make *existence* or *identity* non-univocal).

Throughout the entire book, we will be discussing other deep and articulate links between mereology, existence, and identity.

# Transitivity and Other Features

## 4.1 Is parthood transitive? Yes

It is time to begin applying the methodology we outlined in Chapters 1–3 to the analysis and defense of mereological monism: identify some formal features of parthood and composition on the basis of a selection and systematization of their prototypical instances; use the resulting characterization as a guideline for identifying other literal instances of parthood; dispose of seeming counterexamples to the resulting principles, and discuss a priori arguments in favor of (or against) these principles.

As already noted in the Introduction, CEM consists of three principles (*Transitivity, Uniqueness of Composition,* and *Unrestricted Composition*) and of their logical consequences. Uniqueness of Composition and Unrestricted Composition are the philosophical, controversial core of mereological monism, and we will devote Parts Two and Three to them, respectively. Only in that context all the various aspects of the methodology we outlined will be instantiated.

However, it is advisable to begin our analysis and defense of mereology$_{\text{phi}}$ from the simplest principle: Transitivity. Moreover, in this chapter, we will also discuss the claims made by CEM that parthood is *reflexive* and *antisymmetric*. While these latter claims do not figure as axioms in the presentation of CEM from above, they are nonetheless CEM theorems. Thus, mereological monism is committed to them.

We have already employed and partially discussed Transitivity, that is, the principle that if a thing $x$ is part of a thing $y$ that is part of a thing $z$, then $x$ is part of $z$ as well. In the language of first-order logic, Transitivity is expressed as follows ($P$ is the predicate of parthood):

$$\forall x \forall y \forall z (xPy \land yPz \to xPz) \qquad \text{(Transitivity)}$$

We have seen in Chapter 1 that, when we analyzed occurrences of terms like "part" in English, Transitivity tends to hold when these terms are understood in a nonselective way, while Transitivity tends to fail for selective parthood, which *is not* the subject matter of mereology$_{dis}$.

The counterexamples to Transitivity in the literature also seems to actually concern selective parthood. In some examples, it seems that going nonselective helps. For example, according to Nicholas Rescher,[1] the way in which biologists use the notion of part does not conform to CEM, and in particular does not respect Transitivity. A biologist will consider a mitochondrion to be *a* part of a cell, and the cell *a* part of a tissue, but would deny that the mitochondrion is *a* part of the tissue. In these cases, it seems clear that the biologist has no doubt that the mitochondrion is in the tissue *in a spatial sense*. Due to some features of English which we do not need to speculate about here, the indeterminate article (e.g., "a") tends to elicit a selective reading of "part." If we remove the indeterminate article, the answer of the biologist could change, and obey Transitivity: the mitochondrion is part of the tissue, just because it is in it in a spatial sense.

The spatial sense of parthood (assumed as prototypical) makes Transitivity quite a solid principle. If something is in something that is in turn in something else (where this *being in* is spatial), then it seems quite uncontroversial that the first thing is in the third. As Varzi has argued,[2] the selective varieties of parthood can be seen as *specializations* of general, nonselective parthood. Given parthood, there will be various specialized φ-parthoods, where "φ" is a predicate that restricts the domains of parts (e.g., "direct," "distinguished," "functional").

From the extensional viewpoint, these relations will be *restrictions* of parthood *tout court*. The extension of parthood (which is a binary relation) is a set of ordered couples, such that their first member is part of the second member. But only some of these ordered couples are such that their first member is a *functional* part of the second, or such that their first member is a *direct* part of the second.

The extensions of these specialized relations will be subclasses of the extension of parthood *tout court*: whatever is in the relation of functional, distinguished, direct parthood is also in the relation of parthood *tout court*, but not vice versa. We can say that specialized parthoods are *subrelations* of parthood *tout court*. And there is nothing surprising in the fact that a subrelation of a relation differs from the relation in terms of its formal features, as a very simple abstract reasoning reveals.

Suppose that in its extension a relation *R de facto* includes three couple of objects <*a, b*>, <*b, c*>, and <*a, c*>. Patently these three couples are not counterexamples to Transitivity. Within this extension, it holds that:

$$\forall x \forall y \forall z (x R y \land y R z \to x R z)$$

But now consider *S*, a subrelation of *R*, such that it includes in its extension <*a, b*> and <*b, c*>, but not <*a, c*>. *S* is not transitive. It does not hold that:

$$\forall x \forall y \forall z (x S y \land y S z \to x S z)$$

Rescher's biological examples seem to follow this pattern: nonselective parthood would include the ordered couple <*mitochondrion, tissue*>, and would therefore be a confirmation of Transitivity—not a counterexample to it. The kind of selective parthood elicited by the indeterminate article "a" would exclude the ordered couple <*mitochondrion, tissue*>.

However, in other cases, things are more complicated, and focusing on selectivity risks being insufficient. Let us go back to our example of Kemalists in Chapter 1. The left arm of a Kemalist MP is part of her; the Kemalist MP is part of the parliament. But it seems *definitely wrong* to claim that the arm is part of the parliament. Selectivity should not be blamed for the failure of Transitivity in this case. Sure, the arm is not a selected, *privileged* part of the parliament, for example, because it is not allowed to vote independently. However, nothing changes if we discard these restrictions, and turn to nonselective, pure parthood, as Varzi's methodology suggests. No matter how *pure* parthood becomes, the arm is not part of the parliament.

But is this an instance of parthood at all? The fact that in English it is appropriate to say that an MP is part of the parliament does not *prove* that this is an instance of parthood. We could also say that a member of parliament is (unsurprisingly) *member* of the parliament, and membership is not a mereological notion (it is usually seen as a set-theoretic notion).

We can leave natural language aside and use our methodology. This does not seem to be a *prototypical* case of spatial parthood. By "parliament"—in this context—we do not mean the building where the MPs meet and deliberate, but an institution. While we are not going to delve into the difficult problems of what an institution is, it is perhaps safe to exclude that it has a spatial location, of which the spatial location of our MP is part.

Thus, in the case of the relation between the Kemalist and the parliament, we are outside the domain of prototypical, spatial cases of parthood. By contrast, the relation between the arm and the Kemalist seems spatial and quite standard.

Moreover, it seems that the relation between the Kemalist and the parliament can also be characterized as a set-theoretic notion.

In cases where Transitivity seems to fail, we can *deny* that at least one of the relations involved is parthood. The candidate to be ousted from the domain of mereology is the relation between the Kemalist and the parliament it is a member of. Yes: the Kemalist MP is a member of the parliament, and when we say that someone is part of the parliament, we are not saying anything different from when we say that she is a member of the parliament. Membership is a different kind of relation, and it is not expected to concatenate with the standard, spatial parthood relation between the right arm of the MP and its owner. Thus, there is not a single relation at play, for which we have identified a failure of Transitivity.

## 4.2 Monism, pluralism, and *Ad Hocness*

Someone unpersuaded by the methodology sketched out in the previous chapters could ask: is this move not patently *ad hoc*? It might seem that we have simply got rid of a counterexample by excluding it from the investigation domain. Given an alleged case of a relation $X$ which works differently from our theory of the relation $X$, the mereological monist reacts by claiming that this is not actually a case of the relation $X$. This move—the objector could argue—is *always* possible, and too easy: the mereological monist is restricting the investigation domain to those cases which respect the principles of CEM.

There is certainly a real risk of *ad hoc* moves in these dialectical situations. However, *ad hocness* consists in making an assumption for the sole purpose of obtaining the result one is aiming for. If we have *additional* reasons to make that assumption, then the charge of *ad hocness* is ungrounded.

Indeed, in the specific case under discussion, we have at least one additional reason to argue that the relation between an MP and its parliament is not parthood, but set-theoretical membership. And the reason is that membership (the well-known fundamental relation of set theory) seems to work exactly as the relation between an MP and its parliament. Set-theoretic membership is not transitive (given three sets such that the first is member of the second and the second is member of the third, it does not follow that the first is member of the third).

In general, the charge of *ad hocness* should be taken seriously. The mereological monist is not allowed to expel from the domain of CEM whatever violates its principles. This behavior would be admissible if CEM were considered with an instrumental attitude, as a theory that works *where it works*: a technical framework that can be applied locally, and could be replaced by other frameworks where the relation at stake does not work in that way. But CEM is for the mereological monist (such as me) a true theory about reality as a whole, or at least about a large section of reality (given that formality/generality can come in degrees).

Thus, in order to avoid the charge of *ad hocness*, we need a good enough reason to deny that the same relation connects the arm and the MP in one case, and the MP and the parliament in the other. The legitimacy of rejecting the counterexample to Transitivity rests on the fact that the relation between the MP and the parliament works in another way on its own.

Consider the IPU (Inter-Parliamentary Union): it is a worldwide association of parliaments. Its members are parliaments, including the Turkish parliament of which our Kemalist is a member. Thus, the Kemalist is a member of the Turkish parliament, and the Turkish parliament is a member of the IPU. But the IPU is an association of parliaments only: no person (and thus no MP) can become a member of the IPU. Hence, the kind of membership in question is indeed found to bear a certain resemblance with set-theoretic membership: like the latter, it is a non-transitive relation. In any other similar case, it is upon the mereological monist to show that there are independent reasons to think that a certain relation is not parthood, thereby avoiding the charge of *ad hocness*.

At this point, it is interesting to see how a mereological pluralist could react. In his 2010 paper *Towards a Theory of Part*, Kit Fine presents a very refined form of mereological pluralism. According to him, there are many different relations of parthood, which works in different ways.

Fine presents a very general characterization of parthood, according to which $x$ is part of $y$ if and only if $x$ is in $y$, and the replacement of $x$ with another entity $z$ in $y$ changes what $y$ is or how $y$ is.[3] The notion of being *in* is left intuitive, and is not further analyzed: Fine's idea is that any intuitive judgment that something is in something else should be accepted as evidence, irrespective of its formal behavior.

In the specific case of the Kemalist, Fine would probably insist that the MP patently *is* in the parliament, and that, if the MP were replaced (by another MP), then obviously how the parliament is would change. Analogously, the parliament is in the IPU, and if Turkey were to become a non-parliamentary monarchy, how the IPU is would change. There are two instances of parthood, then, and Transitivity fails. The resulting evidence that the relation in question is non-transitive should lead us to study a non-transitive relation of parthood, and to place it and the transitive relation of parthood studied by CEM side by side within a pluralist mereological framework.

By comparison, we can get an idea of how Lewis's methodology differs: monism settles on a specific characterization of parthood, and offers a guideline for discriminating cases of parthood from other cases. Fine's pluralism accepts any apparent case of parthood as it is: any possible deviance of its behavior is not evidence that the relation is not really parthood; it is evidence that we should enrich our theory of parthood, in order to make room for that variety of parthood as well.

## 4.3 Reflexivity

Among the formal features of parthood, only Transitivity is dictated by a specific axiom in CEM, when CEM is presented from above. But in CEM it is possible to prove that parthood is reflexive and antisymmetric. Thus, the following are theorems of CEM (in the case of Antisymmetry, the language of first-order logic needs to be integrated with the identity predicate):

$$\forall x\, (xPx) \hspace{6cm} \text{(Reflexivity)}$$

$$\forall x \forall y\, (xPy \wedge yPx \rightarrow x = y) \hspace{3cm} \text{(Antisymmetry)}$$

We have claimed that the presentation from above has the virtue of focusing on philosophically perspicuous, substantial principles. And we have seen that Transitivity is precisely such a principle, and provides a sample of the kind of methodology at play in mereological monism. By contrast, *Reflexivity* and (with some important *provisos*) *Antisymmetry* are not sensible topics for a philosophical debate.

Before explaining why this is the case, let us also introduce the relation of *proper parthood*. Something is a proper part of something else if and only if it is a part of it, but is not identical to it. In the following definition *PP* is the predicate for proper parthood:[4]

$$\forall x \forall y\, (xPPy \equiv_{def} xPy \wedge x \neq y) \hspace{2cm} \text{(Proper Parthood–Definition)}$$

Proper parthood is a defined relation. Any occurrence of the predicate "PP" could be eliminated through its definition.

Let us see why it is not very interesting to ask if the relation of parthood is reflexive, that is, if it is such that everything is part of itself. The fact is that CEM actually distinguishes two relations, *P* and *PP*, one easily definable in terms of the other. And one of them is reflexive, while the other is not. The motivations for thinking that parthood is reflexive and those for thinking that is it not reflexive are well served by focusing on one or on the other of the two relations.

The difference between these two relations concerns their extension. The extension of *P* includes any couple whose members are numerically identical. <*Giorgio Lando, Giorgio Lando*>, <*Benny Hill, Benny Hill*>, <*Elizabeth Taylor, Elizabeth Taylor*>, and all other analogously boring couples are among the couples in the extension of parthood. *Identity* is a relation too: its extension includes all and only those couples whose first member is identical to the second. Thus, we could say that the extension of identity is a subclass of the extension of parthood.

By contrast, the extension of *PP* does not include any couple of identical members. The extension of proper parthood has no member in common with the extension of identity. Indeed, quite the opposite holds: proper parthood does not include any couple of identical members.

We have seen above that *PP* can be easily defined in terms of *P simpliciter*. On the other hand, if *PP* were taken as a primitive instead of *P*, then parthood simpliciter could be defined with equal ease:

$$\forall x \forall y (x P y \equiv_{def} x P P y \lor x = y)$$

Thus, the reflexivity of the fundamental relation of mereology simply depends on the choice of *P* or of *PP* as the fundamental relation. Reflexive relations (in general) are those whose extension includes the extension of the identity relation: *P* includes it, as its above definition in terms of *PP* makes clear; *PP* does not include it, as its above definition in terms of *P* makes clear. The definition of *PP* makes it clear that its extension has actually no member in common with the extension of identity, and such relations are called *antireflexive*.

Once either *P* or *PP* is taken as primitive, the other is defined. We could even take both *P* and *PP* as primitives, with a negligible loss of economy. In our own exposition of CEM we would actually use both relations without quibbling about which is more fundamental.

Disputes about what is more *fundamental* are common, and often very interesting in philosophy. According to some philosophers, disputes of this kind are even the privileged subject matter of metaphysics, or perhaps of philosophy in general.[5] But in this case it really seems that nothing profound is at stake. *Proper parthood* is obviously called what it is for a reason. There is a (proper, narrow) sense in which being a part of *x* is incompatible with being *the whole x*. As we have already noted in Chapter 1, if we desire a piece of the cake and we are given the entire cake, our desire can be considered to have been satisfied, but in an extreme, liminal, and *improper* way.

On the one hand, we will see that *PP* figures prominently in CEM (in particular, in the characterization of Extensionalism, an important principle deeply connected to the principle of Uniqueness of Composition—it will be investigated in Part Two), and this could suggest one possible reason to deem it to be more fundamental than *P*. In Extensionalism (as everywhere else) it is obviously possible to replace any occurrence of *PP* with occurrences of *P* through the above definition, but this would increase the complexity of the formula.

On the other hand, one could argue that there is something *less natural* in *PP* than in *P*. What is arguably less natural is precisely the fact of excluding the extension of identity from that of parthood. Consider the case of the cake again, and of one of its crumbs. Imagine a series of increasingly large crumbs; in this series we go through crumbs of increasing size. At a certain point, the pieces are big enough that it would be awkward to call them "crumbs": they are respectable pieces of cake. After that, the pieces of the cake begin to be really big; at a certain point, you obtain a piece of the cake that consists of the whole cake minus a crumb. We continue with our series, and at a certain point we find a piece of the cake that consists of the whole cake minus one glucose molecule. This is definitely a big piece of cake, but it is still both a part and a proper part of the cake. Up to this point, *all* the parts of the cake are both parts *simpliciter* and proper parts of the cake.

Then, not much later in the series, the piece of the cake ends up being the cake itself. You can go further in the series, and involve for example the whole cake plus the piece of paper in which the cake is wrapped (or plus a single molecule of this piece of paper). These further objects (you might wonder if they actually exist, but let us provisionally assume that they do) are obviously not parts of the cake; but still they are in a parthood relation with the cake, namely in an inverted relation. The cake is part of the *cake plus the paper,* and of the *cake plus the molecule of paper*.

Now, we have a series of entities of increasing size each of which (except the cake itself) is involved both in a proper parthood relation and in a parthood relation *simpliciter* with the cake. The cake itself is a part *simpliciter*—and not a proper part—of itself. Is it wise to consider as more fundamental the relation that *excludes* this case, thereby making a seemingly continuous series discontinuous?

Perhaps not. Obviously, the cake is a special, peculiar part of itself, and it is also special among the entities of which the cake itself is a part. But this peculiarity is already expressed by the fact that only the cake, and nothing else in the series, is identical to the cake. This does not make the cake—so to say—mereologically heterogeneous with respect to the other entities in the series. Privileging *PP* over *P* risks cutting the series of parts off at an unnatural joint.

Thus, there are reasons to prefer *P* over *PP*, but also reasons to prefer *PP* over *P* as the fundamental relation in CEM, and no clear winner emerges. We will use both notions in our presentation of CEM, and underline the cases in which the distinction has some bearing. As a result, we will have both a reflexive relation and an antireflexive one at our disposal.

## 4.4 Antisymmetry

The case of Antisymmetry is analogous, but requires some additional care. According to CEM, *P* is an antisymmetric relation. The only case in which there is an *x* and there is a *y* such that *x* is part of *y* and *y* is part of *x* is the case in which *x* and *y* are one and the same thing.

*PP* is not merely antisymmetric, but asymmetric:[6] this means that, according to CEM, there are never an *x* and a *y* such that one is proper part of the other.

$$\forall x \forall y (xPPy \rightarrow \neg yPPx) \qquad \text{(Asymmetry of Proper Parthood)}$$

The Antisymmetry of *P* and the Asymmetry of *PP* are strictly connected. The only case in which *x* and *y* are admitted as mutual parts is the case in which they are the same thing. But if *x* is a *proper part* of *y*, then *x* is not identical to *y*, and mutual proper parthood is ruled out. Thus, insofar as there is no substantial reason to prefer *P* or *PP* as the fundamental relation of mereology or vice versa, there is also no reason to discuss if the fundamental relation of mereology is merely antisymmetric or asymmetric.

From one perspective, however, the case of Antisymmetry is trickier than that of Reflexivity, and in recent years many opponents of Lewis's mereological monism have come to elaborate interesting debates on this. The point is that you could suspect that the fundamental relation of mereology is neither antisymmetric nor asymmetric, and that there are genuine cases of different things that are one part of the other. In the so-called theory of constitution, there would be cases—we will discuss them in Chapter 9—in which two numerically different things are mutual parts.

Thus, how does mereological monism treat these cases and how can it defend the claims that *P* is antisymmetric and *PP* is asymmetric? Let us focus on the realm of prototypical parthood, in which the mereological harmony sketched out in Chapter 1, Section 1.2 holds. In these cases, the reasons to think that there cannot be two different things one of which is part of the other could seem rather clear. Suppose that $x$ is part (part *simpliciter*, the relation expressed by $P$) of $y$ and that $y$ is part of $x$. Then, by mereological harmony, *region(x)* is part of *region(y)*; and *region(y)* is part of *region(x)*.

Now, I am being completely naive about spatial regions and the kind of parthood in which they are involved. I am not committed to any kind of realism about regions of space, or to any claim about the relation of parthood and containment between them. There is a huge variety of philosophical positions about space, which would deserve a book to themselves.[7] My purpose is not to clarify the links between mereology and spatial location, but to illustrate the role of spatial parthood as prototypical literal parthood in the methodology of mereological monism.

At this naive level, *region(x)* and *region(y)*—mutually one in the other—cannot but be a single region of space. At this point, the denier of the Antisymmetry of $P$ is asking us to believe that there are two different things, part of one another, that occupy the same region of space. Well, this is exactly what some deniers of Antisymmetry are willing to do, and it is perhaps even one of the main reasons why they are skeptical about Antisymmetry.

Consider a wood table and the portion of wood of which it is made. And suppose that these are two different entities (we will see in Chapter 7 that there are—highly controversial—reasons to think that they indeed are). Then it is very plausible to think that, at any time in which the table exists, they occupy the same region of space, and that this holds in general for every object and the portion of matter of which it is made.

The principle according to which it is not possible for two distinct individuals to occupy one and the same region of space at the same time is usually called Locke's thesis.[8] This principle is denied by the person who thinks that the table and the piece of wood are different and colocated.

Once this person denies Locke's thesis, she might wonder if there is a mereological relation between the table and the piece of wood; and if she answers this question affirmatively, then she might wish to maintain that they are part of one another and yet different.[9] This would mean that they are actually parts of one another, and violate the Antisymmetry of $P$.

When confronted with this line of opposition to the Antisymmetry of $P$, the mereological monist replies that this is a long and complex reasoning, and that, along it, in order to avoid a certain impression of *arbitrariness* and *shallowness*, some kind of methodology is needed. There are at least three promising ways to avoid this outcome, and preserve the Antisymmetry of $P$ and the Asymmetry of $PP$.

*First*, as we will see in our discussion of Extensionalism in Part Two, it is far from clear whether the table and the piece of wood are different.

*Second*, even if it is conceded that they are different, it is not clear why they should be in a mereological relation at all. The very circumstance that they (allegedly) occupy the same region of space, are distinct, but are not in one another could suggest that the table and the piece of wood *belong to different kinds*, and that in general pieces of material (such as the piece of wood) and artifacts (such as the table) belong to different kinds. Once their spatiotemporal coincidence is not taken as decisive evidence that they are identical, it is not clear either whether it serves as evidence that there is a mereological relation between them.

*Third*, even once it is conceded that there is a mereological relation between them, it is not clear why this mereological relation should be mutual parthood. The reason to distinguish between the table and the piece of wood (and to avoid taking the first way out) is presumably that the table is a *richer* entity, one that instantiates some further properties (for example, some stylistic features—it is in the Art Nouveau style) that the piece of wood lacks. Why should we attribute a *reciprocal* relation to them? We could claim instead that the piece of wood is a proper part of the table, but that the table is not a proper part of the wood.[10]

It is not clear which one of these three ways out the mereological monist should choose (we are going to deepen the analysis of them in our discussion of Extensionalism in Chapter 9). The mereological monist thinks that the Antisymmetry of $P$ and the Asymmetry of $PP$ are constitutive features of parthood in its most standard and less controversial cases. Given this datum, the mereological monist *projects* these features onto the less standard and more controversial cases, such as the relation between artifacts and portions of matter.

This projection offers some guidance. In the specific case under consideration, the projection *precludes* any possible outcome of the philosophical debate about material constitution that violates the Antisymmetry of $P$ (or, equivalently, the Asymmetry of $PP$). Once this outcome is precluded, the three ways out just described remain open. All of them are compatible with mereological monism, and it is good for mereological monism to have several sensible options to choose from.

Since there are many ways of avoiding the violation of Antisymmetry, these alternatives should be preferred. To renounce the Antisymmetry of $P$ or the

Asymmetry of *PP* is a sort of *extrema ratio* that should only be considered if all the other options have been ruled out (but they have not).

Thus, it is pivotal for mereological monism that the Antisymmetry of *P* and the Asymmetry of *PP* are solid principles that stem from the analysis of less controversial cases of parthood. This justifies their projection onto more controversial claims.

Something more can be said about why these are solid principles when less controversial cases are involved. The idea is that parthood, except for the limiting case of improper parthood (i.e., identity), is a relation in which the whole (the second term of the relation) has something more than the part, and the part has nothing more than the whole: nothing in the part lies outside the whole. The piece of the cake cannot include anything that is not in the cake, while the cake *has* to include something that is not in the piece (except in the improper case in which the piece at stake is the cake itself). This idea is more clearly expressed in two principles of mereology (two theorems, when CEM is presented from above), namely *Weak Supplementation* and *Strong Supplementation*. We will be formulating and analyzing these principles in Chapter 9.

Given this idea, the notion of mutual parthood without identity does not make sense. It is impossible for two *different* things *t* and *u* to be such that *u* includes everything that *t* includes, plus something more; and *t* includes everything that *u* includes, plus something more.

It is interesting to note that Kit Fine, perhaps the steadiest opponent of mereological monism in contemporary philosophy, while distinguishing several relations of part, takes Antisymmetry (and the ensuing lack of parthood loops) as a general test for his overall theory of parthood. Fine admits several, formally distinct parthood relations (the one characterized by CEM being only one of them). Given these specific parthood relations, it is possible to define a *general* relation of parthood, which holds between two things if and only if there is a chain of specific parthood relations that goes from one to the other. In order to check the coherence of the resulting overall theory, Fine takes the Antisymmetry of the relation of general parthood as a test.

Fine argues for the Antisymmetry of general parthood in the following way:

> It seems clear [...] that the general relation should be anti-symmetric [...]. For suppose that *x* is a proper part of *y*. There would then appear to be a broad sense of "more" in which it is correct to say that there is more to *y* than *x*. Suppose now that $x_1$ is a proper part of $x_2$ in some specific way, $x_2$ a proper part of $x_3$ in some specific way,..., and $x_{n-1}$ a proper part of $x_n$ in some specific way. There should then be more to $x_2$ than $x_1$, more to $x_3$ than $x_2$,..., and more to $x_n$ than

$x_{n-1}$ and hence more to $x_n$ than $x_1$. Hence $x_1$ and $x_n$ in such a sequence cannot be the same—which is just what is required for the general relation to be anti-symmetric. (Fine 2010, pp. 580–581)

Thus, even a pluralist is in a sense forced to invoke a basic intuition of what parthood is, presumably elaborated from basic cases of parthood. However, mereological monism makes much more of Antisymmetry, and of its status as a constitutive feature of the basic, prototypical instances of parthood. In the above sketch of a typical debate on the relation between an artifact and the piece of matter of which it is made, mereological monism places a constraint on the possible outcomes of the debate: the hypothesis of distinguishing two different things that are mutually part of the other is foreclosed.

As in the case of Transitivity, the method of selecting and systematizing prototypical cases of parthood offers some guidance in dubious cases of parthood. Even the most generous mereological pluralist (such as Fine) seems to need some guidance of this kind. But Fine seems to prefer *minimal* guidance, a sort of core that leaves open a wide space for maneuver: for him, Antisymmetry is the only requisite for a coherent general and pluralistic theory of parthood. By contrast, mereological monism uses Antisymmetry (as much as Transitivity, and other features of parthood and other cognate relations and operations we will be considering) as a powerful tool to discriminate genuine parthood, and refute philosophical theories.

## 4.5 Overlap, Fusion

In CEM, it is useful to introduce by definition other relations, and in particular *Overlap* and *Fusion*. Since they are introduced by definition, the symbols for Overlap and Fusion could always be eliminated from every formula in which they occur, in favor of the more fundamental symbols that are in their *definientia* (such as $P$ and $PP$). However, the definitions (in particular in the case of Fusion) are not mere stipulative, notational shortcuts, but aim to capture intuitive, pre-theoretical notions. The acceptability of the definitions is *constrained* by some pre-theoretical expectations.

Overlap and Fusion will be very important in the discussion of Uniqueness of Composition in Part Two and of Unrestricted Composition in Part Three. These two principles are actually *about* Fusion, and Fusion will be defined in terms of Overlap. Here, it is useful to anticipate the definition of Overlap and to outline the pre-theoretical expectations that Fusion should satisfy.

Overlap is a relation that subsists between those things that have a part in common. It is easily defined from $P$ and standard logical vocabulary. The symbol we will use for Overlap is °.

$$\forall x \forall y (x \circ y \equiv_{def} \exists z (zPx \wedge zPy)) \qquad \text{(Overlap–Definition)}$$

It is a reflexive relation, since everything has with itself at least itself as a common (improper) part. Plausibly enough—we will explain why when discussing Extensionalism in Part Two—everything also has in common with itself all its proper parts, if it has any. It is also a symmetric relation, insofar as the conjunction in the *definiens* is symmetric. Overlap is not transitive: it can happen that $t \circ u$ and $u \circ v$, but not $t \circ v$. It can happen when none of the parts shared by $t$ and $u$ is also one of the parts shared by $u$ and $v$: in this scenario, nothing warrants that $t$ and $v$ have a part in common. Overlap figures prominently in various definitions of mereological Fusion or sum. Perhaps for this reason, Overlap was also used in Nelson Goodman's original presentations of mereology from above (under the label of *calculus of individuals*). Basically, that of Goodman was a different axiomatization of CEM from above. In it, parthood and proper parthood were defined in terms of Overlap.

This is relatively trivial. For example, one could say that $x$ is a part (*simpliciter*) of $y$ if and only if everything that overlaps with $x$ overlaps with $y$ as well:

$$\forall x \forall y (xPy \equiv_{def} \forall z (z \circ x \rightarrow z \circ y))$$

In the improper case in which also the opposite holds—namely, everything that overlaps with $y$ overlaps with $x$ as well—$x$ will be improperly part of $y$, that is, $x$ will be identical to $y$.

This is quite an enlightening way of making explicit the idea that parthood is a matter of complete containment, by proceeding—so to say—by a sort of approximation from outside, from what surrounds them. Consider our example of the red cap of a blue pen (see Chapter 2). The cap overlaps with various things: with the entire pen itself; with the right half of the cap of the pen; with the right half of the entire pen; with the object composed of all the pens in the world; with the object composed of all the caps in the world; with the object composed of all the stationery items within 3 meters from it; with the object covering the entire region of space within a 4-meter radius from it.

It is legitimate to doubt the existence of some of these items (Unrestricted Composition—the principle of CEM we will be discussing in Part Three— will warrant that they all exist). Nonetheless, it seems uncontroversial that, *if they do exist*, then whatever overlaps with the cap of the pen overlaps with the pen too.

Obviously, if I took something not entirely contained in the pen (say, the object composed of the cap and of a cake crumb stuck between the cap and the body of the pen), then this object will overlap with other objects (such as the one composed by all the cake crumbs in the vicinity) that do not overlap with the pen. In order to pinpoint the various parts of the pen (the cap, for example, but not the cap plus the crumb) we need to eliminate anything that overlaps with things with which the pen does not overlap (and this is why the procedure can be characterized as an *approximation from outside*).

The definition of parthood in terms of Overlap does not only deliver the expected cases as instances of parthood; it also excludes those cases that we would expect to be excluded: for example, the pen is not part of the cap. Consistently with our definition of parthood in terms of Overlap, the pen overlaps with objects that do not overlap with its cap: the refill of the pen overlaps with the pen, but not with its cap; the object composed of all the pen refills within one mile from our pen overlaps with the pen, but not with the cap. Thus, we are allowed to say—consistently with the evidence—that the pen is not part of its cap.

We will not discuss any further the presentations of mereology that take Overlap as a primitive. The presentation that takes parthood or proper parthood as a primitive is more common, and is deemed more perspicuous, perhaps simply because the notion of part is more familiar than that of Overlap.

Indeed, there are not many cases, in the prototypical spatial domain, in which we might want to claim that two things have parts in common. As Achille Varzi has suggested,[11] when we distinguish parts in something, it is more common and perhaps clearer to count only nonoverlapping parts (two things that do not overlap are also said to be *disjoint*). When we have to give some examples of overlapping entities, we are forced either to involve spatially scattered and conceptually united objects (such as the object composed of all the pens and the object composed of all the caps in a certain region of space) or relatively remote examples such as Siamese twins (whose shared organs would be the common parts).

In our above discussion of the definition of parthood in terms of Overlap, we have used expressions such as "the object composed of all the pen refills within one mile from our pen," and we have said that it is legitimate to doubt the existence of items of this sort. Once their existence is conceded, it is also unclear perhaps what these objects are. They are mereological fusions or *sums* (henceforth, we will prefer the term "fusion").

This is a very important notion in mereology. We will defer the definition of Fusion to Chapter 11, but it is important to get an idea of what Fusion is expected to be. Fusion is a relation. If CEM is adopted, this relation is also an operation, and in particular an always defined operation.

Let us introduce the notion of operation as a particular kind of relation. A relation having $n$ places is an operation when the first $n - 1$ *relata* determine the last *relatum*. For example, subtraction among natural numbers is a three-place relation between the minuend, the subtrahend, and the difference. It is also an operation, and it is usually called an *arithmetic operation*, since calling it "operation" instead of "relation" is more informative. It is an operation inasmuch as, given two natural numbers in the roles of subtrahend and minuend, it can never happen that two different numbers play the role of difference: the first two *relata* determine the third *relatum*.

As we know, the extension of a 3-place relation is a class of ordered triples. In the extension of operations, there are never two triples with the same first two members. In the extension of subtraction, given two natural numbers (say, 5 and 3), there are not two different triples having those two numbers as first and second element (the only triple in our specific case is <5,3,2>).

Some $n$-place relations are not merely operations, but always defined operations: this means that, given $n - 1$ elements in the domain (roughly, in what we are speaking about), we can be sure that there is an ordered $n$ tuple in the domain of the relation, whose first $n - 1$ elements are those elements of the domain. Subtraction among natural numbers (the set of natural numbers is the domain) *is not* an always defined relation, because given 2 as a minuend and 5 as a subtrahend, there is not a natural number that is their difference. By contrast, addition among natural numbers is an always defined operation: given two natural numbers (say, 3 and 5) as addends, there is always a unique natural number that is their arithmetical sum (in this case, 8).

According to CEM, Fusion is an always defined operation. One could also legitimately ask what the domain of this operation is, and wonder if it is clearly defined as the domain of natural numbers for arithmetical addition and subtraction. We will come back to this problem in Part Three.

In the meantime, let us be content with a provisional characterization of Fusion in terms of our example of the cake. Fusion is a relation between many things and one thing that includes whatever is in these things, and *nothing extraneous* to them. Uniqueness of Composition (the principle to which Part

Two is devoted) makes Fusion an operation. Unrestricted Composition (the principle to which Part Three is devoted) warrants that this operation is always defined.

The labels for both these principles include the term "composition." As it is used in this book,[12] "composition" is coreferential with "fusion," and designates the relation (a relation that, according to CEM, is an always defined operation) between some things and a thing that includes all of them, and nothing extraneous to them.[13]

# Part Two

# Extensionalism

## Abstract

The purpose of this part is to make explicit the role of Uniqueness of Composition and Extensionalism in the ideology of mereological monism, and to defend these principles against several alleged counterexamples, while conceding that other counterexamples indeed require mereological monism to restrict its ambitions of generality. In Chapter 5 we discuss the connection between Extensionalism and nominalism about structure, and explain what structure is in this area of metaphysics. In Chapter 6, we discuss the difference between Uniqueness of Composition and Extensionalism, and between various formulations of Extensionalism. In Chapter 7, we focus on the alleged counterexamples to Extensionalism, which involve a structured entity and the colocated portion of matter. We discuss the strategies to show that the structured entity and the colocated portion of matter are not really different, and the more compelling strategies to show that if they are different, then they have also different parts. In Chapter 8, we focus on the counterexamples in which an abstract entity or a theoretical entity postulated by a philosophical theory seems to violate Extensionalism. We show that in some cases there are promising strategies to make these scenarios compatible with Extensionalism. However, in other cases, these strategies risk distorting or misrepresenting abstract entities that are structured and non-extensional by nature. Finally, in Chapter 9 we investigate and compare some nonclassical, non-extensional mereologies, and we show that, in spite of being technically irreproachable and relatively conservative, these theories are affected by a lack of compelling metaphysical motivations.

# Hyperextensionality and Nominalism about Structure

## 5.1 Extensionalism at the origins of mereology

The second principle of mereology$_{theo}$ we aim to analyze and defend is Uniqueness of Composition. The idea is very simple: given some things, there is at most one thing they compose, or—equivalently (given the way in which we have decided to use "composition" and "fusion" in Chapter 4, Section 4.4)—they have no more than one fusion. Thus, given some things, there is at most one thing that includes them and does not include anything extraneous to them.

Let us use plural constants such as *tt, uu, vv, …* and plural variables such as *xx, yy, zz, …* in order to speak about the many things that are the inputs of the operation of Fusion. The resort to plural constants and variables will be discussed and justified in Part Three (Chapter 10 in particular). In Part Three (Chapter 11 in particular) we will also opt for a specific way of defining Fusion, that is, of capturing the idea of something that includes all the fused entities and nothing extraneous to them.

Uniqueness of Composition can be expressed in plural logic notation in the typical form of a uniqueness claim. For any *x* and for any *yy*, if *x* is the fusion of *yy*, then nothing else than *x* is the fusion of *yy* (we use $\Sigma$ as a relational constant for Fusion):

$$\forall x \forall yy (x \Sigma yy \rightarrow \forall z (z \Sigma yy \rightarrow z = x))$$

(Uniqueness of Composition)

In order to understand and defend the principle, let us make explicit a deep philosophical idea strictly connected to Uniqueness of Composition: *Extensionalism*. The basic idea of Extensionalism is quite simple: there cannot be two distinct things with the same parts. Extensionalism is perhaps the core of the ideology of mereological monism. The philosophers who uphold mereological monism are deeply convinced that there is something metaphysically wrong in the idea of two distinct objects sharing all their parts.

The need to appreciate the importance of Extensionalism is also an occasion for making our picture of the motivations of mereological monism more historically compelling. The picture of the methodology of mereological monism I provided in the previous chapter was not meant as a historically credible reconstruction. I did not mean it as an account of how the idea that CEM is the general, exhaustive theory of parthood became so widespread in twentieth-century philosophy. If we look at the origins of mereology, we do not find philosophers analyzing and systematizing prototypical, spatial cases of parthood, and using the resulting theory as guidance in the application of parthood to other domains.

The methodological picture I provided in Part One is a way to *make sense of contemporary mereology* and of the way in which some philosophers— among whom Lewis has had a decisive influence—have used it as a powerful discriminating tool, for discarding solutions to various philosophical problems. If we look at the origins of mereology in Polish logic or in American philosophy, we find that nothing of the sort occurred. In the case of an often-quoted but nowadays rarely read author such as Leśniewski, his purpose in developing a mereology was to provide an alternative to set theory for the foundations of mathematics. While Leśniewski's foundational project is nowadays scarcely relevant, the relations between mereology and set theory are actually *key* in understanding the ideological importance of Extensionalism in mereological monism.[1]

The foundational role of mereology was later also investigated by Lewis, from a different perspective. In his book *Parts of Classes*, Lewis was moved by the idea that set theory, instead of being replaced by mereology as a foundational tool (as Leśniewski hoped), could be *partially reduced* to mereology, by considering the relation of subset as a case of mereological parthood. This would mean that any set of certain elements can be seen as the fusion of the sets that have only one of these elements as an element: in set-theoretic terminology, any set would be the fusion of the *singletons* of its elements. The reduction was only partial because Lewis found no way to reduce the relation between singletons and their only elements to mereology, and struggled to find a way of making sense of this relation in general.[2]

In this book, we are not going to discuss the prospect of reducing set theory to mereology. Nonetheless, it is important for us to take a closer look at the differences between mereology and set theory, because they help us to understand why Extensionalism is so important in the ideology of mereological monism.

## 5.2 Mereological monism and nominalism

Extensionalism is so important for the ideology of mereological monism, because mereological monism is driven by certain nominalistic motivations, and in particular by *nominalism about structure*. Nominalism can be described, in general, as a family of philosophical claims that some things do not exist: nominalism about universals is the claim that universals do not exist; nominalism about abstract entities is the claim that abstract entities do not exist; nominalism about numbers is the claim that numbers do not exist. Unsurprisingly, nominalism about structure is the claim that *structure does not exist*. What is structure? Structure is construed by philosophers in several different ways, but, in a few pages (and in particular in Section 5.7), we are going to settle on a relatively precise characterization, inspired by Kit Fine's work.

Before that, it behoves me to admit that the connection between mereology and nominalism is sometimes denied in the recent literature. Varzi, for example, writes that the connection between mereology and nominalism was important at the origins of mereology, but there is nothing in mereology that necessarily links it to nominalism:

> while Leśniewski's and Leonard and Goodman's original formulations betray a nominalistic stand [...], there is no necessary link between the analysis of parthood relations and the philosophical position of nominalism.[3]

However, it is far from clear that Varzi, in this very short declaration, disagrees with my account. As I made it clear in the Introduction, the term "mereology" is used in several ways, and, given that Varzi speaks in this passage of "the analysis of parthood relations," it is likely that he is speaking of our mereology$_{dis}$. If so, Varzi is obviously right: there are many ways of construing parthood that are distant and even incompatible with nominalism, and also with nominalism about structure.

Varzi *might* be wrong if he is thinking of our mereology$_{phi}$, or mereological monism. He might be right in any case, because there are many kinds of nominalism, and some of them are extraneous to mereological monism (while—I contend—nominalism about structure is deeply intertwined with mereological monism). As Lewis writes (and, when Lewis speaks of "mereology," there are good chances that he is referring to mereological monism):

> Mereology is silent about whether all things are spatio-temporal. (Lewis 1991, p. 76)

Abstract entities are often meant as entities that are not in space-time. Thus, if mereological monism is silent as to whether all things are spatiotemporal, it is also silent as to whether abstract entities exist, and neutral about the corresponding variety of nominalism.

If Varzi means to claim that mereological monism and nominalism about structure are unrelated, then he is wrong. The link between mereological monism and nominalism about structure is limited only by the proper subject matter of mereology$_{dis}$. Given that the exclusive subject matters of mereology$_{dis}$ are the formal features of the relation of parthood and the identity and existence conditions for wholes, mereology$_{phi}$ is committed to the claim that there are no structures *as far as these subject matters are concerned*. Mereology$_{phi}$ is not committed to the claim that structures do not exist *in general*, but only to the weaker claim that nothing, in the general theory of parthood and composition (mereology$_{theo}$), requires a commitment to structures. In particular, as we will see in this part of the book and in the next, mereological monism dictates that structure has no role in the conditions of identity and existence for complex entities.

In particular, identity conditions for complex entities (that is, entities that are the combination of simpler entities: that are fusions of proper parts, in the language of mereology) are a rather obvious terrain on which evidence in favor of structures could be expected. I can here anticipate how I understand structure: it is the way in which the pieces of something are arranged. The arrangement could consist in their having a certain order, being repeated, or being stratified.

These kinds of arrangements could be suspected of having some bearing on the identity conditions for complex entities: it could matter—the philosopher leaning in favor of structures would say—for the identity of some things how their pieces are arranged. The same three playing cards that are now piled on my table, and compose a pile of cards, could be arranged by wise hands to form the basis of a house of cards. If this happens—the friend of structures could continue—the cards compose something new; and a prima facie sensible account of this difference could be that the cards (the parts) are the same, while their arrangement (the structure of the complex entity) has changed.

Mereological monism can react in three broad ways when confronted with these allegedly explanatory appeals to structures. Against an alleged example of two different wholes sharing all their parts, it can try to show that the wholes *are not really different*, or that the parts *are not really the same*, or that *parthood is not involved at all* in the example. We will be discussing some instances of each of these reactions. Whichever of these strategies they choose, mereological monists are anyway committed to denying that differences between complex items are compatible with them sharing all their parts.


## 5.3 Goodman on hyperextensionality

In order to better appreciate the link between Extensionalism and nominalism about structure, it is useful to go back to the motivations for mereological monism given by its American grandfather, Nelson Goodman. Like Leśniewski, Goodman saw in mereology an alternative to set theory. However, while for Leśniewski the main purpose of this alternative was to free mathematics from the burden of an ontological commitment to sets, Goodman was moved precisely by a kind of nominalism about structure, concerning not only mathematics but also reality in general. Set theory was the most popular framework at the time for representing some entity as including some others in some sense.[4] However, sets were not extensional enough for Goodman's taste: too much structure was relevant for the identity conditions of sets.

You may be surprised to read that *Extensionalism* differentiates mereology and set theory. After all, the classical Zermelo-Fraenkel axiomatization (as well as any other axiomatization of which I am aware) of set theory includes a principle known as the Axiom of Extensionality. This axiom fixes identity conditions for sets; namely, it says that two sets are identical if and only if they have the same elements (X and Y are variable for sets):

$$\forall X \forall Y (X = Y \leftrightarrow \forall z(z \in X \leftrightarrow z \in Y))$$   (Axiom of Extensionality)

However, according to Goodman this was not enough, and his *calculus of individuals* deserved to be called *hyperextensional* precisely in contrast with set theory. In his short 1956 essay *A World of Individuals*,[5] Goodman presents the distinction between extensionality and hyperextensionality. His presentation is a clear and philosophically inspiring introduction to the motivations of mereological monism, but is not exempt from some deficiencies.

First of all, Goodman makes a declaration of nominalism: "For me, as a nominalist, the world is a world of individuals" (p. 197). But he clarifies in what follows that the content of his nominalism is not the denial of the existence of universals (as opposed to particulars), or numbers, or abstract entities. Nominalism is for him the contention that "whatever is admitted as an entity at all be construed as an individual" (p. 199). This kind of nominalism leads to the rejection of sets, because sets are not construed as individuals.

What does it mean to be *construed* as an individual? It means to respect the principles of Goodman's own calculus of individuals (equivalent to CEM), in particular as regards the identity conditions for complex entities. In the calculus of individuals there is no "distinction of entities without a distinction of content."

Now, the entities at stake are complex entities, meant in the above specific sense, and Goodman is saying that nominalism consists in rejecting the existence of different complex entities with the same *content*. Content is what they are ultimately made of: the basic elements from which they are built.[6]

Set theory, in spite of the Axiom of Extensionality, would admit different entities (that is, different sets) with the same content. The Axiom of Extensionality excludes that there may be different sets with the same elements. But the elements of a set are not the ultimate basic elements from which it is made. Indeed, the elements of a set can in turn be sets, with elements of their own. And these elements can be other sets, with yet further elements.

Given some entities (say, $a$, $b$, and $c$) we can "build" several sets from them. The following four sets have the same content (in the sense in which Goodman understands the word "content"): $\{a, b, c\}$; $\{a, \{b, c\}\}$; $\{\{a\}, \{b\}, \{c\}\}$; $\{\{\{a\}\}, \{b\}, \{c\}\}$.

CEM does not admit of different entities with the same content: in this sense it *construes* everything as an individual. For Goodman, to be an individual means to have certain identity conditions: to be such that the identity of content (that is, having the same basic constituents) is necessary and sufficient for numerical identity. For this reason, set theory would be merely extensional, and not hyperextensional: it would admit different entities with the same content.

## 5.4 Hyperextensionality, sets, wholes

Three (mutually intertwined) features of sets seem to stand out as possible culprits for their lack of hyperextensionality. *First*, set-theoretic membership is *not transitive*: the members of a set $a$ can fail to be members of another set $b$ of which $a$ is a member. $a$ is not a member of the third and fourth sets in the above example ($\{\{a\}, \{b\}, \{c\}\}$; $\{\{\{a\}\}, \{b\}, \{c\}\}$), while it is a member of a member of the third set, and a member of a member of a member of the fourth one. This has some bearing on the lack of hyperextensionality, inasmuch as the ultimate constituents of sets (at the end of the chains of parthood relations) are not warranted to be among the elements of the set, in terms of which the Axiom of Extensionality fixes identity conditions for sets.

*Second*, a set with a single member (usually called its singleton) is different from that member: *{a}* is different from *a*, and both of them are different from *{{a}}*. We can envisage an operation that, having *a* has an input, gives its singleton as an output.[7] The iteration of this operation will give us an infinity of entities with the same content: their only ultimate piece is—in our example—*a*.

*Third*, it matters for the identity of a set how the ultimate constituents are grouped. The first two sets in the example (*{a, b, c}*; *{a, {b, c}}*) differ because in the second the basic constituents *b* and *c* are grouped together, while in the first set the members are not grouped at all. We could say that the *structure* of the first set is *flatter* than the structure of the second.

All these three non-hyperextensional features of sets have a connection with structure, and in particular with the fact that the link between the identity conditions for sets and their ultimate constituents is mediated by the way in which the ultimate constituents are stratified in a sort of hierarchy. It *matters*, for example, if the ultimate constituents are members of members, instead of members; it matters if they are encapsulated in singletons; it matters if they are members of sets together with other ultimate constituents.

Nothing of the sort is allowed in CEM. We already know that parthood is transitive according to CEM. The stratification of parts plays no role in the identity conditions for mereological wholes, thanks to Transitivity. As we will see in Part Three, the fusion of a single thing is always that thing itself, not another thing, as in the case of its singleton. Finally, no "grouping" of parts has any bearing on the identity conditions for wholes. Mereological monism is characterized by the idea that no stratification of parts has any bearing on the identity conditions for wholes.

## 5.5 Goodman's approach, atomism, gunk

Goodman's basic idea that mereological monism gives no role to structure in the identity conditions for complex entities is still central in the philosophical debate about mereological monism. However, there are some arbitrary assumptions in Goodman's approach.

The *first* concerns ultimate constituents. Goodman's idea is that both classes and mereological wholes are characterized by a *basic relation*: membership in the case of sets; parthood in the case of wholes. These relations can constitute chains: the members of sets happen to be sets and have members; parts happen to have parts. Thus we can also consider the relation that connects a set with the bottom ends of these chains.[8] In the case of membership, there would be at a certain point members of sets that have no further members (these would be either individuals or the so-called empty set: a special set with no elements). In the case of parthood, we would reach *mereological atoms*.

Mereological atoms are entities that have no proper part. Everything has an improper part (since everything is the improper part of itself), but atoms have *only* improper parts. We can define a predicate *At* for "being an atom" in the following way:

$$\forall x (At(x) \equiv_{def} \neg \exists y (yPPx)) \qquad \text{(Being an Atom–Definition)}$$

The problem is that the application of Goodman's conception of nominalism as hyperextensionality requires the existence of ultimate constituents. What is more, it requires that every entity is *atomic*, that is, it is entirely *decomposable into ultimate constituents.*[9]

Goodman's nominalism does not consider the hypothesis that the chains of membership relations and the chains of parthood relations do not terminate. If in some cases they do not terminate, some sets and wholes do not have a definite domain of ultimate constituents. It would not be possible, then, to establish if two sets or two wholes have the same *content*, since their content—according to Goodman—*consists* in their ultimate constituents. On the contrary, it is *controversial* that sets and mereological wholes have ultimate constituents.

In standard theories of sets, at the bottom of the hierarchy there are either individuals (i.e., members of sets that are not sets themselves), or the empty set.[10] However, there are also nonstandard set theories in which there is no warrant that the chains of membership relations terminate. The application of Goodman's approach to sets requires that we leave these nonstandard set theories aside, but we are not going to assess the costs or the desirability of doing so.

As regards mereology, the problem is that hyperextensionality is difficult to apply to mereological wholes, because nothing in CEM warrants that everything is atomic, that is, that everything has a certain domain of ultimate constituents. CEM is compatible with the hypothesis that everything is atomic, but also with the hypothesis that nothing is atomic, and even with the hypothesis that something is atomic and something else is nonatomic.

The neutrality of CEM over atomism is not *accidental*. It is not a feature of CEM that could be changed (e.g., by adding an axiom according to which everything is decomposable in atoms) without interfering with the *methodology* of mereological monism. The neutrality of CEM over atomism is *material* to the ambition of mereological monism—discussed in Part One[11]—to look at parthood and cognate notions from a formal point of view.

The general and exhaustive theory of parthood, which—according to mereological monism—exists and is identical to CEM, should never dictate that something has or lacks *certain parts*. It is not up to a formal theory—and, more in general, it is not up to philosophy—to establish which parts a car or a biological cell has. The identification of the parts of something requires *topic-specific* competences and inquiries.

Obviously, the choice between atomism and nonatomism is a more general issue than the identification of the parts of a car, or of a cell. However, this higher level of generality is not sufficient to include atomism in the area of competence of philosophical mereology.

The hypothesis that something (or even everything) is such that all its parts have proper parts (so that the chains of parthood relations do not terminate) is considered by mereological monists—most prominently by Lewis—as a *possibility*. Lewis even created a label for it: *gunk*. The motivation for this slightly derogatory label is presumably that something whose parts all have further proper parts would not only be such that no structural consideration has any bearing on its identity conditions, but it would also be without any definite content in Goodman's sense. This would make this kind of nonatomic stuff uninteresting and—so to say—*amorphous*.

The reasons that led Lewis to choose the term "gunk" should not influence us too much. Gunk needs not be something empty or devoid of interest. Actually, many others see gunk as a respectable scientific hypothesis. In the growing literature on it,[12] there is no decisive argument in favor or against its actual existence, and this is a good reason to think that philosophical mereology, which aims to be a formal, topic-neutral doctrine, should avoid presupposing that everything is composed of atoms.

Let us dwell on Goodman's atomistic presuppositions a little more, and explain why it is important to get rid of them in our presentation of mereological monism. One can see in Goodman's way of presenting the nominalistic motivations of mereology, the influence of a sort of old-fashioned mechanistic scientific atomism. During the Scientific Revolution, the idea that any feature of the world can be explained by the features of some small pieces was very important. Forms and structures were seen as remnants of an obsolete metaphysics, broadly in the Aristotelian tradition. In contemporary philosophy, this idea is far from dead. Lewis himself saw in the so-called thesis of *Humean supervenience* a pivotal aspect of his own thought. According to Humean supervenience, every contingent feature of the world supervenes on some intrinsic features of point-sized entities (Lewis dubs these features "perfectly natural properties"), and on the spatiotemporal relations between them.

Supervenience is here understood as a connection between some features B, C, D (the supervenient features) and some other features E, F, G (the basis of the supervenience), such that it is not possible that there is any difference concerning B, C, D, without a concomitant difference concerning E, F, G. The supervenient features here are all the features of the world, while the basis of supervenience is given by the perfectly natural properties of point-sized entities and by the spatiotemporal relations between them.

In an often quoted passage from the "Introduction" to the second volume of his *Philosophical Papers*, Lewis presents Humean supervenience through a metaphorical mosaic:

> All there is to the world is a vast mosaic of local matters of particular fact. [...] We have geometry, a system of external relations of spatiotemporal distances between points. [...] And at those points we have local qualities: perfectly natural intrinsic properties which need nothing bigger than a point at which to be instantiated. [...] All else supervenes on that. (Lewis 1986c, pp. 9–10)

However, Lewis was the same philosopher who coined the expression "gunk" for the hypothesis that there is something whose parts have all further proper parts. This is because Humean supervenience has no direct connection with mereological monism: they simply happen to be two pivotal aspects of Lewis's philosophy, but there is no inferential link between them.[13]

Indeed, there is a considerable distance between Humean supervenience and mereological monism. Humean supervenience for Lewis was not the content of a formal, general doctrine (while mereology was a formal, general doctrine according to him). He meant Humean supervenience as a hypothesis mainly concerning the actual world.[14] As a matter of fact, many contemporary philosophers of science—such as Tim Maudlin[15]—think that Lewis's Humean supervenience is *false*. In any case, even if it were true, there is no reason why it should influence our conception of mereology.

The kind of atomism involved in Humean supervenience is a controversial claim, exposed to the risk of being refuted by science, while mereological monism is a formal claim and is meant to offer some guidance in identifying cases of parthood and composition also outside the domain of prototypical spatial cases. As a result, it should also be compatible with the *negation* of Humean supervenience, and with the hypothesis that there is no bottom level of minimal entities.

As a result, Goodman's way of construing the nominalistic dictum according to which there is no distinction of entities without a distinction of their content is vitiated by the nonformal presupposition that everything is atomic.

## 5.6 Is Goodman's approach circular?

Before looking for an alternative way of construing the nominalistic presuppositions of mereological monism, it is important to discuss a *second* shortcoming of Goodman's approach.[16] There is a risk of circularity in the comparison between mereological wholes and sets.

Why should we assume that the content of a set is given by its ultimate constituents? This assumption is not only a symptom of a sort of old-fashioned atomistic mentality. It also *presupposes* that the relation of parthood that really matters is transitive. Mereological parthood (the fundamental relation in mereology) is transitive, while set-theoretic membership is non-transitive. In order to compare their takes on Extensionalism, Goodman focuses not on these relations, but on the *chains* of membership relations and parthood relations (more technically, on their *transitive closures*).

However, what is the reason for focusing on their transitive closures? The suspicion could be raised that the only reason is the assumption that only transitive relations really matter; that, when we ask what the pieces of something are, a non-transitive relation such as set-theoretic membership cannot be the one we should look at.

This issue is connected with the unsupported atomistic presupposition, yet different from it. Suppose that atomism is granted. Then, Goodman could insist that nominalism is about the impossibility of having more than one complex entity with the same ultimate constituents; and that the set-theoretic Axiom of Extensionality focuses on non-ultimate, superficial constituents (the members of the set), without countenancing what is *in* these superficial constituents. The focus on the transitive closure would be simply motivated by the desire to go as deep as possible.

However, the need to go *deep* into the chains of set-theoretic membership presupposes Transitivity. Without the presupposition that the relation that matters must be transitive, considering the transitive closure would be to go wrong, more than to go deep: it would lead us to count as constituents of entities things that are not such.

In the case of the set *{{a}, {b}, {c}}* for example, it could be objected to Goodman that *a*, *b*, and *c*—far from being ultimate constituents—are not constituents at all.

In order to show that sets are unacceptable, Goodman would be applying to them a notion of ultimate constituent that is tailored for mereology.

Goodman's circular assumption of Transitivity would be dictated by the circular assumption of mereological monism as a whole, that is, by the idea that parthood and related notions work as CEM (under the guise of Goodman's calculus of individuals) prescribes. For example, the simple idea that the constituents of a set are its members would be ruled out for the only reason that membership is not transitive.

As we have already seen in Chapter 2, Section 2.1, Lewis in *Parts of Classes* adopts a somewhat similar stance, and holds that membership is not a relation of parthood "because of a difference in formal character" (p. 5). But the subtle difference is in the methodology. Lewis uses CEM as a guideline for identifying parthood relations: membership does not work as a parthood relation, and as a result does not qualify as a parthood relation. By contrast, Goodman argues that sets are unacceptable entities because they are not extensional enough, on the basis of the fact that they are allowed to be different without having different ultimate constituents, where these ultimate constituents are identified with a mereology-tailored method.

In spite of these two shortcomings (the assumption of atomism, and the risk of circularity in the opposition between mereological wholes and sets), Goodman's ideological motivations for mereological monism in *A World of Individuals* are not far off target. As we will see, it is not difficult to amend Goodman's approach, in order to draw a credible picture of the nominalistic motivations of mereological monism.

## 5.7 Fine's principles of obliteration

Curiously enough, the best way to capture the peculiarities of CEM (and the nominalistic reasons for endorsing mereological monism) has been provided by Fine (he himself a passionate mereological pluralist) in *Towards a Theory of Part*.[17] According to Fine, the peculiarity of mereology is its *blindness to any kind of structure*. The word "blindness" is negatively connoted in Fine's mind: it is the inability of mereology to countenance a decisive aspect of reality. In contrast, a mereological monist could consider mereology's blindness to structure as a virtue of economy and lucidity. If there are no structures, then blindness to structure is a virtue, as much as blindness to ghosts; mereology would not countenance what *should not* be countenanced.

Fine explains what structure is. Perhaps his ontological pluralism helps here: insofar as, in his view, CEM is flanked by other theories of parthood that *are not* blind to structure, Fine is forced to provide a characterization of structure. This characterization ends up being also useful for understanding what CEM is blind to, or—equivalently—about what mereological monism is nominalistic.

Fine distinguishes four *principles of obliteration*. A certain theory of parthood is characterized by the fact that it countenances or disregards (obliterates) certain aspects of structure. If it disregards an aspect of structure, then it respects the corresponding principle of obliteration. If it countenances an aspect of structure, then it violates the corresponding principle of obliteration.

The principles are called *Absorption, Collapse, Leveling,* and *Permutation,* and Fine expresses them as follows (each principle will be analyzed and commented in the subsequent pages):

$$\Sigma(\ldots, x, x, \ldots, \ldots, y, y, \ldots, \ldots) = \Sigma(\ldots, x, \ldots, y, \ldots) \qquad \text{(Absorption)}$$

$$\Sigma(x) = x \qquad \text{(Collapse)}$$

$$\Sigma(\ldots, \Sigma(x, y, z, \ldots), \ldots, \Sigma(u, v, w, \ldots), \ldots) = $$
$$= \Sigma(\ldots, x, y, z, \ldots, \ldots, u, v, w, \ldots, \ldots) \qquad \text{(Leveling)}$$

$$\Sigma(x, y, z) = \Sigma(y, x, z) \qquad \text{(Permutation)}$$

Whereas in a monistic environment $\Sigma$ expresses mereological Fusion, in Fine's pluralistic approach $\Sigma$ is meant to express a generic operation that has some parts as inputs, and a whole as output.

In each principle of obliteration the same variables are found on both sides of the identity sign. The values of the variables correspond to Goodman's *content* of a complex entity. However, they are not expected to be ultimate constituents. They can be at any level of application of $\Sigma$ within the complex entity.

According to Fine, sets are wholes whose parts are their members. Indeed, as we know, Fine adopts a very broad characterization of parthood, according to which $x$ is a part of $y$ if and only if $x$ is in $y$ and the replacement of $x$ in $y$ with another entity $z$ would change what $y$ is or how $y$ is. And it is uncontroversial that if we replace a member of a set with something else, we obtain another set.

Sets and mereological wholes are far from exhausting the variety of Fine's pluralism. Actually, sets are less blind to structure than mereological wholes only from some points of view. Sets are stratified entities in which it matters how many times an entity is encapsulated in a set (as a member of it, or as a member of a member of it), and how elements at a certain level are grouped together. By contrast, the order and the repetition of elements do not matter for the identity of a set.

Other wholes could instead be such that these kinds of arrangements bear on their identity conditions. For example, *multisets* are entities analogous to sets in which the multiple occurrences of members make a difference (but their order does not matter). *Sequences* could be seen as entities in which the order of entities in the sequences matters.

The four principles of obliteration allow us to distinguish various kinds of wholes in terms of their attitude toward various aspects of structure. It is not always a matter of listing various complex entities for which a formal framework is already available (as is the case with mereological wholes, sets, multisets, and sequences). We can even foresee unexpected combinations of attention and disregard for various aspects of structure.

CEM is *blind to everything*. It respects all the four principles of obliteration. In order to obtain an analysis of the radical kind of nominalism about structure that motivates mereological monism, it is important to be explicit about the aspect of structure of which each principle dictates the obliteration.

The principle of *Absorption* obliterates (i.e., sanctions the irrelevance of) the *repetition* of parts in the whole.

$$\Sigma(\ldots, x, x, \ldots, \ldots, y, y, \ldots, \ldots) = \Sigma(\ldots, x, \ldots, y, \ldots) \qquad \text{(Absorption)}$$

It does not matter if something occurs two or more times in a whole. Mereological wholes and sets obey Absorption, while multisets violate it.

The principle of *Collapse* obliterates a kind of *stratification*: the kind that could obtain when we make a whole out of a single part.

$$\Sigma(x) = x \qquad\qquad\qquad\qquad\qquad\qquad\qquad\qquad \text{(Collapse)}$$

Sets (as well as multisets, but from now on we will leave multisets aside) violate Collapse, because for every $x$ the singleton of $x$ ($\{x\}$) is different from $x$. As we will explain in Part Three, CEM respects Collapse, because for any $x$ the fusion of $x$ ($\Sigma(x)$) is identical to $x$.

The principle of *Leveling* obliterates another kind of *stratification*, which happens when some parts of the entities are *grouped* and *encapsulated* in a *subwhole*.

$$\Sigma(\ldots, \Sigma(x, y, z, \ldots), \ldots, \Sigma(u, v, w, \ldots), \ldots) =$$
$$= \Sigma(\ldots, x, y, z, \ldots, \ldots, u, v, w, \ldots, \ldots) \qquad \text{(Leveling)}$$

In Fine's formulation of the principle above, this grouping is expressed by the two "internal" occurrences of $\Sigma$. Sets violate Leveling, which is why, for example, the set $\{\{a, b\}, \{c, d\}\}$ is different from the set $\{\{b, c\}, \{a, d\}\}$. Mereological sums respect Leveling.

The fact that CEM respects Collapse and Leveling accounts for the common observation that mereology gives a *flat* picture of reality, in which no stratification of entities has an impact on the identity conditions of complex entities. Jointly, Collapse and Leveling embody the difference between mereological fusions and sets that was at the core of Goodman's distinction between set-theoretical extensionality and mereological hyperextensionality. This distinction could be traced back to the transitivity of mereological parthood and to the non-transitivity of set-theoretic membership. Fine frames the same distinction within a larger picture of what structure is.

Finally, the principle of Permutation sanctions that the order of the entities in the whole does not matter.

$$\Sigma(x, y, z) = \Sigma(y, x, z) \qquad \text{(Permutation)}$$

Both mereological sums and sets respect Permutation. In the case of sets, $\{a, b, c, d\}$ and $\{d, b, c, a\}$ are the same set; "$\{a, b, c, d\}$" and "$\{d, b, c, a\}$" are referential expressions denoting the same set, to the point that they can be considered mere notational variants.

Goodman's opposition between sets and mereological wholes failed to underline that both frameworks ignore the order of parts (as well as the repetition of parts). However, in the debate on mereological monism, the blindness of CEM to order is an important aspect. In particular, when mereology is applied to some philosophical debates, Permutation can be perceived as an especially heavy constraint by the enemies of mereological monism (or as a powerful principle by its friends).

Suppose, for example, that I wished to admit *facts* in my ontology, and that I expect facts to make true sentences and beliefs.[18] Consider the sentence "Marseille is to the south of Paris." What in the world makes it true, that is—at a very rough approximation—necessitates its truth? The sentence is not made true by Marseille and Paris collectively, since it seems possible that they exist, while being in a different geographical relation. Nor it is made true by Marseille, Paris, and the relation of *being to the south of* collectively, since the relation could exist[19] and yet be instantiated only by other towns. In order to fill this role, some philosophers have introduced the category of facts. The sentence "Marseille is to the south of Paris" would be made true by the fact that Marseille is to the south of Paris.

According to Armstrong (1989) (among others), facts are complex entities made of the individuals and the universal involved (Armstrong actually prefers to call facts *"states of affairs"*). In the example, its constituents are Marseille, Paris, and the relation of *being to the south of*. Facts seem to be the result of applying *an operation* to some individuals and one universal. What kind of operation? It seems that it is an operation that violates Fine's Permutation, because the order of the constituents matters for the identity of a fact. We can suppose that the fact that Marseille is to the south of Paris results from $\Sigma$ (*Paris, at the south of, Marseille*); in any case, it is different from the fact that Paris is to the south of Marseille, which could result from $\Sigma$ (*Marseille, at the south of, Paris*).

Lewis, when reviewing Armstrong (1989) in Lewis (1992), assesses Arsmtrong's theory of states of affairs from the viewpoint of mereological monism. From this viewpoint, CEM tells the entire truth about composition. Any violation of Permutation is a violation of CEM (more in particular, it runs counter to mereological Extensionalism). The circumstance that a theory contradicts a principle of CEM is a *sufficient* reason to *reject* that theory.

In his review, Lewis observes that Armstrong's facts seem to violate also another principle of CEM, namely Unrestricted Composition (it will be discussed in Part Three). Indeed, two individuals and a binary relation may exist, yet fail to compose a fact. Consider David Cameron, Boris Johnson, and the relation of love: they do not compose any fact, inasmuch as Cameron does not love Johnson, and Johnson does not love Cameron.

Both the violation of Extensionalism and the violation of Unrestricted Composition are for Lewis two good, individually sufficient reasons to think that there is something wrong in Armstrong's theory. He writes (remember that Armstrong's "states of affairs" are what we have called "facts"):

> To me, it is mysterious how a state of affairs is made out of its particular and universal constituents. We may not think of it as the composition of a whole out of its parts: first, because different states of affairs may have the very same constituents; and second, because the existence of the constituents by no means entails the existence of the state of affairs. It is some sort of unmereological composition, and to my mind, that is a contradiction in terms. (Lewis 1992, p. 216)

CEM—that is for Lewis the formal, general, exhaustive theory of composition—respects Permutation and has Unrestricted Composition as one of its principles. Armstrong's theory of composition is incompatible with mereological monism (that is, with the thesis that CEM is the general, exhaustive theory of composition).

The analysis of mereological Extensionalism provided by Fine's principles of obliteration gives us a rather definite picture of what mereological monism is nominalistic about. Structure (to which mereological monism is proudly blind) is not (only) an opaque leftover of anti-materialistic strands in the history of philosophy, but is a collective label for the stratification, grouping, repetition, and order of constituents.

It is worth stressing that, as a result, the blindness to structure of mereological monism cannot be justified by pretending that structure is an intractable notion, for which we lack a formal tool. Set theory is a very well-developed tool, which is abundantly legitimized by its importance outside of philosophy, mainly in the foundations of mathematics; and, by violating Collapse and Leveling, it offers a very reliable way to make sense of stratification and grouping. Frankly, there is nothing opaque or flimsy in multisets and sequences either, for which repetitions and order make a difference in identity conditions.

Therefore, the reason for endorsing mereological monism and be blind to structure is not that structure is an obscure or unintelligible notion. The reason is that, even if structure is perfectly understandable, it *does not play any role* in the identity conditions for complexes. The epistemic desirability of mereological monism we discussed in Chapter 2 plays a role here: if there are no good counterexamples to Extensionalism, then Extensionalism is a *desirable* philosophical thesis, because it enables us to refute philosophical theories and narrow down the range of eligible solutions to some philosophical problems.

Thus, counterexamples are the crucial test bed, and Chapters 7 and 8 will be devoted to them. I will anticipate here that there are two main kinds of potential counterexamples. Some alleged counterexamples concern entities whose existence and involvement in parthood relations *is not* controversial; but, as we will see, it is far from clear that these cases set forth a real exception to Extensionalism. These cases will be discussed in Chapter 7. Some other alleged counterexamples concern entities whose existence and involvement in parthood relations is highly controversial. This is the case of facts, and of many abstract entities. Many contemporary philosophers think that there is no good reason to introduce in our ontology the category of facts, and the existence of abstract entities is the subject of persistent philosophical controversies. Moreover, for all these entities, the suspicion can be raised that they have no parts, but are simple entities, so that CEM would have nothing to say about their identity conditions.

Nonetheless, we will see in Chapter 8 that this second group of counterexamples is actually more insidious for Extensionalism, and could even require mereological monism to restrict its ambitions of generality.

# What Extensionalism Says

## 6.1 Uniqueness of Composition and Extensionalism

At this stage, we have acquired at least some idea of the ideological content of Extensionalism: it is a way of endowing complex entities with identity conditions such that only their parts matter; nothing else matters—in particular, the arrangement (stratification, grouping, repetition, order) does not matter. We have seen that it is misleading to focus on ultimate parts as Goodman did. It is misleading also because, according to mereological monism, the stratification of parts does not matter, and thus focusing on the lowest level of parts does not make much sense: the mereological picture of reality does not attach importance to the distinction between various levels of reality. Indeed, Extensionalism does not discriminate between different levels of parts. It simply says that complex entities (that is, entities with proper parts) are identical at the necessary and sufficient condition of having the same proper parts.

In the language of first-order logic, we can express Extensionalism as follows:

$$\forall x \forall y((\exists z(zPPx) \wedge \exists z(zPPy)) \rightarrow (\forall z(zPPx \leftrightarrow zPPy) \leftrightarrow x = y)) \quad \text{(Extensionalism)}$$

Also Uniqueness of Composition (the axiom of CEM directly connected with Extensionalism) does not discriminate. According to it, you can take any entities: no matter whether they are sparse, whether they overlap or not, or whether they have different or similar sizes, they can have one fusion at most.

$$\forall x \forall yy(x\Sigma yy \rightarrow \forall z(z\Sigma yy \rightarrow z = x)) \quad \text{(Uniqueness of Composition)}$$

Uniqueness of Composition and Extensionalism do not intuitively say the same thing, and they are not equivalent. Extensionalism provides identity conditions for complex entities. Uniqueness of Composition is about Composition/Fusion, and warrants that it is an operation.

As a matter of fact, Uniqueness of Composition is *stronger* than Extensionalism: Uniqueness of Composition implies Extensionalism, but not vice versa. Its major strength makes Uniqueness of Composition suitable for the simple axiomatization from above of CEM, which is the focus of this book (in which Transitivity, Uniqueness of Composition, and Unrestricted Composition are the only axioms). Extensionalism would not be strong enough.

However, it often happens in mereology$_{theo}$ that the difference between non-equivalent principles is philosophically negligible, because the scenarios in which the weaker principle holds and the stronger does not are implausible and uninteresting. This is one of those cases. As Achille Varzi has shown,[1] the scenarios in which Extensionalism holds but Uniqueness of Composition does not are quite deviant.

It is rather obvious why Uniqueness of Composition implies Extensionalism: any object with proper parts is the fusion of *all* its proper parts; it has each of its proper parts as parts, and it does not include anything extraneous to them (otherwise, it would have *other* proper parts). In the other direction, why does Extensionalism fail to imply Uniqueness of Composition? It is because there are *fake* ways of respecting Extensionalism, which consist in adding intermediate levels of proper parts. These ways violate Uniqueness of Composition.

It is useful to make these scenarios explicit, in order to leave them aside in what follows. Once this move is made, it will be clear that the main role of Uniqueness of Composition for mereological monism is to imply Extensionalism, thereby providing identity conditions for complex entities. Extensionalism will also be the crucial test bed for Uniqueness of Composition: any interesting counterexample to it is also a counterexample to Extensionalism, and in the rest of Part Two we will focus on counterexamples to Extensionalism.

In order to picture the deviant scenarios in which Uniqueness of Composition and Extensionalism diverge, let us introduce Hasse diagrams. These diagrams are often used to picture *models* for mereology. Each diagram consists of a tree, whose *nodes* represent entities in the domains of mereology, and *upward* segments represent parthood relations. The two important conventions about Hasse diagrams are that:

(a) each node represents a different entity;
(b) an entity $x$ is part of another entity $y$ if and only if the node representing $x$ is connected to the node representing $y$ through a series of upward segments.

As a consequence of convention (a), only *proper parthood* is explicitly represented in Hasse diagrams. As a consequence of convention (b), Hasse diagrams are suitable for representing only *transitive* relations (such as proper parthood is according to CEM): if $x$ is connected to $y$ by an upward segment, and $y$ is connected to $z$ by an upward segment, then $x$ cannot fail to be connected to $z$ by a series of upward segments.

The following is a Hasse diagram that violates Uniqueness of Composition while obeying Extensionalism:

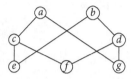

Focus on $a$ and b. These two different objects have different proper parts. Indeed, $c$ is a proper part of $a$, but not of $b$; $d$ is a proper part of $b$, but not of $a$. Thus, $a$ and $b$ *obey* Extensionalism. In contrast, a problem emerges for Uniqueness of Composition: for $a$ is a fusion of $e$, $f$, and $g$, because it has them as proper parts (each of them is connected to $a$ by a series of upward segments) and it does not include anything extraneous to them ($c$ is not extraneous to them: it is simply the fusion of $e$ and $f$); and, for analogous reasons, also $b$ is a fusion of $e$, $f$, and $g$. Thus, $e$, $f$, and $g$ have two fusions, and violate Uniqueness of Composition.

However, does this diagram illustrate a metaphysically interesting model? Not much. $c$ has the exclusive role of isolating $e$ and $f$ from $g$, and $d$ has the exclusive role of isolating $f$ and $g$ from e. Given that parthood is transitive, they do not play any real role, except for signaling that $e$ and $f$ (but not $g$) are grouped together within $a$ (but not within $b$), while $f$ and $g$ (but not $e$) are grouped together within $b$ (but not within $a$). These groupings are a kind of structure in Fine's understanding of structures discussed in Chapter 5, Section 5.7, one of those things mereological monism is proudly blind to.

At this point, one might think that the distinction between Extensionalism and Uniqueness of Composition is actually important: only Uniqueness of Composition—and not Extensionalism—respects Fine's Leveling, thereby *obliterating* a certain kind of structure. Fair enough.

However, it should be noted that the kind of structure at stake is not very interesting: if you have already conceded that proper parthood is transitive, why should you postulate entities such as $c$ and $d$? What could motivate the ontological commitment to such *intermediate* "groups" of parts? It seems that if we already have $e$ and $f$ (or $f$ and g) as parts of $a$ (or of $b$, respectively), then there is no reason to include *also* $c$ ($d$) among the parts of $a$ ($b$).

Thus, it seems that Uniqueness of Composition does actually express a stronger kind of nominalism about structure than Extensionalism. However, the kinds of structure that it obliterates in addition to Extensionalism are not very interesting. Indeed, the scenarios we are going to discuss in the rest of Part Two are potential counterexamples both to Extensionalism and to Uniqueness of Composition. No metaphysically promising scenario is a counterexample to Uniqueness of Composition only.

## 6.2 Why Extensionalism is thus formulated

The difference between Uniqueness of Composition and Extensionalism is rather dim. Moreover, the philosophical importance of both these principles lies in the fact that they provide identity conditions for complex entities, and Extensionalism does this more explicitly, as the proposed formulation makes clear:

$$\forall x \forall y((\exists z(zPPx) \land \exists z(zPPy)) \to (\forall z(zPPx \leftrightarrow zPPy) \leftrightarrow x = y)) \qquad \text{(Extensionalism)}$$

For these reasons, henceforth we will be focusing on Extensionalism.

Why is Extensionalism formulated exactly in this way? In particular, why does it involve proper parts instead of parts, and why is it restricted to entities with proper parts? Both these choices can be convincingly justified.

Suppose that we drop the restriction to entities with proper parts. If we simply removed the antecedent of Extensionalism, we would obtain the claim that two entities whatsoever (including mereological atoms) are identical if and only if they have the same proper parts. But then every two mereological atoms would be trivially identical: since, by definition of what an atom is, they have no proper parts at all, whatever is a proper part of an atom is also a proper part of any other atom. Thus, there would be at most one atom. This consequence is unintended and utterly undesirable.

One might wonder why Extensionalism cannot be formulated simply in terms of *P*, instead of *PP*, perhaps as follows:

$$\forall x \forall y(\forall z(zPx \leftrightarrow zPy) \leftrightarrow x = y)$$

This formulation could allow us to drop the restriction to non-atoms. Two atoms have trivially the same proper parts, but do not have the same parts *tout court*: given two atoms *u* and *v*, *u* is part of *u* (but not of *v*), and *v* is part of *v* (but not of *u*). The risk of unacceptably identifying all atoms would be avoided.

Actually, there is *nothing wrong*, from the point of view of CEM, in the above formulation of Extensionalism in terms of *P*, and without the restriction to non-atoms. It is a theorem of CEM, and it follows from rather weak principles of CEM. However, this is exactly what makes it unsuitable to the role of substantial and philosophical principle expressing mereological monism's take on the identity of wholes, a role which by contrast Extensionalism plays.

In particular, unrestricted Extensionalism in terms of *P* is a consequence of the Reflexivity and Antisymmetry of *P*. Suppose that two things *t* and *u* share all their parts. Given the reflexivity of *P*, *t* is a part of *t* and *u* is part of *u*. But *t* and *u*, by hypothesis, share all their parts, including their improper parts. As a consequence, *t* is part of *u* and *u* is part of *t*. *P* is antisymmetric: the only case of reciprocal parthood is the improper one, in which one and the same thing is part of itself. Thus, *t* = *u*. In brief, it is not surprising that it is sufficient for two things to have the same parts in order for them to be identical, if these parts include improper parts. To have the same improper parts is to be identical to the same things.

In Chapter 9, we will see that Antisymmetry can be targeted as the source of Extensionalism, and that it is possible to get rid of it if we are unconvinced by the nominalistic motivations and by the arguments in defense of Extensionalism we will be illustrating. However, this concerns only the *alternatives* to CEM. If you are a mereological monist, you want a formulation of Extensionalism that embodies its controversial, desirable content, and goes beyond the mere consequences of the Reflexivity and Antisymmetry of parthood. The formulation of Extensionalism I will focus on *is not* a mere consequence of Reflexivity and Antisymmetry. It provides *controversial* identity conditions for every complex entity.

However, what is controversial is not the entirety of its content. The consequent of the conditional in Extensionalism is a biconditional, according to which things have the same proper parts *if and only if* they are identical. This biconditional can be disassembled in its left-to-right direction, according to which if they have the same proper parts, then they are identical; and in its right-to-left direction, according to which, if they are identical, then they have the same proper parts.[2] The left-to-right direction provides a sufficient condition for identity, while the right-to-left direction provides a necessary condition for identity.

The left-to-right direction is a substantial and *controversial* claim. The opponents of mereological monism wish to deny it; they wish to show that two entities can share all their proper parts, and yet be different in virtue of their structure—that is, of the ways in which their parts are arranged. By contrast, the right-to-left direction is hardly controversial: it is simply an instance of a basic principle in the logic of identity, namely the Indiscernibility of Identicals or Leibniz's Law (but as several metaphysical principles have been dubbed "Leibniz's Law," we will prefer the former label).

The Indiscernibility of Identicals is a very solid principle. It claims that if two things $x$ and $y$ are identical, then it does not happen that one of them instantiates a property or a relation while the other fails to instantiate it. A standard view of identity (usually attributed to Quine) characterizes identity as that relation which anything has with itself and with nothing else. Equivalently, identity can be characterized as the smallest reflexive relation on the universal domain: everything is self-identical, and—obviously—nothing is identical with something else.

As a consequence, it would be hard for anyone to put forward a counterexample to the Indiscernibility of Identicals. It would amount to claim that $x$ is identical to $y$, but instantiates a property or a relation which $y$ does not instantiate (or that $x$ does not instantiate a property or a relation that $y$ instantiates). But this would be tantamount to saying that one and the same thing does and does not instantiate a property or a relation: a plain contradiction. Thus, at least if this standard view of identity is adopted,[3] the Indiscernibility of Identicals is as solid as the Law of Non-Contradiction, and there is nothing surprising or controversial in the fact that identical things have the same parts, have the same proper parts (as the left-to-right direction of Extensionalism claims), overlap with the same things, and so on.

Thus, there is nothing controversial from a mereological viewpoint in the right-to-left direction of Extensionalism. I have taken up the whole formulation of Extensionalism as an object of discussion mainly because it makes it clear that CEM provides *identity conditions* for complex entities, but what is exposed to counterexamples is only the left-to-right direction. An additional reason for considering the entire formulation of Extensionalism is that, as we will see in Chapter 7, Section 7.7 in particular, some scenarios that could be mistaken for serious counterexamples to Extensionalism turn out to actually be counterexamples to its left-to-right direction, and thus can easily be disposed of.

## 6.3 Extensionalism, atoms, and verbal tricks

Before discussing the potential counterexamples to Extensionalism, it is useful to reflect on its *expected generality*. The external universal quantifiers in Extensionalism are expected by mereological monists to be unrestricted. However, the explicit limitation to entities with proper parts—a limitation which, as we have seen, is needed in order to avoid unintentional consequences about atoms—already sets an explicit limitation to the generality of the provided identity conditions.

Consider again *facts*: as we know, Armstrong's facts seem to disobey Extensionalism. They fail to respect Fine's Permutation (the order of their parts *matters* for their identity conditions). The fact that Romeo loves Juliet is different from the fact that Juliet loves Romeo, but seems to have the same proper parts. Lewis's reaction is to say farewell to facts: nothing violates Extensionalism; thus, Armstrong's facts do not exist. But a mereological monist might prefer a different reaction: she could deny that facts have proper parts at all. Facts could be *mereological atoms*.

This move does not amount to a restriction of the quantifiers of Extensionalism. Facts would continue to be in the domain of quantifiers, but, insofar as they have no proper parts, they would respect Extensionalism in a trivial way (the antecedent of Extensionalism would be false). Extensionalism would not provide identity conditions for them.

The exclusion of atoms from the range of what Extensionalism provides identity conditions for does not determine what is an atom, and what is not an atom. In order to avoid the ensuing aura of *ad hocness* and arbitrariness, the thesis that facts are mereological atoms should not be endorsed *with the only purpose* of ensuring compatibility with Extensionalism. It should be endorsed for independent reasons within the theory of facts: given the expected explanatory duties of facts, should we expect them to have proper parts, or not?

We are not going to answer this question in this book. It is enough to underline that it is important to bring into play *independent motivations* when taking these decisions. A general principle is that if you want to be really faithful to mereological monism, you are not entitled to *verbal tricks*. You should not insist that facts are *atoms*, while endowing them with *pieces* under another label. You should not say that facts are partless, but have bits, components, or constituents.

After Lewis's criticism of Armstrong's theory of facts, the latter went ahead to claim that the composition of facts is a kind of *non-mereological* composition.[4] As a result, Armstrong had the burden of showing how this kind of non-mereological composition works, and, as a matter of fact, he has been rather elusive on this subject.

What matters for our characterization of mereological monism is that lexical prudence—that is, the mere avoidance of the word "part," or the apposition of "non-mereological" to "composition"—is not enough to reconcile mereological monism with an exception to Extensionalism. You need to be *serious* in arguing that facts—or propositions, or events, or any other entities that risk clashing with a principle of CEM—are partless. Your stance will forbid you to explain features of those entities in terms of the parts, pieces, bits, and so on, they have.

In other words, if you have good independent reasons, then you can elude Extensionalism for certain entities while continuing to be a mereological monist, by declaring that those entities are atoms. However, with this move, you are renouncing the explanatory power of parthood notions: you are denying yourself the opportunity to connect facts, propositions, events, and so on, with something simpler that could be in them, such as individuals, relations, concepts, and so on.

By contrast, if you shun CEM and *deny* mereological monism, then it is upon you to clarify in another way the varieties of parthood, overlap, and fusion you are employing: you have the burden of characterizing these relations in an alternative way, and also of explaining why precisely this alternative characterization of such relations *fits* facts, propositions, or events.

# Extensionalism and Concrete Entities

## 7.1 A multiplicity of extensional (non-fuzzy) mountains

Concrete entities are typically involved in prototypical, spatial parthood relations. Thus, in the light of the picture of the methodology of mereological monism we drew in Part One, the potential counterexamples from the realm of concrete entities are the most serious menace to Extensionalism—as well as the most widely discussed one in the literature.

The most common kind of counterexample to Extensionalism in this area involves an artifact (typically, a statue) and the colocated portion of matter (typically, a lump of clay or bronze). The literature on these examples is huge. In order to start relatively afresh, it is useful to discuss these kinds of counterexamples by changing some of their inessential features. In particular, I am going to replace the artifact made of a homogeneous material with a natural entity composed of heterogeneous materials. I am going to consider an entity which is more often discussed with reference to other philosophical problems (such as vagueness): a mountain.[1]

Consider a mountain in the Eastern Italian Prealps: *Monte Grappa*. The metaphysics of mountains is not simple: it is not easy to determine where mountains begin and end, and how they are separated from the other mountains, hills, and plains that surround them.

Some philosophers (e.g., Lewis 1993) would argue that there are many things that are candidate to be the referent of the referential expression "Monte Grappa." There are many ways to delimit the portion of terrain that is that mountain, and each of these many ways determines a candidate to the role of referent of "Monte Grappa." These many things are—as Lewis claims—"almost one," and this is why nobody would say that there are *many mountains* there, in spite of the fact that there are many candidates to the role of referent of "Monte Grappa." The difference between the various candidates does not matter in any ordinary circumstance.

Thus, the answer to the question "how many mountains are there?" is undoubtedly: "one." By contrast, the answer to the much more philosophical questions "how many things are there?" or "how many entities are there?" (suppose that "there" is uttered while pointing out in a map an area that bears the name "Monte Grappa") seems to depend on a specific theory.

Lewis's above-mentioned solution—according to which there are as many things as ways of delimiting the mountain, but this plurality of things is irrelevant for most practical purposes and counting practices about mountains—is highly desirable for a mereological monist. Given a certain way of delimiting the mountain, some things are included in the mountain, while others are excluded: some fields, rocks, and snowy expanses are in, others are out; at a much more microscopic level, some microphysical particles are in, others are out. Once the limits are traced, the identity conditions for the mountain have to countenance only the proper parts that fall within the mountain (for the moment, let us leave aside the issue that the mountain changes over time, and focus on a single moment; we will come back to temporal change later).

Each of these objects (the candidates to be the referent of "Monte Grappa") can be seen as a mereological whole, for which Extensionalism holds: they are identical if and only if they share all their proper parts. There are actually many mereological wholes, one for each way of delimiting the mountain from what surrounds it. The existence of these wholes is warranted by Unrestricted Composition (which we will discuss in Part Three): given any choice whatsoever of microphysical particles (as well as of fields, rocks, and snowy expanses), there is their fusion; some of these fusions are candidates to the role of referent of "Monte Grappa." Thus, the identity and existence conditions for the things involved are perfectly in line with mereological monism.

A mereological monist is not forced to agree with Lewis's claim that the many things are "almost one." According to a position that can be attributed to Williamson (1994), there is a single mountain there, with precise limits, but we ignore its precise boundaries: we do not know which microparticles and more macroscopic parts are in it, and which are instead out of it, but there is a single thing, with definite boundaries, that is, the mountain. However, this does not rule out the existence of many other compounds, with different boundaries, that *are not* the mountain. Also from this perspective, for all the objects involved, the identity conditions can conform to Extensionalism, without any reason to deviate from it.

In the context of a Williamson-like solution to the metaphysics of mountains, one might wish to separate Unrestricted Composition from Extensionalism.

One could say that there is only that single mountain whose boundaries we do not know, while different choices of microparticles, fields, rocks, and snowy expanses *have no* fusion.

This would collide directly with Unrestricted Composition (composition would happen only in the case of the single mountain), but Extensionalism could be preserved: you can consistently continue to hold that the single mountain is such that its identity conditions do not need to consider any kind of structure, but only its proper parts. In Fine's terms, every aspect of its structure can be safely obliterated, also if the composition of mountains is restricted.

Thus, Extensionalism is prima facie compatible with a certain variety of metaphysical views about mountains. Where does the menace to Extensionalism come from? The most serious problems for Extensionalism arise from a different kind of multiplicity: not from the abundance of candidates to the role of referent of "Monte Grappa" in Lewis's theory; but from a kind of *duality* that can be spotted in Monte Grappa (as well as in many other concrete things).

However, before analyzing the potential problems arising from such duality, and seeing that also in that case there are several, promising, nominalistic strategies to defend Extensionalism, we should admit that a reason to doubt Extensionalism could come precisely from the difficulty of establishing the boundaries of the mountain.

Suppose that we agree with Williamson that there is a single referent for "Monte Grappa," but disagree with him that this single reference is a well-defined object, having precise boundaries, about which we are epistemically ignorant.[2] Suppose that, according to us, the only thing at stake has imprecise boundaries. There are some microparticles and even some fields, rocks, and snowy expanses of which it is objectively, ontologically indeterminate whether they are in or out of the single mountain.

From within mereological monism as it is, it is difficult to account for this philosophical stance—whose other merits and difficulties cannot fully be assessed here. The imprecise, underdefined mountain *does not have* a definite domain of proper parts. More exactly, some proper parts will be perhaps definitely in the mountain (presumably, those in the vicinity of the summit), and other things will definitely be out of it; however, some other things still would be neither definitely in nor definitely out.

If we think that there are so-called *fuzzy objects* of this kind, mereological monism is not the way to go. As we will see in Part Three, a certain tension between mereological monism and certain approaches to vagueness is confirmed—and escalates—when Unrestricted Composition is at stake. It is important to note that fuzzy objects raise *lots* of philosophical problems and that, while it is easy to say that their identity conditions cannot conform to Extensionalism inasmuch as they do not have a definite domain of proper parts, it is not at all easy to say which identity conditions they could have instead.

The problem with fuzzy objects is not that some aspects of structure should be countenanced: since they lack a domain of proper parts, any possible reference to the ways in which these parts are arranged is not going to help. One could even wonder if identity between fuzzy objects is definite or vague, and whether it makes any sense at all to apply identity to them.[3] In any case, let us count the difficulty of dealing with fuzzy objects among the potential *costs* of mereological monism: if you are a mereological monist, you are better off renouncing the intrinsically controversial doctrine of fuzzy objects. This book does not aim to convince its readers that this doctrine is wrong, but simply concedes that this doctrine is incompatible with mereological monism and remarks that there are very attractive alternatives to it in the literature, such as Lewis's contention that there are many things—but almost one—that are candidates to the role of referent of "Monte Grappa."

## 7.2 A kind of duality

The most serious problems for Extensionalism do not stem from the intrinsically controversial hypothesis of fuzzy mountains, but from a kind of duality. What is in the spatial region which the maps label as "Monte Grappa" could be seen in two ways, quite independently of the way in which its boundaries are assessed. One of the ways to see what is there is to consider the mountain. Another is to look at it as a portion of matter. The matter in that spatial region is far from homogeneous: it includes rocks, soil, some vegetables, and occasionally some snow. At a more microscopic level a wide variety of chemical elements are to be found.

The kind of duality that is at stake here is between the mountain—Monte Grappa—and the total portion of heterogeneous matter colocated with the mountain. Let us call this portion of heterogeneous matter *Mountmatter*. Some philosophers think that Monte Grappa and Mountmatter violate Extensionalism; that they are two different complex entities, with the same proper parts. Both of them would be made of the same proper parts at any level of complexity: same fields, rocks, and snowy expanses; same molecules, and same physical microparticles. Still, they would be different.

Their difference would be proved by the fact that they instantiate different properties. If they instantiate different properties, then a quite uncontroversial principle about identity, namely the Indiscernibility of Identicals, leads to the conclusion that they are different. Indeed, the principle, in its second-order formulation, says that identical things instantiate the same properties:

$$\forall x \forall y (x = y \rightarrow \forall P(Px \leftrightarrow Py)) \qquad \text{(Indiscernibility of Identicals)}$$

To be more precise, the deniers of mereological monism invoke the converse of this principle:[4]

$$\forall x \forall y (\exists P(Px \wedge \neg Py) \rightarrow x \neq y)$$
$$\text{(Indiscernibility of Identicals–Converse)}$$

They point to properties which would differentiate Monte Grappa from Mountmatter, and then apply the converse of the Indiscernibility of Identicals in order to conclude that they are not one and the same thing.

## 7.3 Modal properties and counterpart theory

The allegedly differentiating properties are basically of two kinds: (a) *modal properties*; and (b) *aesthetic (and other kinds of axiological) properties*. In this section we discuss the case of modal properties, while aesthetic properties will be discussed in the next section. The modal properties at stake have to do with the possibility of surviving a certain kind of change. Time and change are sometimes mentioned as a general source of skepticism about Extensionalism; but, as we will see later in the chapter (Section 7.7), this source of skepticism can be dealt with by adopting some general and independently motivated stances in the philosophy of time.

However, here the problem is the *possibility* of existing also after a concurrent change, and it can be made sense of without mentioning time at all. It is a matter of imagining a *counterfactual* scenario in which the situation would be different from the way it actually is.

Consider two plausible modal differences between Monte Grappa and Mountmatter.

(a1) Suppose that a single piece is lacking. We can imagine this single piece as a cubic meter of snow in the snow expanses on Monte Grappa's slopes. Monte Grappa would survive this loss; Monte Grappa would be still Monte Grappa also without that cubic meter of snow. Please note that, in itself, this is no objection to

Extensionalism, inasmuch as Extensionalism does not say that things necessarily have the parts they have: thus, the fact that the mountain would be the same without a proper part (such as the cubic meter of snow) is not a problem for Extensionalism.

However—the opponents of Extensionalism would claim—Mountmatter would not survive the loss of any of its proper parts, and this is a problem for Extensionalism. The portion of matter, which is seen by these philosophers as being more indifferent to structural conditions than the coinciding mountain, would be a *different* portion of matter if some of its matter—namely, the snow in the cubic meter cube—were to disappear. The idea seems to be that a portion of matter, quite independently of Extensionalism and other CEM principles, has essentially the parts that it has.

Thus there would be two things which have the same proper parts, but a different modal property.

(a2) Now suppose that a falling meteorite hits that region, and that all the portions of rock, field, and snow are dissipated across a larger and discontinuous region in Northern Italy. Suppose that this disruptive event is, a bit paradoxically, rather conservative: that no piece of matter disappears due to it. All the pieces are simply taken apart.

The composite portion of matter would survive, would be *itself*, quite indifferently to the fact that the various sub-portions are not compact or cohesive anymore, but are widely disseminated. By contrast, Monte Grappa would be destroyed and cease to exist. Thus, Monte Grappa would disappear in these circumstances, while Mountmatter would not. Thus, again, these two things would have the same proper parts, but a different modal property.

Modal properties are a highly controversial topic in themselves, and an application of the Indiscernibility of Identicals to modal properties inherits these controversies. Moreover, there are independently motivated accounts of modal properties in which the apparent sources of discernibility between Monte Grappa and Mountmatter could be explained away. Suppose, for example, that we were to interpret modal ascriptions through Lewis's counterpart theory.

A counterpart of $x$ is—at a very rough approximation—a thing, typically in another possible world, that is sufficiently similar to $x$. Then, "Possibly $Px$" would be interpreted as "There is a $y$ such that $y$ is in a possible world $w$, $y$ is a counterpart of $x$, and $Py$." Then, to survive in a certain counterfactual scenario would be to have at least a counterpart in the possible worlds in which that counterfactual scenario comes true.

Given counterpart theory, one can reconstruct (a1) and (a2) both from an anti-extensionalist perspective and from an extensionalist perspective. Let us begin with the anti-extensionalist perspective. One could claim that, as regards (a1), Monte Grappa has counterparts in possible worlds where the cubic meter of snow has no counterparts, whereas Mountmatter has no counterpart in such worlds. As regards (a2), the anti-extensionalist could claim that, in possible worlds in which the counterparts of the pieces of the mountain are disconnected and spread across a large region, Monte Grappa has no counterpart, while Mountmatter has counterparts. Then, these differences in counterparts make the mountain and the composite portion of matter discernible and, through the Indiscernibility of Identicals, different.

On the other hand, the extensionalist could reply that one of the major advantages of counterpart theory is a certain flexibility. The kind of similarity required by counterparthood is not written in stone, nor is the level of similarity required by counterparthood. One could say—and Lewis would have agreed[5]— that these choices depend on the context or the viewpoint from which we look at a thing.

Thus—the extensionalist could say—there is actually a single thing (Monte Grappa is identical to Mountmatter), but we can look at it from different perspectives, and these different perspectives select different counterparts. These different counterparts correspond to a different modal profile: thus, according to the perspective from which we look at the mountain, we are inclined to claim that the single thing would survive the annihilation of a cubic meter of snow, or to deny that it would survive it (a1); and to claim that the single thing would disappear if its parts were scattered across a large region, or that it would survive (a2). There would be a single object to which we can attribute different modal profiles.

## 7.4 Aesthetic properties and metalinguistic negation

Given the controversies surrounding modal properties (with respect to which counterpart theory is neither the only nor the dominant approach), the opponents of Extensionalism often focus on different examples, which involve *aesthetic*—or in any case *axiological*—properties (b).

Monte Grappa is a relatively frequent and enjoyable subject for local photographers. We could plausibly claim that it is *photogenic*. But it seems strange, or far-fetched to claim that a composite portion of matter is photogenic.

Monte Grappa is also a challenging and desirable target for mountain climbers. We could say that it is *a dream* for many climbers. But—the anti-extensionalist argues—Mountmatter, the colocated composite portion of matter, is not a dream for any climber (or perhaps for anyone at all).

Photogenicity and the property of being a dream for many climbers *do not look like* modal properties, and counterpart theory or other approaches to modality are unlikely to be relevant there. The anti-extensionalist applies the converse of the Indiscernibility of Identicals to this property, and concludes that Monte Grappa and Mountmatter are a counterexample to Extensionalism.

However, the line of criticism to Extensionalism that stems from (b) is exposed to a general perplexity. It is a perplexity that is actually so general that it involves virtually any application of the principle of Indiscernibility of Identicals in metaphysics, as Benjamin Schnieder has clearly shown.[6]

First of all, one could suspect a certain circularity in the claims of discernibility. The anti-extensionalist propensity to claim that only Monte Grappa is photogenic and a dream for many climbers, while Mountmatter is not, *depends* on the propensity to distinguish these two entities. If the mountain and the portion of matter are two distinct things, then it is plausible to claim that it is the mountain—and not the portion of matter—that possesses aesthetic and other axiological properties.

By contrast, if you do not presuppose that there are two things there, you can simply insist that a single thing bears these properties. You do not need to deny that, when considering photogenicity and its role in the dreams of many climbers, it is *more appropriate* to refer to that single thing with the proper name "Monte Grappa" than with the proper name "Mountmatter," or with a description such as "the composite portion of matter colocated with Monte Grappa." These questions of appropriateness—Schnieder argues—should not lead to an application of the converse of the Indiscernibility of Identicals.

Schnieder points to other cases—quite independent of the debate on Extensionalism—in which a certain predication is most appropriately combined with a certain denomination of its subject. These cases should not commit us to a proliferation of entities through applications of the converse of the Indiscerniblity of Identicals.

Suppose that an assistant professor in Philosophy, whose name is "Petra Sambunjak," is also a passionate mountain climber. Due to her professional activity, Petra spends most of her time reading and writing research papers; she performs these activities mostly indoors, at home or in her university room, in order to better concentrate and interact with students and colleagues. At university, she is usually called "Professor Sambunjak." In other contexts, given her agility on rocks, her friends and fellow mountaineers call her "Petra the chamois."

Now, it is quite clear that only one woman is involved in this story. I might feel the need to distinguish various viewpoints in relation to her, and connect these viewpoints to her different appellations ("Professor Sambunjak" and "Petra the chamois"). For example, I might want to assess if she spends too much time indoors. I could say that, inasmuch as she is a university professor, she does not spend too much time indoors: the amount of time she spends indoors is perfectly adequate to the effort, concentration, and involvement required by academic research. In the context of this claim, it is natural to call her "Professor Sambunjak." But I could also claim that, inasmuch as she is a talented and passionate mountain climber, she spends too much time indoors: if she went out in the mountains more often, she could develop her talent, and achieve greater results.

Thus, I could claim that Petra the chamois spends too much time indoors, and that Professor Sambunjak does not spend too much time indoors, without thereby incurring a contradiction. However, it would be unwise to infer that Professor Sambunjak is discernible from Petra the chamois, and to apply the converse of the Identity of Indiscernibles to the conclusion that there are actually two women involved: a scholar and a climber.[7]

The most obvious thing to do is to *better specify* the property that we were tempted to attribute and deny to one and the same person. We could say that a single woman, Petra, is a university professor and climber, and enjoys *both* the property of *spending more time indoors than it is advisable for a climber and* the property of *not spending more time indoors than it is advisable for a university professor*. These properties, once appropriately relativized to a role, *are not* incompatible.

One may insist to ask if Petra is or is not spending too much time indoors, *absolutely*, given that Petra is both a university professor and a talented climber. And the answer could balance the respective importance of Petra's two roles, and perhaps reach the conclusion that she is not spending too much time indoors, because her profession (academic research) is more important than her passion (mountain climbing). Otherwise, one could also conclude that there is no definite answer to the question whether Petra spends too much time indoors *tout court*: the questions about spending too much time in some activity—one could argue—should always be evaluated with respect to a need or role. In any case, there is more than one reasonable way to avoid attributing to the professor a property which the climber does not instantiate, and concluding that they are two different people.

It is well-known that *negation* in natural language is used in several ways, and does not always express the conviction that the content of the negated sentence is false. Some instances of negation are *metalinguistic* in character, and are used to express the fact that the negated sentence is a *lexically or pragmatically inappropriate* way of talking.

Schnieder makes the example of the following dialogue:

> "What the heck is this cur doing?" speaker *x* barks. "This is not a cur, it is my dog," speaker *y* replies. (Schnieder 2006, p. 45)

What speaker *y* wants to convey with the negation in "This is not a cur" is that it is inappropriate and impolite to call her lovely pet a "cur."[8] Something of the sort could be happening in our case. It is inappropriate or impolite to call Petra "Petra the chamois," when you are claiming that she spends too much time indoors, because in such claim you are implicitly presenting a consequence of her academic job, with reference to which she should be referred to as "Professor Sambunjak," and not "Petra the chamois."

The extensionalist can argue that the case of Monte Grappa and Mountmatter is actually quite similar to that of Professor Sambunjak and Petra the chamois. Let us go back to (b), an alleged source of discernibility between Monte Grappa on the one hand, and Mountmatter on the other. It is not difficult to adapt Schnieder's metalinguistic interpretation of negation to this case. When I use the name "Mountmatter"—which has been introduced to refer to the mountain, inasmuch as it consists of a portion of matter—it would be *inappropriate* to express features strictly connected to the morphology, aesthetic value, or cultural relevance of the mountain. It is much clearer to use its specific, widely known name "Monte Grappa." It is so inappropriate to use "Mountmatter" that it is quite natural to signal the inappropriateness by saying "Mountmatter is not photogenic," as well as "Mountmatter is not a dream for most climbers."

In making this claim, I do not wish to argue that the thing in question (the referent of "Mountmatter") lacks the features that would qualify it as photogenic and as a dream for most climbers. What I wish to claim is that, when attributing those features to it, it is inappropriate to call it "Mountmatter."

Metalinguistic negation is a great tool at the disposal of mereological extensionalists, for the purpose of negating that Monte Grappa and Mountmatter are actually discernible, and of blocking the ensuing application of the converse of the Indiscernibility of Identicals. Nonetheless, it should be conceded that the dialectical situation of (b) is not completely on a par with that of Petra Sambunjak's case. In Petra's case, it is basically undisputed from the start that only one person is at stake. Nobody in the discussion is seriously denying that only one person is a philosophy professor and a talented climber (since this example is fictional, we have actually *assumed* from the start that Petra is a single person). Given that it is undisputed that only one person is involved, the Indiscernibility of Identicals is invoked in its *direct* form: given that Petra the chamois *is* identical to Professor Sambunjak, she must be indiscernible from herself. We only need to decide how to dispel the wrong impression—given by certain pieces of natural language—that the two are discernible. Metalinguistic negation *manages* to dispel this patently wrong impression.

By contrast, in the case of Monte Grappa and Mountmatter, it would be illegitimate to *presuppose* uniqueness. What the extensionalist and the anti-extensionalist *disagree* upon is precisely whether Monte Grappa is identical to Mountmatter, or not. In the philosophical dialectics, one side (the anti-extensionalist side) wants to show that there are two things. In order to prove this thesis, this side of the dialectics accepts the apparent source of discernibility as such. Then, it applies the *converse* of the Indiscernibility of Identicals, and concludes that there are two things. At this point, the other side of the dialectics (the extensionalist side) needs to show that the alleged sources of discernibility are not such, and that there are good reasons to interpret them differently, perhaps as the effect of a metalinguistic kind of negation.

In this case, the extensionalist has the *burden* of showing that the best semantic analysis of the specific cases to which the anti-extensionalist applies the converse of the Indiscernibility of Identicals does not deliver any real case of indiscernibility. It would be unacceptably circular for the extensionalist to presuppose that Monte Grappa and Mountmatter are identical, and to apply the Indiscernibility of Identicals in its direct form. The same move, which is perfectly legitimate in Petra Sambunjak's case, risks being inadmissible in this case.

Given this additional difficulty, the extensionalist could support his analysis of the aesthetic properties by means of an analogy. Just as it is strange to refer to a professor—attributing to her typically professorial features—as "Petra the chamois," it is strange to refer to something endowed with a value (such as photogenicity and desirability for climbers) with a generic, aseptic, connotation-free term such as "Mountmatter."

However, this kind of debate is likely to end in a stalemate. What for the extensionalist is an improper—but ultimately *true*—sentence ("Mountmatter is photogenic") about the *single* thing at stake is for the antiextensionalist a *false* sentence about *one of the two things* at stake.

## 7.5 Different things, with different parts: Extensionalism vindicated

It is possible to sidestep this stalemate, and make some progress in the debate about Extensionalism, by paying attention to another aspect. The extensionalist could simply concede that no decisive reason is going to resolve the debate on the alleged modal and/or aesthetic discernibility of Monte Grappa and Mountmatter.

This leaves open the possibility that Monte Grappa and Mountmatter are discernible and, as a consequence, different. However, this amounts to a counterexample to Extensionalism only if the two allegedly different things are complex entities *with the same proper parts*.

Extensionalism claims that complex entities (i.e., entities with proper parts) are identical if and only if they have the same proper parts. Thus, given a potential counterexample that involves complex entities, one of the following four scenarios will apply:

(i)   same proper parts, two different wholes;
(ii)  same proper parts, a single whole;
(iii) different proper parts, two different wholes;
(iv)  different proper parts, a single whole.

Only (i) is a counterexample to Extensionalism. (ii) is obviously a confirmation of Extensionalism. (iv) would be a counterexample to the *uninteresting*, right-to-left direction of Extensionalism, and is ruled out by the Indiscernibility of Identicals itself, as we remarked in Chapter 6, Section 6.2: if two things have different proper parts, then they are discernible already for this reason, and this is enough to conclude that they are different; thus, scenarios of type (iv) are impossible.

What about (iii)? (iii) is not problematic for Extensionalism at all. It is the case in which Monte Grappa is *different* from Mountmatter, and the proper parts of Monte Grappa are also *different* from the proper parts of Mountmatter. As Varzi has shown,[9] there are good reasons to think that the cases involving an entity and the colocated portion of matter (such as the case of Monte Grappa and Mountmatter) are scenarios of type (iii). These good reasons are provided— quite surprisingly—by the anti-extensionalist herself.

The anti-extensionalist indicates some modal and aesthetic sources of discernibility between Monte Grappa and Mountmatter. However, the reasons that lead the anti-extensionalist to accept these sources of discernibility for the wholes seem to *apply to the parts as well*. It would be arbitrary to limit these sources of discernibility to the wholes, because any reason you can provide for them at the level of the whole can be reiterated at the level of its proper parts.

Indeed, suppose that, as in (a1), actually only Monte Grappa—but not Mountmatter—would survive the annihilation of a cubic meter of its snow. And focus on one of the expanses of snow on Monte Grappa (one of the proper parts of Monte Grappa), which includes more than a cubic meter of snow. Would this expanse of snow survive the annihilation of a cubic meter of snow? If you believe that Monte Grappa would survive the annihilation of a cubic meter of snow, then you should extend this belief to the expanse of snow.

The same happens for the valleys, fields, and forests that are proper parts of Monte Grappa. For each of these proper parts of Monte Grappa one might want to distinguish it from a colocated portion of matter, insofar as they would be discernible. Focus on a forest: would it survive the annihilation of a cubic centimeter of wood in one of its trees? Sure. In contrast to the forest, the corresponding portion of matter would not survive the annihilation of that cubic centimeter of wood; "portions of matter" are, so to say, completely defined by the matter they include, so that the lack of any of it (and thus, in the specific case, the lack of the cubic centimeter of wood) would destroy it.

Obviously, you could also suspect that these different modal profiles depend on the flexibility of counterparthood. Or that it is lexically inappropriate to say that the *portion of matter* survives, because we are discussing a scenario in which the matter changes. In this scenario it would be more appropriate to call it "forest," and it is possible to signal the inappropriateness with a metalinguistic negation: "the portion of matter would not survive the annihilation of that cubic centimetre of wood." *If* these approaches are legitimate at the level of the forest, then they are equally legitimate at the level of the mountain. Thus, either there are two things whose forest parts are different or there is a single thing with the same forest parts. In both cases, Extensionalism is untroubled.

The anti-extensionalist might hope to block this outcome in the case of *less natural* parts, for which there is no so-called sortal term, such as "forest," "mountain," or "expanse of snow." Focus on the composite of a half-wood with a half-field. Or focus on a cubic meter of snow in one of the expanses of snow. The anti-extensionalist could argue that her own anti-extensionalist argument cannot be applied to these gerrymandered entities. She could argue that in these cases there is nothing more than a portion of matter.

Let us consider the two proposed cases.

1) In the case of the composite of a half-wood and a half-field, the anti-extensionalist could try to argue that nothing located there would survive the annihilation of a cubic meter of snow. The anti-extensionalist is—*au fond*—a denier of Fine's principles of obliteration of structure. Mountains and forests are structured entities for her, and their structure has an impact on their identity conditions, and also on their survival conditions. But when we move from the level of structured entities downwards to simpler things, at a certain point structure would not matter anymore. In particular, half-woods (in contrast to woods), half-fields (in contrast to fields), and their composites would be such that structure would not matter for them, and for their survival conditions.

However, this line of reasoning is not compelling. It assumes that there are some things for which structure matters, and for those things it postulates a distinction between them and their colocated portions of matter. After that, it *excludes* other things from this distinction: half-woods, half-fields, and their composites would be identical to portions of matter. This asymmetry is pivotal in delivering the violation of Extensionalism. Indeed, there is a violation of Extensionalism if and only if there are two complex things with the same proper parts. And we obtain this result if and only if both the following conditions hold: in some regions of space (those occupied by allegedly structured entities) there are two things (the structured entity and the colocated portion of matter); in some other regions of space (those occupied by allegedly *unstructured* entities) there is only one thing.

The problem is that the distinction between structured entities and unstructured entities is controversial and blurred. First of all, the entities we have discussed are all involved in the problem of vagueness we discussed in Section 7.1. It is far from clear that there is a single entity which is the mountain, and another single entity which is the forest. According to Lewis's approach in "Many, But Almost One," there are a lot of candidates to the role of referent of "Monte Grappa," and the same for any name of the forest. This suggests that there is nothing special at the specific granularity level of mountains (or of forests), such that only at that level there are two colocated things. Also in a Williamson-like solution, such that there is a unique thing that is the mountain but we are epistemically unable to pinpoint it, it is not clear that the metaphysical privilege attributed to this single thing could consist in the fact that it is the only one to be colocated with a portion of matter different from it.

More generally, if you are convinced that structure matters for the identity conditions of things, there is no sensible reason to exclude half-forests, half-fields, half-expanses of snow, and their composites from the scope of your conviction. From the physical point of view, a half-expanse of snow has all the chemical and physical complexity that an entire glacier has; and the biological and descriptive complexity of a half-forest is very similar to that of an entire forest. It seems that the distinction between two levels of things to which the anti-extensionalist is committed (on one level, two wholes; on the other, the same proper parts) is completely unsupported.

2) Consider the cubic meter of snow. Obviously, from the point of view of the specific property in (a1), it cannot be distinguished from the portion of matter colocated with it. Neither the cubic meter nor the portion of matter would survive the annihilation of a cubic meter of snow. If a cubic meter of snow were annihilated in a cubic meter of snow, *nothing* would remain.

However, this is not a good way to argue that the proper parts of Monte Grappa are identical to those of Mountmatter. First of all, the cubic meter of snow is only one of the proper parts at stake. For other proper parts (such as the forests), it seems that they should be distinguished from the colocated portions of matter for the same reasons why the whole mountain should be distinguished from the colocated portion of matter.

Moreover, the hypothesis of the annihilation of a cubic meter of snow is only *one* source of discernibility, where the entities at stake have a cubic meter of snow as a *proper* part of them: but—proper parthood being antireflexive—the cubic meter of snow is not a proper part of itself. Thus, in the case of the cubic meter of snow, we should identify a proper part of it and ask what would happen to the cubic meter of snow if this proper part were annihilated; for example, if a *snowflake* in the cubic meter were annihilated. Would that cubic meter of snow survive the annihilation of one of its snowflakes?

The answer to this question could be influenced by the referential expression "that cubic meter of snow." We can argue that its reference would not survive the annihilation of one of its snowflakes: for the annihilation of any spatial part of it would change at least to some extent the volume of the amount of snow; and, if the volume of a cubic meter of snow decreases, obviously there is no longer a cubic meter of snow there. But this simply suggests that referential expressions that include a reference to dimensions (of the form "that cubic metre of," or "that metre of") usually refer—from an anti-extensionalist viewpoint—to the portion of matter, and not to the structured thing. But this does not mean that there is not *also* a colocated, structured thing there.

Suppose that that cubic meter of snow is the subject of a scientific experiment: some chemical substance is injected in it, in order to assess if the chemical substance, when in contact with snow, generates enough heat to partially melt the snow. The snow that is involved in the experiment is called "Champion." Suppose that the experiment fails: after the injection, the snow does not melt at all. But obviously this is metaphysically contingent, and in another, counterfactual scenario, some of the snow would melt. In this counterfactual scenario, we would not have a cubic meter of snow (the portion of snow would be smaller); but Champion would be still there, though partially molten. Thus, the anti-extensionalist, if coherent with her methodology, should conclude that Champion and the portion of snow colocated with Champion are modally discernible, since only Champion would survive the annihilation of one or more snowflakes.

Also in this case, if the anti-extensionalist wishes to distinguish two wholes, then for the sake of coherence she should distinguish its proper parts too. Conversely, if she does not wish to distinguish its parts, then she should not have distinguished the wholes in the first place.

The anti-extensionalist could perhaps try to focus on *mereological atoms*. She could concede that for mountains, forests, half-forests, quarters of fields, and every recombination of such parts, a sort of dualism holds: there is the structured entity *and* there is the colocated portion of matter. By contrast, at the level of atoms a kind of monism should be endorsed.

The anti-extensionalist could argue in favor of such a differential treatment of atoms in the following way. The ways in which proper parts are arranged *matter*—according to her—for the identity conditions of complex entities. They should not be obliterated, while extensional CEM obliterates them. By contrast, at the level of atoms, *there is nothing* that could be structured or arranged: no proper parts can be ordered, or repeated, or stratified, since the atoms have—by definition—no proper part.

One could even argue that, at the level of atoms, sources of discernibility such as (a1) and (a2) do not arise, because no proper part of an atom can be annihilated (an atom has no proper part at all) and it is not possible to spread the proper parts of an atom across a large region of space (for the same reason). Thus, the anti-extensionalist could hold that at every level—except for the level of atoms—there is a kind of dualism between entities and the portions of matter colocated with them.

As Varzi has shown,[10] the resulting metaphysical picture is bizarre and arbitrary: at the level of atoms, a unique domain of atoms would be the basis for both structured entities and for their colocated portions of matter; but from that level upwards, for any location, there would be two colocated things. The failure of Extensionalism would be quite local. First of all, failures could happen only in domains in which things are decomposable into atoms. In the case of so-called gunk (which, as we have seen in Chapter 5, Section 5.5, CEM does not rule out, and is considered by many as a respectable scientific hypothesis), everything is such that all its parts have still further proper parts, and these further parts could be arranged in some way, and these arrangements could be relevant for the identity conditions, according to the anti-extensionalist viewpoint.

Moreover, even if we forget gunk and concede that atomism holds, the only entities for which anti-extensionalism would fail would be the entities whose proper parts are all atoms. Consider any whole $x$ with at least one proper part $y$ that is not an atom. Both $x$ and $y$ would be different from their portions of matter $m(x)$ and $m(y)$, but then $x$ and $m(x)$ would not be a counterexample to anti-extensionalism, because $x$ would have $y$ (but not $m(y)$) as a proper part, while $m(x)$ would have $m(y)$ (but not $y$) as a proper part.

Thus, the only things for which Extensionalism would fail would be—so to say—*quasi-atoms*, that is, *things whose proper parts are all atoms*. Not even the fusion of three atoms is a quasi-atom, because its proper parts are not only the three atoms, but also the three fusions of two of those three atoms. Ultimately, only the fusions of two atoms would be exceptions to anti-extensionalism. The resulting metaphysical picture attributes to atoms and quasi-atoms an exceptional status, for which—no matter how hard I try to put myself in the anti-extensionalist's shoes—I am unable to imagine independent justifications.

## 7.6 A role for structures in Extensionalism

The moral to be drawn from Varzi's argument in defense of Extensionalism is that Extensionalism and mereological monism are not the real focus in the philosophical discussion on cases such as that of Monte Grappa and Mountmatter. In these discussions, the main philosophical debate is between a kind of *monism*—according to which there is a single entity in that region of space— and a kind of *dualism*—according to which Monte Grappa and Mountmatter are two, genuinely different entities in that region of space. The kind of monism that is here at stake should not be confused with *mereological monism*: the kind of monism here at stake does not directly concern parthood and composition, but rather the relation between structured entities and their colocated portions of matter.

As we have seen in Sections 7.3–7.4 the dialectics between monism and dualism risks ending in a stalemate. However, Extensionalism is not really put at risk by this stalemate. On the one hand, monism is the most obvious and common stance for extensionalists in these cases. On the other, as shown in the previous section, dualism, when consistently developed, is *fully compatible* with Extensionalism: portions of matter are parts of portions of matter, structured entities are parts of structured entities, and you never find two things with the same proper parts. Only the attribution of peculiarities to the level of atoms could lead to a failure of Extensionalism, but such attribution would be hard to justify.

This leads us to an important point: structured entities, that is, entities that are characterized by having their parts arranged in a certain way, are not *as such* a problem for Extensionalism. It is quite obvious that an entity, in order to qualify as a mountain (or as a forest, or as a field), needs to have its proper parts arranged in a certain way. It is not easy to say how they should be arranged, but it is quite obvious, for example, that if all the proper parts of a geographical entity $x$ are coplanar (i.e., if they lie on the same plain), then $x$ is not a mountain. But this obvious claim does not show that there are two complex things with the same proper parts, and does not falsify either Extensionalism or any other aspect of mereological monism.

As we have seen in considering Fine's principles of obliteration of structure in Chapter 5, Section 5.7, Extensionalism obliterates structure only in the sense that it attributes to complex entities identity conditions in which structure plays no role. Extensionalism does not dictate that the parts of everything are like an amorphous amount of unmatched puzzle pieces. If it were to dictate such a claim, it would be inconsistent with the austere delimitation of the explanatory duties of mereology$_{dis}$, according to which mereology$_{dis}$ is only about formal features of parthood, and about existence and identity conditions for wholes. Mereology$_{dis}$—according to this austere understanding, endorsed by mereological monism—is not about the mutual relations between parts, or about the conditions at which a whole falls under certain predicates, such as "mountain" or "forest." Extensionalism simply says that, *as regards identity*, only the pieces matter.

The distinction that the dualist wishes to draw between entities and their portion of matter may or may not be legitimate, and this should be decided by considering the methodological and substantial problems raised by the application of the converse of the Indiscernibility of Identicals to these cases. But what *consistent dualism* points to is the idea that reality has two overall layers (the layer of structured entities and the layer of the portions of matter), and this is not a problem for Extensionalism at all.

This is perhaps made clearer by those theories which draw a sharp distinction between the level of entities and the level of matter, as is the case in so-called *stuff ontologies*, endorsed for example by Henry Laycock and Thomas McKay.[11] According to stuff ontologies, matter (also called "stuff") is something radically uncountable, and is the typical referent of so-called mass terms, such as "water" or "snow." It would be misleading to speak of stuff as a kind of entity, because "entity" is a countable term. Even more wrong would be our previous talk of "portions" of snow or other matter: when matter is divided into portions, it is turned into something countable, and this already brings us on the side of structured things. By contrast, matter/stuff would be so unstructured that it would not be possible to count it. The dualist approach of stuff ontology seems to make it clear from the start that there are two globally separate layers of reality.[12]

Finally, there is another sense in which dualism could be a problem for Extensionalism. When dualism is endorsed—and even if dualism is consistently developed and concerns any level of complexity—one needs to characterize the relation between the structured entity and the colocated matter or portion of matter in some way. What kind of relation connects $x$ and $m(x)$? Is it a mereological relation, namely a relation of parthood? If so, further problems could arise for Extensionalism. It should be noted that, according to some philosophers, such as Judith Thomson and Aaron Cotnoir,[13] the reason for deviating from Extensionalism lies in the study of *this* relation: the reason for abandoning Extensionalism would be not the admission of two colocated wholes with the same *smaller* proper parts, but the fact that colocated wholes are mutual parts of one another. We will come back to their proposals in Chapter 9, and show that, even from a dualist perspective, it is not clear that the study of the relation between a structured entity and the colocated matter or portion of matter is among the explanatory duties of mereology$_{dis}$.

## 7.7 Extensionalism and time

In order to complete our analysis of Extensionalism in the realm of concrete entities, we need to consider what happens when we factor in time and change. Indeed, up to now we have treated Monte Grappa as a static entity that *could* change, but does not actually change. Obviously, however, like virtually all other concrete entities, Monte Grappa *does change* over time. The snow melts away in spring and summer, the vegetation changes its shape and color from season to season, and long-term geological phenomena gradually—yet dramatically— change the overall morphology of the mountain.

One could have the vague impression that extensional mereology is radically *unfit* to deal with time and change. The thesis that complex entities are identical at the condition of having the same proper parts does not look change-friendly: one of the most obvious cases of change over time is the change of parts.

The change of parts has been scrutinized several times in the history of philosophy: the problem of the Ship of Theseus is well-known from the times of Plutarch, and it is a case of change of parts. During a voyage all the parts of a ship are gradually replaced: is the ship at its arrival identical to the ship that departed? Given that Extensionalism connects identity with the sharing of every proper part, it might seem to dictate the conclusion that at every change of a single part the ship becomes a different one, so that the voyage would actually be made by a succession of several different ships.

Undeniably, the Ship of Theseus, together with many other ingenious thought experiments involving change and time, has been the object of many important philosophical reflections and controversies. However, the impression that these controversies primarily concern mereology, and in particular Extensionalism, is wrong.

First of all, as we have seen in Chapter 6, the controversial component of Extensionalism is its left-to-right direction, that is, the claim that the sharing of all proper parts is a *sufficient* identity condition for complex entities; or, equivalently, that if two complex entities share all their proper parts, then they are identical. By contrast, the right-to-left direction is much less controversial and *is not specifically mereological*: it is the claim that the sharing of proper parts is a necessary identity condition for complex entities; or, equivalently, that if two things are identical, then they share all their proper parts. This second claim is simply an instance of the Indiscernibility of Identicals in its direct form: in general, identical things have all their properties and relations in common.

The issue of change in parts, as presented in the Ship of Theseus problem, raises the question of whether *one and the same thing can have different parts*: it does not concern the *controversial* aspect of Extensionalism. When it is not integrated within a more complex framework, the simple claim that the Ship of Theseus is identical throughout its voyage would lead us to conclude that in order for two things to be identical, it is not necessary for them to share all their parts. And this is simply a rejection of the Indiscernibility of Identicals, a move that—as we have seen—makes us slip into contradiction.

There is no specifically mereological problem here. We can imagine that the Ship of Theseus also undergoes *non-mereological* changes during its voyage: its color and shape could change, for example, because it gets repainted and renovated, or due to spontaneous corrosion. Let us suppose that it is brown when it departs, and gray when it arrives; thus, it is not gray when it departs, and it is not brown when it arrives. Now, if you claim that the ship at departure time is identical to the ship at arrival time, then you are saying that one and the same thing is and is not brown, and is and is not gray.

Obviously, the philosophy of time offers several ways to avoid the ensuing contradictions. The two most famous, broad solutions are the following, and can be applied to mereological change as well as to other kinds of change (such as the change of color and form).

The *first*, broad option is to deny that there is inter-temporal identity, and claim that at every stage of the voyage there is a different entity. The different stages have a sort of causal continuity, but are strictly speaking different. Then, it is possible to claim that the ship is the sum of these stages, or that each of the stages is the ship at a certain time. The resulting treatment of time and change is usually called *perdurantism*.[14]

As far as the issue of discernibility is concerned, the advantage of these approaches is that the properties of being brown and of not being gray are attributed to the ship at departure time, while the properties of being gray and of not being brown are attributed to the ship at arrival time. According to this approach, the ship at departure time is different from the ship at arrival time, thus the mentioned properties make *different things discernible*, and this is perfectly compatible with the Indiscernibility of Identicals. At any moment in its voyage, Theseus's ship will have some properties, *as well as some proper parts*. At any moment, there is not a single ship with different properties, or with different proper parts. Thus, mereological change too will be reconciled with Extensionalism.

I could also direct my attention to temporally extended wholes. In other words, instead of limiting my attention to instantaneous entities, I could consider *intertemporal* mereological fusions of various stages of the ship. Also in this case, no problem ensues for Extensionalism. The resulting intertemporal fusions will have, as proper parts, the stages, the proper parts of the stages, and any recombination of these things. The various stages of the ship will be called *temporal* parts of the spatially extended ship.

The notion of temporal part is highly interesting and problematic, but its problems concern the philosophy of time, not mereology$_{dis}$, and in particular not Extensionalism. In the doctrine of temporal parts, there are no temporally extended objects with the same proper parts, nor can it ever be the case that— in contrast with the Indiscernibility of Identicals—a single whole has different proper parts. The fact that temporal parts work as ordinary parts may be regarded as an advantage of the doctrine of temporal parts.

This is probably why many mereological monists, such as Goodman and Lewis, have endorsed a four-dimensionalist position and the doctrine of temporal parts: the doctrine of temporal parts is an application of mereology, an application that aims to solve the potential tension between temporal change and the Indiscernibility of Identicals. But the affinity between mereology and the doctrine of temporal parts *does not imply* that a mereological monist is *forced* to adopt perdurantism over its alternatives.

The *second* broad option is to insist that the ship is one and the same throughout its voyage, and reconcile change and inter-temporal identity with the Indiscernibility of Identicals in another way: namely, by relativizing properties, or the instantiation of properties, to times. Let us focus on the relativization of properties. One could call $t_d$ the time at which the ship departs, and $t_a$ the time at which the ship arrives. The ship is brown at $t_d$, non-gray at $t_d$, gray at $t_a$, and non-brown at $t_a$. But being gray at $t_d$ and being gray at $t_a$ are two different properties. The ship is of a single color each time. Every color property should be relativized to a specific time, and thus there is no property that the ship instantiates and fails to instantiate.

Also in this case, this general approach to temporal change (usually dubbed *endurantism*) can be applied to mereological change as well: the relation of parthood (and, with it, proper parthood, overlap, and fusion) should be relativized to a time. Thus, at a certain $t_m$, the Ship of Theseus will have some proper parts, and at a certain other time $t_n$ it will have some other proper parts. There is no discernibility stemming from having a certain proper part at $t_m$ and not *having* it at $t_n$, because being proper part at $t_m$ and being proper part at $t_n$ are different relations.

Endurantism—in contrast with perdurantism, which leads to an application of mereology$_{theo}$ to the temporal domain—could require some adjustment in mereology$_{theo}$ itself. Indeed, the strategy for coping with the apparent violations of the Indiscernibility of Identicals consists in relativizing the mereological relations to times. But this relativization can be expected to be general. This additional difficulty is perhaps an additional reason why mereological monism is more often conjoined with four-dimensionalism.

In this book, we will not discuss the ways in which mereology$_{theo}$ can be relativized to times,[15] but one can legitimately wonder if, in our formulation of Extensionalism, a three-dimensionalist should relativize the occurrences of the predicate *PP*. The most promising way to do so is to quantify universally over times: two things will be identical on the sufficient condition of having, at every time, the same proper parts.

It is a very conservative modification: every occurrence of *PP* is replaced by an occurrence of $PP_t$[16]; in the antecedent, there is an existential quantification over times, in order to limit the principle to entities that have proper parts at least at one time; in the consequent, the sufficient condition includes a universal quantification over times, so that entities with the same proper parts at every time are identical.

$$\forall x \forall y ((\exists t \exists z (z PP_t x) \wedge \exists t \exists z (z PP_t y)) \rightarrow (\forall t \forall z (z PP_t x \leftrightarrow z PP_t y) \leftrightarrow x = y))$$

This principle would be disobeyed by two different complex things that share all their proper parts at every moment. Potential counterexamples of this kind would be similar to those in which an object is distinguished from its colocated matter or portion of matter due to modal or aesthetic properties. We have seen in Section 7.5 that the motivations for drawing these distinctions tend to *propagate* from wholes to parts, without ever determining a compelling exception to Extensionalism.

Thus, Extensionalism is perfectly compatible with four-dimensionalism. Three-dimensionalism could require a reformulation of CEM in which parthood and other mereological relations are relativized to times. In this reformulation also Extensionalism should be reformulated accordingly, but this in no way affects the reasons in favor or against Extensionalism: all the arguments in defense of Extensionalism we discussed in the previous chapters will still be available after a relativization to times. Time and change are not a matter of special concern for Extensionalism, and for mereological monism in general.

# Extensionalism and Abstract Entities

## 8.1 A different scenario

The abstract counterexamples to Extensionalism are less commonly discussed than concrete counterexamples. They deserve a separate discussion, since they raise different and interesting methodological concerns. In many cases, these counterexamples involve entities whose *existence* is controversial; and even when their existence is conceded, their *nature* is controversial.

Many of the abstract entities at stake are commitments of philosophical theories. Thus, it is not clear whether mereological monism can be used to rule them out, or whether they rule mereological monism (and, in particular, Extensionalism) out. We have real evidence against the absolute generality of mereological monism only if: (a) we have good reason to think that the abstract entities at stake exist; (b) independent reasons make it unavoidable or preferable to construe these abstract entities in such a way that two of them are allowed to share all their proper parts while being different.

At the opposite extreme, it should be noted that there is a *trivial* way to clash with Extensionalism. It is not difficult at all to imagine or to *postulate* that a kind of abstract entity violates Extensionalism, and is such that its identity conditions countenance structural aspects, thereby violating Fine's principles of obliteration.

Some descriptions of CEM as the *logic* of parthood—sometimes provided by mereological monists themselves, in an effort to clarify the alleged formal, topic-neutral status of mereology, in analogy with the formal status of logic, as we have seen in Chapter 3—can be easily overrated: it is not *logically* deviant or difficult to set up a characterization of parthood that violates Extensionalism. The so-called nonclassical mereologies are relatively well-developed frameworks that are not so called because they need to adopt a nonclassical logic.

They are called "nonclassical" simply because they deviate from CEM.[1] While this book is a presentation and philosophical defense of mereological monism (that is, of the contention that CEM tells all the truth about parthood and cognate notions), we will occasionally take a look at nonclassical mereologies (in particular, at non-extensional mereologies in Chapter 9), and we will see that they do not present any special logical or technical difficulty. Their main deficiency—which for their supporters is probably a virtue—is that they are less powerful than CEM, and in particular do not provide identity conditions for the entities they are about.

This lack of power is not a technical difficulty in formulating them. For analogous reasons, when we look at non-strictly mereological theories—that is, at theories that are not about parthood and composition, but in which parthood and composition are or can be applied—it is very easy to meet theories that are incompatible with mereological monism, and with Extensionalism in particular.

However, it is at least dubious that they respect the two conditions (a) and (b) above. The options either to deny that the entities at stake exist (*contra* (a)), or to deny that they are involved in the parthood relations, or to revise the application of parthood to them in an extensionalist-friendly way (*contra* (b)) are in some cases attractive, and in others not definitely foreclosed. Let us discuss some examples before drawing a general conclusion about the two different ways in which mereological monism applies to concrete and abstract entities respectively.

## 8.2 Facts and propositions

Many theories of so-called facts and propositions seem to violate Extensionalism in a blatant way. We have already mentioned Armstrong's facts. These are complex entities, expected to make sentences and beliefs true, and are composed of some individuals and a universal (either a property or a relation). In the case of asymmetric relations, there would be two facts with the same proper parts: the fact that Romeo loves Juliet and the fact that Juliet loves Romeo are different facts (they are the truth makers of different sentences), but Juliet, Romeo, and the relation of *loving* would be the only proper parts of both facts.

Propositions are often taken to be what sentences express and the object of so-called propositional attitudes, such as belief. They raise analogous problems, if they are meant as structured entities, in a tradition that dates back to Russell.

Suppose that Jim believes that Berlin is west of Paris. Then, we could think that the object of Jim's belief is a structured entity whose parts are the city of Berlin, the city of Paris, and the relation of *being west of*. This structured entity is not a fact, since it is not a fact that Berlin is west of Paris (the sentence "Berlin is west of Paris" is false). The proposition that Berlin is west of Paris is also different from another structured proposition of the same category, namely the (true) proposition that Paris is west of Berlin. However, the two structured propositions that Berlin is west of Paris and that Paris is west of Berlin would share all their three proper parts. A counterexample to Extensionalism ensues.

Armstrong's facts and Russellian propositions violate Extensionalism. But a quick look at the enormous and fractured literature on facts, truth-making, propositions, and attitudes reveals that tons of things could have gone wrong in the above train of thought that would lead one to reject Extensionalism.[2]

In the case of facts, the role of truth makers could be played by other entities, such as individuals, tropes, or relations. Alternatively, there could be *no need* for truth makers at all. Even if truth makers are needed and facts are assumed as the best candidates for this role, it is not clear that facts have parts, or that these parts should be a universal and some individuals for which order matters.

As far as propositions are concerned, it is controversial that belief and other so-called propositional attitudes have objects at all (for example, according to adverbialism, belief is not a relation, but a property of its subject[3]); and, assuming that something must indeed play the role of the object of belief, propositions compete with sentences, utterances, and mental contents as the best candidates for this role. Even if propositions turn out to be the best candidates, they are meant in a variety of ways. In the semantic proposals of Hintikka and Montague, propositions are actually sets of possible worlds, and it is far from clear—as we will see below—that sets violate Extensionalism.

All these controversies surrounding facts and propositions are largely beyond the scope of this book. Obviously, the mere observation that it is controversial to admit these kinds of entities and to construe them in an anti-extensionalist way *is not* an argument for Extensionalism: it leaves open the possibility that the right solution to these controversies is precisely to admit that in some cases the order of entities—or other structural features of wholes—*should not* be obliterated, and thus that the identity conditions provided by CEM are wrong.

Nonetheless, the existence of these controversies makes it clear that, when Extensionalism is confronted with these "philosophical" kinds of entities, its fortunes depend on other philosophical debates. The decisions as to whether facts and propositions exist and about their natures *do not belong* to mereology$_{dis}$.

Still, mereology$_{dis}$ could and should interact with the different theories that are in charge of dealing with facts and propositions.

The ideal procedure should be roughly as follows. In semantics, philosophy of mind, and perhaps epistemology, some scholars propose facts or propositions as the best candidates for some roles to be filled. They characterize them through some principles. When the theories are developed formally, these principles might take the form of axioms, and provide an implicit definition of what a fact or a proposition is. The debate about the theories themselves is expected to determine whether these roles should really be filled, whether those candidates are really the fittest, and whether they should really be construed in a non-extensional way.

If—in at least one case—a positive answer is given to all these scrutinies, then we have an argument for anti-extensionalism. Mereology$_{dis}$ *does play* a role in this procedure. It plays it as a matter of fact, since appeals to mereology are very frequent in the debates about the existence and the nature of these kinds of entities. According to Lewis—as we know—facts do not exist, insofar as, if they existed, they would instantiate a non-mereological kind of composition.

There are good reasons why mereology$_{dis}$ plays this role. In particular, the intrinsic theoretical desirability of the simple and clear-cut identity conditions provided by CEM, through Uniqueness of Composition and Extensionalism, has an important role in these debates. It is an intrinsic advantage to adopt a theory in which parts determine what is identical to what and—as a result—how many things there are. As we will see in Chapter 9, non-extensional mereologies— while formally unproblematic and relatively well-developed—do not replace Extensionalism with different identity conditions for complex entities.

It is a great merit of Fine to have shown that identity conditions that are sensible to structure are not bound to be *cans of worms*. Structure is not a mysterious, intractable notion: we can have a sensible and manageable conception of structure, in which various kinds of arrangements of parts are classified and systematized.

Nonetheless, even the seemingly most innocent and desirable kind of structure—namely the order of the parts, as this is involved in structured facts and propositions—makes our theory *significantly* more complicated. Identity conditions will be topic-specific. Facts and propositions actually require us to countenance both the order and the repetition of parts. For example, the fact that Narcissus loves himself is expected to be composed by the binary relation of love and by Narcissus *twice*. This might lead us to think that parts fill slots in a structure, so that one and the same thing can fill two slots in a same structure.[4]

The idea that order matters is also connected with the idea that relations have a certain ariety: a number of places or slots to be filled.

Thus, the rejection of some principles of obliteration of structure (Absorption and Permutation in this case) entails the need to enrich and complicate our ideology with new notions. Again, this does not prove that this enrichment is *worthless* (less so that it is technically arduous, or formally flawed). Nonetheless, in the context of the typical cost-benefit analyses of philosophical investigations, increased complexity is a cost, and not a minor one either. While in this context I cannot establish whether propositions and facts exist and are structured, anti-extensional entities, mereological monism makes it clear that structured facts and propositions are a philosophically committing, expensive option.

## 8.3 Extensionalism and stipulation

Could we *stipulate* that facts and propositions are in a certain way? Or are they something out there, endowed with an objective nature of some kind? When philosophical entities are at stake, it seems as though the fate of Extensionalism could be settled with a stipulation. The same suspicion arises with respect to nonphilosophical abstract entities (such as sets, or structures employed in formal semantics for the interpretation of a formal language), when these abstract entities are attributed some parts and mereology is applied to them.

It is difficult to generalize claims about such a wide and diverse domain of things, but—at least in some cases—it seems plausible that it is a matter of choice and stipulation whether to be extensionalist or not.

In the debate about concrete entities (as in our example involving Monte Grappa and Mountmatter in Chapter 7), it seems that the discernibility intuitions are a datum; we are not free to stipulate that Mountmatter *would* survive the annihilation of a molecule, or that it is photogenic; we can only interpret some data in various ways. By contrast, nothing similar happens in the case of abstract entities, because there is no discernibility intuition at play. The entities at stake are philosophical constructions that can be designed to violate Extensionalism.

Why are facts and propositions often stipulated in an anti-extensionalist way? The reason for this relatively common—though controversial—choice seems to lie in language. Facts have the main theoretical role of making sentences true; propositions are the objects of so-called propositional attitudes, and attitudes are attributed by complex sentences, in which smaller sentences figure in the so-called *that-clauses*.

The fact that Paris is west of Berlin is conceived as a sort of metaphysical mirror of the sentence "Paris is west of Berlin," which the fact would make true. The (false) proposition that Berlin is west of Paris is conceived as a sort of metaphysical mirror of the sentence "Berlin is west of Paris," which is included in the that-clause of the belief ascription "John believes that Berlin is west of Paris."[5]

This mirroring can be identified as the source of the anti-extensionalist trends in the metaphysics of facts and propositions. It is because these entities are construed as metaphysical "shadows" of natural language that order and repetition matter in them: we can refer to the same thing twice, and it matters—for the syntax and for the truth conditions of a sentence—whether a referential expression is the subject or the direct object of a predicate. In the literature about facts and propositions, this is a major source of perplexity about them: after all, why should we think that there are structured entities in the world that mirror the structure of linguistic entities?

Here we cannot decide whether facts and propositions exist, and whether it is sound to construe them as structural mirrors of sentences. It is enough to reiterate that, when these kinds of theoretical entities are at stake, some decisions and stipulations about them *must* be adopted, and that, in the context of such stipulations, the intrinsic desirability of structure-free, content-only identity conditions should be countenanced as a benefit in favor of *extensionalist* options.


## 8.4 Extensionalism and language


Language is the primary origin of anti-extensionalist theories of facts and propositions. However, it is important to remark that language, by itself, does not provide any compelling evidence against Extensionalism.

This remark is important because, while facts and propositions are theoretical entities whose existence is doubtful and whose nature could involve a stipulative element, sentences, words, letters, and analogous linguistic entities are not such that their existence can simply be denied. We have (more in linguistics than in philosophy) lots of evidence about their existence and nature. Thus, if language offered clear exceptions to Extensionalism, Extensionalism would be in *serious* trouble.

The statement that language does not offer any evidence against Extensionalism may sound surprising. Prima facie, language displays many violations of Extensionalism. However, the more we analyze these seeming violations, the more we see that they depend on philosophy-laden, controversial assumptions. Basically, the apparent violations of Extensionalism in language depend on taking language as something *metaphysically extraordinary*. If, by contrast, linguistic items are taken as down-to-earth, standard, concrete items, then linguistic items are no less Extensionalism-friendly than mountains, statues, persons, and other concrete items.

Already Lewis was aware that language is a major source of prima facie attractive anti-extensionalist examples. These examples may involve letters and words, since it seems that different words can have the same letters as parts:

> It might be said, for instance, that the two words "master" and "stream" are made of the same six letters.[6]

Other examples involve words and sentences: the sentence "Romeo loves Juliet" seems to have the same words as parts as the different sentence "Juliet loves Romeo."

These latter examples are closely linked to anti-extensionalist sentence-like conceptions of facts and propositions: in the case of facts, for example, the fact that Romeo loves Juliet will be thought to have the same parts as the different fact that Juliet loves Romeo, as much as the sentence that Romeo loves Juliet would have the same parts as the different sentence that Juliet loves Romeo.

Linguistic entities, at several levels of complexity (letters, syllables, words, syntagms, sentences, and so on), can be viewed in two very broad ways. They can be seen as *tokens*: these tokens can be concrete inscriptions, with a specific spatial location, or sounds, that occur at a certain time. Let us focus on written tokens: "master," "stream," and "master" are *three* word-tokens. In each of these word-tokens, there are six letter-tokens.

The three word-tokens are mutually mereologically disjoint: they do not share *any* letter-token. Token-words do not usually share token-letters: in usual English notations, token-words are sharply separated. The same happens with sentences: the token-sentences "Romeo loves Juliet" and "Juliet loves Romeo" *do not have* the same token-words as constituents; by contrast, they do not share any token-word.

However, letters, words, and sentences can be seen as types, as well: linguistic types would be abstract, repeatable entities, of which each token is an instance. In this sense, the word-type "master" would include the same letter-types included by the word-type "stream"; and the sentence-types "Romeo loves Juliet" and "Juliet loves Romeo" would include the same word-types.

Is Extensionalism doomed? Only if some highly controversial choices are made. Sure, we tend to say that "master" and "stream" are made of the same letters, and we have the impression that this claim is true. By contrast, if the claim is meant to refer to linguistic tokens, then it should be false. But what we mean by that allegedly true claim is far from clear.

If what we mean is that "master" and "stream" are two word-types that include the same letter-types, we would be inclined to claim that also "master" and "masters" (as well as "stream" and "streams") are made of the same letters. But the inclination to assent to this latter claim is much weaker: it would be reasonable to object that "master" and "masters" *are not* made of the same letters, because "masters" includes a letter which "master" does not include. This objection cannot but concern letter-tokens (and, in particular, the additional token of "s" in "masters"). Nonetheless, there is no evidence of any ambiguity between types and tokens between the claim that "master" and "stream" are made of the same letters and the claim that "master" and "masters" are not.

A solution might be to interpret the claim that some words are made of some letters in terms of tokens and similarity. "Master" and "stream"—the two token-words—are made of six token-letters each: there is a one-to-one correspondence between their constituting token-letters such that each token letter is similar to the corresponding one in the other word. The fact that we tend to use the expression "same letters"—instead of "similar letters"—could be explained as an appeal to *qualitative* identity: the token-letters would be numerically different, but still so similar in terms of their linguistically relevant features as to be regarded as "the same letter"—a bit like when we say that Venus and Mars are the same celestial body, and we mean that they share enough features to be both planets, in spite of the fact that they are obviously numerically different.[7]

Thus, we have a way to explain why we say that different words are made of the same letters, without incurring in an exception to Extensionalism. Given that this explanation does not involve linguistic types at all, we could keep it as an indication that linguistic types *do not exist at all*, and *a fortiori* cannot determine an exception to Extensionalism. However, this would be a far-fetched and hazardous conclusion: it seems correct to say that the English alphabet is made up of twenty-six letters, and it would be *awkward* to insist that it is made up of twenty-six concrete inscriptions. Analogously, when a dictionary provides the definition of a word, it seems that it does not give the definition either for a single token or for a definite plurality of tokens: the definition is expected to be valid also for future tokens, that is—from the most straightforward viewpoint—for new instances of the abstract type.

Getting rid of linguistic types is a challenging (and fascinating) nominalistic project—endorsed in various ways by mereological monists such as Goodman and Quine, and in a different context by Wilfrid Sellars.[8] The kind of nominalism that is here at stake is not the nominalism about structure that is entangled with mereological monism, but nominalism about linguistic types. It can be motivated by a radical form of naturalism about language, according to which—at least at the syntactic level—language should consist only of concrete, perceivable, down-to-earth entities; or by a more general kind of nominalism, according to which any commitment to repeatable entities, universals, or possibly abstract entities in general, is best avoided.

However, if Extensionalism were to rely on nominalism about linguistic types, it would inherit all its difficulties. There are several alternatives. First of all, in the philosophy of language there is a lively debate about what linguistic types are. According to an influential proposal by David Kaplan, linguistic types *are not* abstract, repeatable entities, but standard *continuants*, that is, entities that persist through time.[9] Different tokens would be *temporal parts* of types. A token would count as a part of the same type of a previously uttered or written token if and only if it is uttered or written with the *intention of repeating* the previous token.

Kaplan's proposal is independently motivated. Kaplan has no apparent interest in preserving mereological Extensionalism. The main reason for Kaplan's proposal is that *similarity* is a poor guide to linguistic types: we classify linguistic word-tokens such as "Phosphorus" and "Fosforus" as belonging to the same type, in spite of their patent notational difference; we classify some written and oral linguistic tokens as belonging to the same type, in spite of the fact that it is not clear at all in which sense a sound is similar to a written sign. By contrast, in all these cases—according to Kaplan—there is a sort of *causal* link between different tokens of a same type; and the unifying element of each type would be the intention to repeat previous tokens.

If linguistic types are standard, concrete continuants, then they do not raise any specific concern for Extensionalism. They can be reconciled with Extensionalism through the strategies we discussed in Chapter 7, Section 7.7.

Kaplan's metaphysics of linguistic types is attractive, but this is not the place for a full assessment of its merits and problems. However, even assuming that linguistic types exist and that, *contra* Kaplan, they are repeatable, abstract universals, Extensionalism can be defended in other ways. As we have seen, it is possible and quite reasonable to admit linguistic types, while at the same time denying—as in the above case—that we are referring to linguistic types when we say that different words (sentences) have the same letters (words) as parts.

Nonetheless, quite independently of what we mean when we say that different types have the same parts, we should decide whether linguistic types have parts at all, and—if so—what parts they have. We could construe them as mereological atoms, but this would be strange, since there is a clear sense in which words are in sentences, and letters are in words.

At this point, we might attempt to claim that word-types are parts of sentence-types, and that letter-types are parts of word-types, but that there are other parts as well. As observed by Varzi,[10] it is highly anomalous, and in open contrast with CEM, to exclude from the domain of the parts of something the fusions of its parts. More specifically, why should syllable-types, and in general arbitrary combinations of consecutive letter-types in a word, not be parts of word types? And why should syntactically complex units (such as the combination of a predicate with its direct object) not be parts of sentence-types? If we admit these different parts, then "master" and "stream"—even if regarded as types—share some parts (the letter-types), but differ in many other parts (only "master" has "ma" as part, and only "stream" has "str" as part); as a result, they do not deliver any exception to Extensionalism.

However, this solution too is anomalous: if the order does not matter (if CEM obliterates it), it should not matter even when establishing what combinations of letters are admitted as parts of words (or what combinations of words are admitted as parts of sentences). The restriction to combinations of *consecutive* letters is unmotivated, and, once it is dropped, both "ma" and "str" end up being parts of both "master" and "stream." Since the letters are the same in both words, also any combination of letters will be the same in both words.

A better solution (a solution we need *only if* we insist that linguistic types exist and are abstract entities, and not standard continuants as Kaplan has proposed) is to concede that linguistic types are not mereological fusions of other linguistic types, but sets. As Lewis says about "master" and "stream,"

> then indeed two things are generated set-theoretically out of the same six members. (Lewis, 1991, p. 71)

The idea—which Lewis does not detail any further—is not that "master" and "stream"—as types—are sets whose members are the six letters, because in that case they would be the same sets: according to the Axiom of Extensionality (endorsed by any set theory), two sets are identical if and only if they have the same members. By contrast, linguistic types would be *more complex* sets, in which the order and the repetition are codified, for example by marking the parts with a natural number.[11] The word "master" would be the set *{{m,1}, {a,2},* *{s,3}, {t,4}, {e,5}, {r,6}}*, while "stream" would be the different set *{{s,1}, {t,2}, {r,3}, {e,4}, {a,5}, {m,6}}*.

This set-theoretic understanding of linguistic types might seem artificial, or even arbitrary: there are many other ways of codifying order set-theoretically (instead of inserting numbers in subsets, we could mark the order by including each letter in different levels of singletons).[12] This risk of arbitrariness in set-theoretical interpretations of entities which are not prima facie sets is widely discussed in the philosophy of mathematics: numbers too can be identified with different sets, and there seems to be no clear motivation for preferring some sets to others.[13] How are we supposed to choose between them? In the linguistic case, if word-types, sentence-types, and so on are expected to exist, and to be a primary object of linguistics, how can their nature be *arbitrary*?

One could here resort to some of the replies usually given in the philosophy of mathematics: for example, one could say that words are a certain kind of set (perhaps the one with natural numbers of which we gave two examples above), and that our lack of reasons to choose that specific kind of set over another is simply a matter of ignorance (due to contingent facts or to the constitutive epistemic limits of human beings); if we knew better, we would know that words are things of that kind.

Perhaps it is better to acknowledge that *abstract* linguistic types (if they exist at all, and if they are really abstract, *contra* Kaplan), as much as other abstract or theoretical entities (such as facts and propositions), are connected with a kind of *stipulation*; and that, if we stipulate them in an anti-extensionalist way, then they will violate Extensionalism. When we decide what an abstract word-type is (as well as when we decide what a fact or a proposition is), we can make it extensional or not: the price of making it non-extensional is that we lose an economic and general way of providing identity conditions for word-types.

Thus, the only linguistic entities which constitute a danger for mereological Extensionalism are linguistic types, *if* their existence is conceded and *if* they are construed as abstract entities, and not as standard concrete continuants, as Kaplan has proposed. Abstract linguistic types *can* violate Extensionalism, if the stipulations about them violate Extensionalism. This makes them quite similar to other abstract entities, such as sets.

There is no specific danger for Extensionalism in language. Linguistic counterexamples to Extensionalism apply only if the ontology of language hosts abstract entities, such as abstract linguistic types. While I do not claim to have shown that the ontology of language should not host such things, it is important to keep in mind that it is not clear or evident that there are abstract linguistic types. Even if abstract linguistic types are admitted, the problems they raise for Extensionalism are simply an instance of the general problems raised by abstract entities. We are going to discuss these problems in the next two sections.

## 8.5 A limitation for Extensionalism

It seems that in certain cases the fate of Extensionalism can be decided with a stipulation. After all, Extensionalism consists in the obliteration of structure, but it is perfectly possible to introduce *structured* abstract entities in mathematics or in semantics. Some of these entities are even called *structures*, as is the case in algebra and in formal semantics. Mereology$_{phi}$ cannot *forbid* these stipulations, and it would be wrong and presumptuous for philosophers to claim that there is something technically wrong in them.

I will propose that, in certain cases, the mereological monist should simply concede that there are counterexamples to Extensionalism in the realm of abstract entities, and restrict its ambitions of formality/generality to the realm of concrete entities. This distinction might correspond to a general difference between abstract and concrete entities: abstract entities can be created by stipulation, while concrete entities cannot. Thus, Extensionalism would concern those entities in relation to which it cannot be violated in a too simple, stipulative, *fiat* way.

The nature of the structured abstract entities at stake (those which could violate Extensionalism) is strictly constrained by specific theories. This is the case with *sets* themselves, whose nature is expected to be completely determined by some axioms. However, even once these axioms are established, it seems that some stipulations can concern the application of mereological concepts to sets, and determine whether sets obey Extensionalism or not.

Consider again the two sets with which in the previous section we have identified the word-types "master" and "stream": $\{\{m,1\}, \{a,2\}, \{s,3\}, \{t,4\}, \{e,5\}, \{r,6\}\}$ and $\{\{s,1\}, \{t,2\}, \{r,3\}, \{e,4\}, \{a,5\}, \{m,6\}\}$, respectively. The ultimate constituents of these two sets—which Goodman, as we know, considered to be the *content* of these sets—are the same six letters and the natural numbers from *1* to *6*: *m, a, s, t, e, r, 1, 2, 3, 4, 5, 6.* These "basic" constituents are differently arranged, stratified in the two sets.

So do sets ultimately violate mereological Extensionalism or not? It depends again on the stipulation, as seems to be generally the case when abstract or theoretical entities are confronted with Extensionalism. Here the crucial stipulation does not concern the nature of sets, but the way in which parthood is applied to sets.

Goodman saw sets as essentially anti-extensional items, and devised his own calculus of individuals as a *more* extensionalist (hyperextensional), nominalistic (in the sense of nominalism about structure) alternative to set theory. However, it is possible to look at sets and Extensionalism from a different viewpoint, and reach a different conclusion. From a pluralistic perspective, Fine focuses on the operation of *set-building*, which connects elements of a set to the set itself. This operation—in opposition to mereological Fusion—violates Collapse and Leveling (two of the principles discussed in Chapter 5, Section 5.7). This means that members—and not ultimate members—are taken as parts of sets. And, from this perspective, the set-theoretical Axiom of Extensionality warrants that there are not two sets with the same elements: if the parts of a set are its elements, then sets *respect* Extensionalism after all.

By contrast, Lewis takes the fact that set-theoretic membership is not transitive as a reason to think that membership is not parthood, and claims that the parts of a set are its subsets. As a result, $\{\{m,1\}, \{a,2\}, \{s,3\}, \{t,4\}, \{e,5\}, \{r,6\}\}$ (the set with which the type "master" would be identified) and $\{\{s,1\}, \{t,2\}, \{r,3\}, \{e,4\}, \{a,5\}, \{m,6\}\}$ (the set with which "stream" would be identified) would have different parts: for example, $\{\{a,2\}, \{s,3\}\}$ would be part of "master," but not part of "stream"; $\{\{e,4\}, \{m,6\}, \{s,1\}\}$ would be part of "stream," but not of "master."

Thus, Goodman, Fine, and Lewis *disagree* on what is part of a set: ultimate elements, for Goodman; set-theoretic elements, for Fine; subsets, for Lewis. As a consequence of these decisions, the sets with which the word-types "master" and "stream" are identified will respect or fail to respect Extensionalism: for they have the same ultimate elements, but different set-theoretic elements, and different subsets.

By contrast, when concrete entities are at stake, we are not "free" to decide what is part of what, and the fate of Extensionalism cannot be determined by such decisions. It would be viciously *ad hoc* to deal with potential concrete counterexamples to Extensionalism by selecting the parts of something in a specific way. In the case of abstract entities, these kinds of decisions should be taken in any case, and it is legitimate, and not *ad hoc*, to identify parts of them—"parts of classes," as the title of Lewis's book runs—so as to respect Extensionalism.

Lewis would probably disagree with this reconstruction of his work; he would *deny* that subsets are parts of classes *because of* a stipulation. He would claim that subclasses—and neither members nor ultimate members—are parts of classes because membership is not transitive and it is possible for two classes to have the same ultimate members. But in this way Extensionalism is simply assumed, instead of being argued for.

Unfortunately, when abstract entities are at stake, it is difficult to do any better. The stipulations that can be made about abstract entities and about the application of parthood to them are simply free to violate Extensionalism. The mereological monist could staunchly deny that structured abstract entities exist, by embracing fascinating and arduous nominalistic programs (in which the nominalism at stake *is not* nominalism about structure, but nominalism about abstract entities); or insist in preferring Extensionalism-friendly stipulations about what parts they have. As we have seen, Lewis's idea that the parts of sets are their subsets (instead of their elements, or fundamental elements) prevent sets from being counterexamples to Extensionalism.

Does this strategy for defending Extensionalism in the case of abstract entities always make sense? A very general perplexity one could voice is that the strategy in question aims to make extensional entities that were *designed* to be non-extensional. Suppose that we find a more or less bizarre way of "extensionalizing" *structures*, that is, those algebraic entities defined by a set (the domain of the structure) and some operations and relations on such domain. Structures are usually employed in formal semantics to provide an interpretation of a formal language. The idea behind structures is precisely that *one and the same set* can be the domain of different structures: the role of operations and relations in a structure is precisely to specify how the elements of the domain are *arranged*.

Suppose that we found a way to extensionalize structures. There would be something really curious and ironic in this operation: we would take entities whose usual name ("structure") suggests—rather correctly—that the arrangement of what is in them *matters*, and we would show that, given a certain way of construing them and applying mereological concepts to them, they respect mereological Extensionalism. It seems that we would have simply found a way to *hide* the arrangement of entities in a structure. Moreover, our decisions and stipulations would be unashamedly driven by our need to respect Extensionalism, without any attempt to be faithful to the real nature of structures themselves.

In general, Extensionalism about abstract entities raises different issues from those raised about concrete entities in Chapter 7. It seems that we can *stipulate* structured abstract entities that prima facie violate Extensionalism; and that, in many cases, it is *de facto* very useful to stipulate such entities (the myriad of applications of sets and structures is strong evidence of the usefulness of the respective stipulations). After that, we can make further stipulations about the way in which mereological concepts should be applied to them, in order to safeguard Extensionalism. However, in some cases—such as the case of structures—these further stipulations risk *clashing* with the motivations for thinking that those entities exist.

Given these difficulties, the mereological monist is better off *withdrawing* her pretense of *absolute* formality or topic-neutrality. The peculiar connection between abstract entities and stipulations always leaves the possibility of violating Extensionalism open. There are various strategies to reconcile the apparent exceptions to Extensionalism with Extensionalism, but some lead to disappointing results, which seem to apply mereological concepts to non-extensional entities in a way that is in strident contrast with the expected nature of these entities.

## 8.6 Why it is reasonable to exclude abstract entities

The decision to limit Extensionalism (and hence the claim of adequacy for the identity conditions provided by CEM) to concrete entities may seem painful. It is a limitation for mereological monism on the whole: in the realm of abstract entities, parthood and composition are allowed to work in a different way. However, there are two main reasons why this cost does not divest mereological monism of its interest and *raison d'être*.

*First,* the categorical distinction between abstract and concrete entities is expected to be definite (that is, exempt from vagueness) and modally rigid (what is abstract is necessarily non-concrete, and what is concrete is necessarily nonabstract).[14] This means that, after the restriction, mereological monism still holds for a precisely delimited—and patently very wide—domain of entities.

However, it is important to remark that not all kinds of entities I have discussed in this chapter are abstract. Some of them (in particular facts) are theoretical entities—they are introduced in a philosophical theory, in order to play some explanatory roles and given an appropriate cost-benefit analysis—but are not abstract. Facts are thought by their supporters to be constituents of the world: according to Wittgenstein's famous motto in the *Tractatus Logico-Philosophicus*, "the world is the totality of facts."[15] As a result, facts are expected to have some kind of spatial and temporal location. According to some epistemologists, facts are the primary objects of knowledge.[16] Facts could also be involved in causal links and scientific laws.

Facts are really a risky bugbear for Extensionalism: a metaphysics of facts is a picture of *concrete reality* (about which no stipulation is expected to settle what there is) in which the order and the repetition of constituents matter, and should not be obliterated. Even once it is conceded that Extensionalism and mereological monism *do not hold* for abstract entities, facts cannot be disposed of in this way.

Nonetheless, extensionalists still have some attractive ways out at their disposal. First of all, facts could be entities without parts, or could be identified with sets of possible worlds (as it is more often done with propositions).[17] In this latter hypothesis, they would be classified as abstract entities, and would quit the expected domain of application of mereological monism. Second, one could deny that facts exist. There is nothing like a consensus about the commitment to facts in contemporary metaphysics. For any of the above-listed theoretical roles, there are alternatives to facts (tropes, relata-specific relations, events).

Finally, the line of reaction we have suggested above for mereological monism is more plausible in the case of facts than it is in the case of properly abstract entities, such as sets and structures. In the case of sets and structures, we have seen that they are plausibly introduced with the accompanying specific intention to account for certain kinds of arrangements of what is in them (stratification for sets, a much richer array of structural features for structures); and that—as a consequence—it is undesirable to be forced to apply mereological concepts to them in a structure-obliterating way.

Facts are different: facts are introduced in order to play the roles—among others—of truth makers and objects of knowledge but this in itself does not require them to be structured. The hypothesis that they have no parts, or are sets of a certain kind, is prima facie left open by their roles. From this viewpoint, facts are a special case: it is not easy to make another example of plausibly concrete entities that—according to a certain conception of them—threaten to undermine Extensionalism. Thus, it is not surprising that the mereological monist needs a specific treatment in this case: either a rejection of facts also on the basis of Extensionalism itself, or a deliberately extensional conception of them, or the thesis that facts are—*contra* expectations—abstract.

*Second*, we have seen that one major advantage of mereological monism— an advantage warranted by Extensionalism—is the provision of clear-cut and simple identity conditions for every entity. Now, suppose that the mereological monist is forced to restrict its ambitions, and in particular to admit that sets and other abstract entities are not extensional in the mereological sense. This would be a *significant* concession, but the concession would concern entities which can be expected to have definite and clear identity conditions *quite independently of mereological monism.* In other words, the great merit of Extensionalism is to provide definite and clear identity conditions; but abstract entities do not need them, because their respective theories already provide definite and clear identity conditions for them.

Consider sets: the Axiom of Extensionality claims that sets are identical if and only if they have the same members. Thus, sets have definite, explicit identity conditions, no matter how mereology is applied to them and whether they obey mereological Extensionalism or not. These identity conditions also display a certain level of formality or topic-neutrality (which, as we know, is a gradable feature): no matter what kinds of things the elements of these sets are (they may be other sets, individuals, universals, or anything else), sets have their identity conditions dictated by the Axiom of Extensionality.

Structures are no different: structures are identical if and only if they have the same domain and the same relations and operations on that domain. Moreover, structures are usually represented as ordered sets whose elements are their domain, a set of operations on it, and a set of relations on it. Thus, structures would be nothing but complex and stratified sets, and would enjoy the clear and definite identity conditions dictated by the Axiom of Extensionality.

The overall picture suggests that it is not by chance that the contraposition of mereological wholes and sets is a recurring element in the philosophical history of mereology (from Goodman to Lewis, up to pluralist approaches *à la* Fine). The sensibility to structure, which abstract entities (through their identity conditions) are often stipulated to have, can be expressed in set-theoretical terms. Set-theoretical elementhood and the operation that connects the elements of a set to the set itself could be thought to play in the realm of abstract entities the role played by parthood and Fusion in the realm of concrete entities.

The idea of a double-tier reality—concrete mereological wholes on the one hand and abstract sets on the other, connected by those instances of set-theoretic membership in which a concrete entity is member of a set—is far from new. Also Lewis in *Parts of Classes* points to it, quite independently of his attempt to distinguish what is mereological in set theory. His "Division Thesis" runs as follows:

*Division Thesis:* Reality divides exclusively into individuals and classes. (Lewis 1991, p. 7)

To claim that every abstract entity enjoys the identity conditions of sets is a bold claim, which I do not aspire to prove in the present context. But even if one doubts this claim, it is reasonable to assume that every abstract entity, even if it is not a set, is such that a theory provides identity conditions for it. If so, and if the strategies to reconcile abstract entities with Extensionalism are deemed unsatisfying, the mereological monist has a way out: she could opt for a strategic and well-motivated retreat from the domain of abstract entities.

# The Alternatives to Extensionalism

## 9.1 Motivations for a non-extensional mereology

In this book, we are focusing on a specific mereology$_{theo}$: CEM. According to mereological monism, it is the right one. In the literature—particularly in the recent literature—several other, nonclassical kinds of mereology$_{theo}$ are to be found. These are often motivated by the need of eschewing Extensionalism.

In some cases, the need for a non-extensional mereology$_{theo}$ is not motivated by the explicit conviction that *reality* violates Extensionalism, but by the need to have a framework for managing fictional or scientifically controversial scenarios.

The typical fictional example[1] involves Borges's *Aleph*:

> I saw the Aleph from all points. I saw the earth in the Aleph and in the earth the Aleph once more and the earth in the Aleph [...].

The Aleph would have everything as a proper part (including the Earth). As other claims in Borges's story would show, also the Earth would have everything as a proper part, including the Aleph. This is *not* directly a (fictional) counterexample to Extensionalism, because the Aleph and the Earth *do have* different proper parts: only the Aleph—and not the Earth—has the Earth as a proper part; only the Earth—and not the Aleph—has the Aleph as a proper part. Nonetheless, it is a scenario incompatible with classical mereology, and in particular with the Asymmetry of proper parthood: the Aleph and Earth are different, mutual proper parts.

None of the fictional and parascientific examples in the literature are uncontroversially counterexamples from reality, and thus show that Extensionalism or other CEM's theorems are false metaphysical theses. Nonetheless, they are useful as a source of inspiration for alternative frameworks, in particular if these frameworks are taken with an instrumental attitude (remember that in this book my attitude toward CEM *is not* instrumental: to my mind, CEM is the sound and complete doctrine of parthood and composition for concrete entities).

In Chapter 8, Section 8.6 we have seen that abstract entities do not really require *an alternative* to CEM, because—so to say—*they are* an alternative to CEM, at least as regards identity conditions: their respective theories provide them with clear identity conditions.

Thus, the two major motivations for exploring non-extensional theories of parthood are: an instrumental attitude, according to which it is useful to have a technical framework for non-extensional scenarios, possibly motivated by fictional or parascientific examples; the steady belief that Monte Grappa and Mountmatter are different and have the same proper parts. This belief is steady because it resists all the *monist* attempts to show that Monte Grappa is identical to Mountmatter (Chapter 7, Sections 7.3 and 7.4), as well as the arguments suggesting that, if they are different, then their proper parts too are different (Chapter 7, Section 7.5).

Before making a couple of examples of non-extensional mereologies, let us briefly discuss another scenario that belongs to the same group as Borges's Aleph. However, this is not a *literary* example, but a sort of thought experiment inspired by the literature on time travels. Suppose that I want to build a wall with a single brick, but with a time machine at my disposal. At a certain time $t_m$ I take my brick back to a previous time $t_n$, and I put my transported brick next to the brick that was already at $t_n$. Now I have an initial fragment of a wall that has the size of two bricks, but the two bricks are numerically identical, by hypothesis. I could iterate the procedure at many other times after $t_m$, thereby obtaining an entire wall made of a single, multilocated brick.[2]

The example presupposes that time-travel is possible—and this is a presupposition that I am not going to discuss.[3] However, this is not the only controversial presupposition: another is that when the brick is moved back to a time in which it already existed, it is possible to put it *next to itself*. This kind of example would point to a supposed failure of Fine's principles of Absorption. While, to my mind, no concrete counterexample to Extensionalism is compelling, what is interesting about these counterexamples is that they point to different kinds of arrangement of parts in a whole. Fine's analysis of what structure is can be usefully compared with these alleged counterexamples. Various non-extensional mereologies correspond to the violation of some of Fine's principles of obliteration, while usually abiding by—or staying neutral about—other principles.

Nonetheless, the sensibility to some kinds of structural arrangement can be more easily matched with the sensibility to some other kinds of structural arrangement. We know that sets violate both Collapse and Leveling (since they are sensible to the stratification of what is in them), while they respect Absorption and Permutation. Correspondingly, the reasons for violating Absorption (and thus to countenance repetition) usually match the reasons for violating Permutation (and thus to countenance order).

The common root in this latter combination (the violation of both Absorption and Permutation) is the idea that it matters for the identity of the wholes what role or roles a part plays. The specification "for the identity of the whole" is—as always—*pivotal* in order to capture the real disagreement with mereological monists: mereological monists *do not deny*—at least *qua* mereological monists and extensionalists—that in a qualitative description of a whole it is often important to give an account of the relations between the parts, their respective position, their functional roles, and so on. They deny only that these aspects have any bearing on the identity conditions of wholes; and, due to their narrow understanding of mereology$_{dis}$, mereological monists think that it is not the business of mereology$_{dis}$ to account for what *does not matter* for the formal features of parthood, or for the identity and existence conditions of wholes. Anti-extensionalists disagree inasmuch as, according to them, structural features matter for the identity conditions of wholes.

## 9.2 Roles, forms, Extensionalism

If you care about roles and positions, you will be inclined both to admit that a single thing can play more than one role, or cover more than one position, and to admit that two wholes can differ simply because two of their parts have their role switched in them, even if they have all their parts in common. Thus, for example, in a non-extensional, structural theory of parthood sketched by Karen Bennett,[4] wholes have *slots*: roles to be filled by parts. The same part can fill more than one slot in a whole. An obvious consequence of Bennett's approach is that there can be two wholes that have the same slots and the same parts, but are nonetheless different because the slots are differently occupied.

Other kinds of non-extensional mereologies$_{theo}$ are more directly motivated by concrete cases such as that of Monte Grappa and Mountmatter, or by fictional and parascientific examples, such as those of the Aleph and of the wall made of a single brick. Consider the case of Monte Grappa and Mountmatter again.

As we have noted in Chapter 7, Section 7.6, there is a gap in the kind of dualism that stems from Varzi's reading of the debate. According to Varzi, the coherent dualist thinks that, at every level of complexity, there is a structured entity and a colocated portion of matter. In this thorough form of dualism, there are some relations that still lack an explanation: the relations between each structured entity and the colocated portion of matter.

Is it a mereological relation, which our mereology$_{theo}$ should characterize in some way? Due to my strong monist inclinations, I have difficulties in making my mind up about this supposed relation between Monte Grappa and Mountmatter. Perhaps dualists should simply construe the relation between Monte Grappa and Mountmatter as colocation, and colocation should be dealt with by a theory of spatial location.

An alternative is to say that the portion of matter is in the object, but not vice versa. This idea comes from a broadly Aristotelian *hylomorphist* tradition, according to which the object is a substance—that is some kind of compound of form and matter. The matter is in the substance, but not vice versa.

Hylomorphism is a relatively popular doctrine in contemporary philosophy, in particular among so-called Neo-Aristotelian philosophers.[5] Hylomorphists tend to disagree with mereological monism, but also among themselves. The differences among them hinge in particular on the role of *form* in a substance. Some of them (Fine for example) deny that the form is a part of a substance, while others (Kathrin Koslicki) disagree with Fine, and believe that the form *is* part of a substance. The inclusion of form among the parts of a substance *solves* the problem with Extensionalism, because the object and the portion of matter end up having different parts: the substances (Monte Grappa, the forest, and all their parts) have their forms as parts, while the colocated portions of matter (Mountmatter and all its parts) have no forms as parts.

One problem with Koslicki's *extensional* variety of hylomorphism is that the purpose of form should be to embody the structure of the parts, and it is not clear if this role can be played by an *additional* part. It seems that the structuring role of form as an additional part could end up consisting in the mutual arrangement of form and the other parts. But then form would not really explain or embody the structure: the real structure would consist in the way in which form structures the material parts. A *regress* seems to ensue.

Structure should consist in a net of relations, in which material parts can be in a certain order, appear multiple times, and at various levels of complexity. This is what structure is, and adding a further part named "form" could be a superfluous step, and could ignite a regress. One could reply that form as an additional part is not superfluous, because it helps to reconcile dualism about objects and portions of matter with Extensionalism; but if this is its only function, then the move seems viciously *ad hoc*.

## 9.3 Dropping Weak Supplementation

If form is not introduced as an additional part, the relation between Monte Grappa and Mountmatter can hardly find a mereological representation *within CEM* as it is. One could insist that Mountmatter is in Monte Grappa. In these cases, the word *constitution* is sometimes used (while in some other cases "constitution" is synonymous with "composition," and some *xx* constitute/compose a *y* if and only if *y* is the fusion of *xx*): Mountmatter would constitute Monte Grappa.

Is constitution a parthood relation? If it is not, then it bears no consequence for the theory of parthood. If it is, then the claim becomes that the portion of matter is part of the object, but different from it. This would mean that the portion of matter is a *proper part* of the object. But, insofar as form is not a part of the object, nothing else would be part of the object.

This needs a departure from CEM. It is not immediately clear that it is a departure from Extensionalism, because Monte Grappa is deemed to be different from Mountmatter, but has also a different proper part: Mountmatter is a proper part of Monte Grappa, but Mountmatter is not a proper part of itself (proper parthood is irreflexive). However, something else in CEM must be dropped. Among the principles of CEM, Uniqueness of Composition should be dropped. Both Monte Grappa and the colocated portion of matter would count as the fusion of all the smaller portions of matter (or of any selection of portions of matter such that nothing—so to say—is left over). Thus, two allegedly different things would be the fusions of the same things.

When a principle of CEM "seen from above"—as in Lewis's formalization—is dropped, one needs to look at weaker principles that can be retained. And, as we have seen in Chapter 6, while Extensionalism is weaker than Uniqueness of Composition, the choice of dropping Uniqueness of Composition while preserving Extensionalism is not very promising, because it ends up introducing unmotivated, intermediate "groups" of parts (see Chapter 6, Section 6.1 in particular).

Moreover, this route does not meet the needs of a dualist, for whom the portion of matter is a proper part of the colocated object, but not vice versa. Thus, while this case does not directly disobey Extensionalism, it disobeys another CEM theorem, which in the presentations of CEM *from below* is often taken as an axiom, and deemed to be *constitutive* of what parthood is:[6] Weak Supplementation.

The idea behind Weak Supplementation is that, if *x* is a proper part of *y*—instead of being an improper part of *y*, that is, *y* itself—it is because there is *something more* in *y*: this something more is a part of *y* that does not overlap with *x* (i.e., this part of *y* has no part in common with *x*):

$$\forall x \forall y (xPPy \rightarrow \exists z (zPy \wedge \neg z \circ x))$$                    (Weak Supplementation)

The reason why Weak Supplementation is often taken for granted is that, if a whole includes nothing more than one of its proper parts, then that proper part is—so to speak—suspiciously improper. But if we look at the kind of dualism we are assessing, it seems clear that it consists in a *systematic violation* of Weak Supplementation, such that every substance has a proper part (the colocated portion of matter), but no other part disjoint from it.

Nonetheless, the sheer and isolated denial of Weak Supplementation does not seem, in itself, a desirable strategy.[7] If the formal features of *P* (Reflexivity, Antisymmetry, Transitivity) and *PP* (Irreflexivity, Asymmetry, Transitivity) are preserved, the rejection of Weak Supplementation brings with itself the failure of Extensionalism, that is to say of the way in which CEM provides identity conditions for the entities it is about. Moreover, it also delivers an unsatisfying concept of *proper part*. In CEM, "proper part" is meant to designate a part *different* from the whole, and, if Weak Supplementation alone is dropped, this difference is left completely unexplained: mereology would not explain the alleged difference between Monte Grappa and Mountmatter at all.

If this is the outcome, it would have been much better to retain Extensionalism and the full power of CEM, and a consistent, global dualism in which the relation between objects and portions of matter is not explained at all: the reason why we went further was that we sought to *explain* the relation between Monte Grappa and Mountmatter in mereology. Getting rid of Weak Supplementation leaves us without the explanation we were expecting to find.

## 9.4 Reciprocal proper parts

The anti-extensionalist, at this point, might wish to get rid of the neo-Aristotelian idea that the portion of matter is *in* the more structured object, but not vice versa. This idea of a *one-directional* mereological relation between

Mountmatter and Monte Grappa was ultimately rooted in the presence of *form*, which was expected to explain the difference between Monte Grappa and Mountmatter. In Koslicki's variety of hylomorphism, form is actually a part among others, and explains the difference between Monte Grappa and Mountmatter, while at the same time triggering a regress. If, by contrast, *form* is not a part, then there is no *mereological* explanation of the difference between Monte Grappa and Mountmatter, and the need for this explanation was the only motivation we had to depart from the kind of consistent, extensionalist dualism in which the difference was left unexplained (at least as far as mereology$_{dis}$ is concerned).

An alternative is to think that the mereological relation between Monte Grappa and Mountmatter is not one-directional, but *reciprocal*. Actually, if we go back to the alleged sources of discernibility between Monte Grappa and Mountmatter, there is nothing in them to suggest a one-directional mereological relation between them; it is not clear why Mountmatter should be in Monte Grappa, but not vice versa (this idea simply slipped into the dialectics through a confrontation with Aristotelian hylomorphism). Only one of them (Monte Grappa) would survive the annihilation of a cubic meter of snow; and only one of them (Mountmatter) would not be destroyed if the various pieces of it were disseminated across a vast tract of land by a violent volcanic eruption. In scrutinizing these reasons, with which the dualist motivates her stance, it is not easy to understand why one of the two should be *before* or *after* the other in the kind of order that the relation of parthood is for its domain.

A promising kind of non-extensional mereology$_{theo}$ set forth by Aaron Cotnoir[8] admits reciprocal parthood. This requires Cotnoir to modify a formal feature of parthood: for, in CEM, parthood is antisymmetrical, and proper parthood is asymmetrical; no parthood relation is allowed to hold reciprocally between two entities. Cotnoir, as we will see, drops the Antisymmetry of parthood, and redefines proper parthood.

Before assessing the details of Cotnoir's proposal, it is worth remarking that it coheres with the *spirit of dualism* about objects and portions of matter. According to the spirit of dualism, *at a single level* of mereological complexity there are *two* things. Thus, dualism finds its most appropriate expression in a theory of parthood only if this theory allows—as Cotnoir's non-extensional mereology$_{theo}$ does—two different things to be in a reciprocal relation of parthood.

Cotnoir's revision consists in dropping the Antisymmetry of parthood, while redefining proper parthood; given the redefinition, the Asymmetry of proper parthood is preserved. When applied to the case of an object and the colocated portion of matter, this results in the claim that Monte Grappa and Mountmatter are reciprocal parts.

The redefinition of proper parthood distinguishes it from parthood *tout court*, by excluding just the cases of mutual parthood, instead of excluding specifically the identity case.

$$\forall x \forall y (x P P y \equiv_{def} x P y \wedge \neg y P x)$$

(Proper Parthood—Cotnoir's Redefinition)

The identity case (that is, the hypothesis that something is a proper part of itself) is excluded nonetheless, given that the new definition of proper parthood makes it explicitly asymmetric and, as a consequence, irreflexive.

As Cotnoir underlines,[9] the resulting kind of theory of parthood is an attractive kind of anti-extensionalism. The Antisymmetry of parthood could be seen as a sort of Extensionalism for *improper* parthood, so that it is ideologically consistent for the anti-extensionalist to reject it. Antisymmetry is the claim that, if some things have the same improper parts (that is, the same things that occupy the same mereological level for the same portion of reality), then they are identical; thus, the anti-extensionalist should reject it, because her own anti-extensionalism can be understood as the claim that two different things *can* occupy the same mereological level.

What happens to identity? Cotnoir's mereology$_{theo}$ does not provide identity conditions for wholes. Nonetheless, it can specify a relation of *mereological similarity*.[10] Mereological similarity is an equivalence relation that connects those entities that occupy the same level of mereological complexity; Monte Grappa and Mountmatter are mereologically similar; any other concrete entity is mereologically similar to the colocated portion of matter. Mereological similarity *is not* identity: it is a sort of *mereological indiscernibility* that comes without any accompanying generalized indiscernibility: mereological indiscernibles may still be discernible in relation to non-mereological features. Thus, Monte Grappa and Mountmatter may differ in modal and aesthetic features, as expected by dualists.

It is important to remark that the general picture of reality that stems from a mereology$_{theo}$ of this kind is largely undetermined: the reasons to think that Monte Grappa and Mountmatter are numerically distinct and mereologically similar are not given by Cotnoir's mereology$_{theo}$ itself. As far as Cotnoir's mereology$_{theo}$ is concerned, monism about constitution could be true. Or there could be three, or four, or any other number of colocated things. This does not mean that this kind of anti-extensionalism *is committed* to an indefinite multiplication of entities, but that it *does not rule out* an indefinite multiplication of entities. The appeals to discernibility and indiscernibility do not replace mereological Extensionalism in its role of a guide as to how many things there are.

Indeed, in general, discernibility/indiscernibility arguments are reliable guides to diversity, but not to identity. The converse of the Indiscernibility of Identicals allows us to infer diversity from discernibility; since it is a relatively uncontroversial principle, discernibility can be considered a reliable guide to diversity. By contrast, indiscernibility *is not* a reliable guide to identity, because the principle of Identity of Indiscernibles (according to which things that share all their properties are identical) is a highly controversial metaphysical doctrine.[11] As a result, the fact that the modal and aesthetic properties we discussed in Chapter 7 lead us to distinguish—if the dualist is right—two colocated things (instead of three, or more) does not imply that there are *only* two things there. Cotnoir's non-extensional mereology$_{theo}$—in contrast with CEM—does not provide identity conditions for the entities it is about.[12]

From an anti-extensionalist viewpoint, the fact that a mereology$_{theo}$ does not provide identity conditions for wholes is likely to be seen as a virtue: anti-extensionalism *is* the claim that the identity conditions should countenance not only parts, but also the way in which these parts are structurally arranged. Thus, the identity conditions should countenance features which do not belong to the subject matter of mereology$_{dis}$.

## 9.5 Strong Supplementation and Extensionalism

A virtue of Cotnoir's non-extensional mereology$_{theo}$ is its relative conservativity with respect to CEM. The rejection of the Antisymmetry of parthood brings with itself the rejection of Extensionalism and Uniqueness of Composition, but other important principles are preserved.

Weak Supplementation holds for the redefined *PP*. But also another pivotal theorem of CEM is preserved: Strong Supplementation. Strong Supplementation is prima facie a very reasonable principle. It is a claim about the cases in which something (*x*) is not a part of something else (*y*). In some of these cases, *x* is completely outside of *y*. In others, *x* and *y* overlap, but *x* is not entirely in *y*, and thus it is not a part of it; in some of these latter cases, *y* is actually a proper part of *x*. In all these cases, there is something in *x* (a part of it) that is completely outside of *y*, that is, that does not overlap with *y*. The principle can be formalized as follows:

$$\forall x \forall y (\neg x P y \rightarrow \exists z (z P x \wedge \neg z \circ y))$$ (Strong Supplementation)

In order to understand why Strong Supplementation is a very reasonable principle, it is useful to reflect on its converse. According to the converse, if no part of $x$ is disjoint from $y$, then $x$ is part of $y$. Nothing in $x$ makes it external—so to say—to $y$, and so it is reasonable to conclude that $x$ is part of $y$.

There is an ideological connection between Strong Supplementation and Extensionalism: according to Extensionalism, there is no numerical difference without difference in parts; according to Strong Supplementation, there is no non-parthood between $x$ and $y$ without an allotted ground in $x$ (namely, the part of $x$ that does not overlap with $y$).

Indeed, given Strong Supplementation and the Antisymmetry of parthood, Extensionalism follows. But what should an anti-extensionalist reject? As we have seen, the rejection of Antisymmetry, in particular if coupled with a redefinition of proper parthood, is a well-motivated move from the viewpoint of dualism about constitution (and dualism about constitution is the pivotal motivation for anti-extensionalism about concrete, nonfictional, non-intrinsically controversial entities): it allows for a mereological representation of the relation between an object and its colocated portion of matter.

By contrast, the link between the rejection of Strong Supplementation and the motivations of dualism is less transparent. The following is a Hasse diagram representing a failure of Strong Supplementation:

Here, the relation between the two wholes ($a$ and $b$) is not represented at all. $a$ and $b$ are not part of one another, and this is exactly the reason why $a$ and $b$ violate Strong Supplementation in both directions: $a$ is not part of $b$, $b$ is not part of $a$; but $a$ has no part that does not overlap with $b$, and $b$ has no part that does not overlap with $a$.

Thus, a non-extensional mereology$_{\text{theo}}$ in which Strong Supplementation fails is not motivated by the need to represent the relation between objects and their colocated portions of matter mereologically. Quite the opposite is the case: a mereology$_{\text{theo}}$ in which Strong Supplementation fails *does not* characterize the relation between objects and their colocated portions of matter mereologically.

Indeed, the kind of anti-extensionalism stemming from the denial of Antisymmetry is significantly different from the one stemming from the denial of Strong Supplementation. The former is better suited to characterizing internally a kind of dualism about constitution, because it does not leave the mutual relation between an object and its portion of matter unexplained.

By contrast, if the inclination toward anti-extensionalism comes from the general conviction that the arrangement of parts matters for the identity conditions of wholes, then perhaps it is better to leave the relations between different wholes with the same parts *out of* the explanatory target of mereology$_{theo}$: in this case, the initial motivation is precisely that this difference *cannot* be captured in terms of parthood, and thus not even by mutual parthood.

This difference reveals an important *dichotomy* between motivations of anti-extensionalism. *On one side*, some anti-extensionalists are convinced by counterexamples to Extensionalism, and by alleged sources of discernibility between entities and colocated portions of matter. On this terrain, it is worth repeating that: (1) there are good ways to dispel the discernibility intuitions (such as counterpart theory and metalinguistic interpretations of negations, Chapter 7, Sections 7.3 and 7.4); (2) discernibility intuitions lead to dualism, and not directly to anti-extensionalism; Varzi has shown that when dualism is consistently endorsed at every level of complexity, there is no reason at all to endorse anti-extensionalism (Chapter 7, Section 7.5). However, if (1) and (2) are not accepted as sufficient reasons to endorse Extensionalism, then the dualist discernibility intuitions are better served by a rather conservative kind of anti-extensionalism, such as Cotnoir's rejection of Antisymmetry of parthood and redefinition of proper parthood.

*On the other side of the dichotomy*, anti-extensionalism is sometimes motivated by the sheer conviction that the arrangement of parts *matters* for the identity conditions for wholes. When confronted with this attitude, the mereological monist should always make sure that her anti-extensionalist opponent is aware that what is at stake in the debate are *only* the identity conditions. Extensionalism *is not* committed to denying that in an adequate description of reality the relations between parts have a pivotal role. As a matter of fact, many twentieth-century mereological monists are nominalists *also* about properties and relations, and might prefer a characterization of reality in which only spatiotemporally located individuals play a role. However, while mereological monism is deeply entrenched with nominalism *about structure*, its links with other kinds of nominalism are looser, and of a mainly historical character. There is no inconsistency in endorsing mereological monism (Extensionalism included), while being realists about relations.

The inarticulate impression that mereological monism provides a flat picture of reality, and that every mereological whole is a sort of inert heap, should not be

overrated: mereological monism is content with denying that the arrangement
of parts has some bearing on the identity and existence conditions for wholes
(we will discuss existence conditions in Part Three). It does not dictate that
the arrangement of parts is *not important*. Conversely, the mere insistence
on the importance of structures or relations in reality falls short of falsifying
mereological monism, and Extensionalism in particular.

# Part Three

# Unrestricted Composition

## Abstract

This part of the book analyzes and defends the principle of Unrestricted Composition, according to which given some things—no matter how many and how disparate they are—their fusion exists. In order to formulate this principle, we need a way of speaking collectively of a plurality of entities whose number can vary indefinitely. Chapter 10 shows that plural quantification is the best tool for this purpose, and in particular that it is preferable to quantification over sets and to schematic formulations of mereological principles, mainly due to reasons of philosophical perspicuity. Chapter 11 discusses the definition of Fusion, and compares it with another plausible yet non-equivalent definition. Chapter 12 analyzes various cases of problematic fusions which, according to some scholars, make Unrestricted Composition a counterintuitive principle, and shows that they are substantially different from one another. Chapter 13 scrutinizes the so-called Lewis-Sider argument in support of Unrestricted Composition, as well as some previous versions of it by Quine and Williams. The philosophical gist of the Lewis-Sider argument is shown to consist in the idea that mereology should be a neutral tool, and this idea is closely associated with a Quinean understanding of existence. Finally, in Chapter 14, I discuss the impact on Unrestricted Composition of the adoption of a non-Quinean metaontology. In particular, I show that some considerations in favor of Unrestricted Composition can be reformulated in an interestingly different way, if Fine's so-called postulationism or expansionism is adopted.

# Mereological Fusion and Plural Logic

## 10.1 Mereological monism and ontological economy

Is it true that mereological monism delivers ontological economy? In Part Two, we have seen that Extensionalism rules out the existence of multiple wholes with the same proper parts. But one could observe that this does not warrant a great *overall* ontological economy because it leaves open the possibility that there are a lot of parts, and a lot of wholes. In Chapter 7, we have seen that Extensionalism is actually compatible both with monism and with dualism about material constitution: the consistent dualist will be committed both to objects and to colocated portions of reality, at each level of reality. The resulting kind of extensionalist dualism seems to be rather deficient from the viewpoint of *absolute* ontological economy.

However, the keyword here is "absolute." Only the sheer denial of the existence of certain entities or kinds of entities warrants absolute ontological economy. Mereological monism is not about that: it is a philosophical thesis about parthood and cognate relations, and it can warrant economy only within the limits of its subject matter. Extensionalism warrants that two different things have the same proper parts, but does not warrant any economy about parts.

Given the general nominalistic motivations for mereological monism we have discussed in Chapter 5, it is perhaps more ideologically coherent to combine mereological monism with other kinds of doctrines which care about ontological economy (insofar as nominalists usually consider ontological economy an important theoretical virtue). This is perhaps the reason why Lewis—for example—was a *monist* about material constitution, and why I have strong monist inclinations myself. But these links are only a matter of ideological coherence: no *inferential* link leads from mereological monism to absolute ontological economy.

There is another reason—a reason quite independent of Extensionalism, and altogether more important—why the link between mereological monism and ontological economy can be doubted: Unrestricted Composition, the principle of CEM to which this part of the book is devoted. Unrestricted Composition warrants that, given some entities, there is a fusion of them. In the language of plural logic:

$$\forall xx \exists y (y \Sigma xx) \qquad\qquad \text{(Unrestricted Composition)}$$

Does Unrestricted Composition really go against the kind of ontological economy which nominalism aspires to? Before investigating the philosophical significance and the reasons for and against Unrestricted Composition and its bearing on ontological economy, we need to clarify two potential controversies about its formulation. The first controversy concerns the resort to plural quantification in the formulation of Unrestricted Composition. The second concerns the definition of Fusion ($\Sigma$).

Both these controversies might seem to also concern Uniqueness of Composition, since plural quantification and the relational constant for Fusion appear in the formulation of Uniqueness of Composition as well. However, we have seen in Chapter 6 that the interesting philosophical content of Uniqueness of Composition is expressed by Extensionalism, and Extensionalism does not require plural quantification or the constant for Fusion in any of the formulations we have discussed. Thus, the possible problems concerning plural quantification and the operation of Fusion do not concern the philosophical core of Uniqueness of Composition.

I am going to suggest that these problems do not really concern what is at stake with Unrestricted Composition either, but it is important to prevent the opposite doubt that they matter, given that plural quantification and Fusion *do* figure prominently in the formulation of Unrestricted Composition. The problems concerning the application of plural quantification in mereology$_{theo}$ will be discussed in the remainder of this chapter, while the definition of Fusion will be the subject matter of Chapter 11.

## 10.2 Plural quantification

First, why is plural quantification employed in the formulation of Unrestricted Composition? Fusion is a multi-one relation. The number of its inputs is not fixed: it can vary from one to infinity. The values of a plural variable are *some* objects in the domain of quantification, from one to infinity. Thus, plural quantification seems to be the perfect tool for expressing mereological Fusion, and it is used not only in Uniqueness of Composition and Unrestricted Composition, but already in the definition of Fusion/Composition.

The definition, which we will analyze and justify in Chapter 11, says—in accordance with the provisional characterization of Fusion set forth in Chapter 4, Section 4.4—that something is a fusion of some things if and only if each of those things is part of the fusion and each part of the fusion overlaps with at least one of those things. Thus, it includes plural variables for the fused entities both in the *definiendum* and in the *definiens*, and the predicate *is one of* (<)—which is distinctive of plural logic—in the *definiens*.

$$\forall x \forall yy (x \Sigma yy \equiv_{def} \forall z(z \prec yy \to zPx) \wedge \forall z(zPx \to \exists w(w \prec yy \wedge z \circ w)))$$

(Fusion–Definition)

We cannot replace the plural variable with a plurality of variables in the definition of Fusion (as well as in Uniqueness of Composition and Unrestricted Composition) and make Fusion a more than binary predicate, because there would not be any *right* number of argument places for it. This is not a merely technical problem: it is a symptom of the fact that, when in an operation the number of inputs is variable, we *need* a symbol for these variably numerous entities. We are talking about them *collectively*, and not distributively: when we say that a chair is the fusion of four legs, a back, and a seat, this does not imply that the chair is also the fusion of the seat only, or of only three or four legs. The kind of predication we make about the fused entities concerns them all as a totality, and not each of them separately.

Plural quantification fits the bill perfectly. A quick look at the growing literature about plural quantification shows that its introduction is often motivated by the need to express *collective* predication (in cases such as "the besiegers surrounded the building," in which none of the besiegers individually surrounded the building).

However, there are several long-standing philosophical and technical controversies about the admissibility and the understandability of plural quantification.[1] Moreover, there are presentations of CEM in which—often out of the conviction that plural quantification is a controversial tool, which should be avoided whenever possible—plural quantification is not used. Thus, it is unavoidable for us to take a look at these controversies, in order to make sure that the adoption of plural quantification really is the best option at our disposal in formulating CEM.

Some of the controversies about plural quantification do not matter at all for us, such as those concerning the link with quantification in predicative position and the interaction with modal logic, and we will not discuss them. However, the seemingly most heated controversy about plural quantification concerns its so-called *logicality*, and this controversy could be suspected to have a bearing on the application of plural quantification in mereology$_{theo}$. Is plural logic *really* logic? This could be perceived as a relevant aspect from the viewpoint of mereology itself.

*If mereology were logic*, it would be undesirable to use nonlogical language in defining one of its core notions (Fusion), which appears in two of its axioms. However, this worry is less important than it seems. Indeed, *mereology is not logic*. Let us qualify and discuss this claim in the next section, before examining (in Section 10.4) the *alternatives* to plural quantification in the definition of Fusion, and in axioms such as Unrestricted Composition.

## 10.3 Mereology is not logic

The claim that mereology is logic is sometimes attributed to the twentieth-century fathers of mereology, but in some cases the attribution is unconvincing, while in others it relies on an extremely broad, obsolete notion of logic, which by design ends up including also metaphysical doctrines.

Goodman, for example, never qualified his calculus of individuals as logic: he understood it as a true, general, nominalistically motivated metaphysical doctrine (and this even though he never used the word "metaphysics"—a rather unpopular term at the time—in this context). Leśniewski saw mereology as a fragment of a larger project, which he would probably have qualified as "logic," but which was expected to concern also classical metaphysical problems, such as the nature of instantiation.

From a contemporary perspective, neither mereology$_{dis}$, nor mereology$_{theo}$, nor mereology$_{phi}$ are logic, according to any interesting contemporary understanding of logic. Mereology$_{theo}$ can be formulated in a logical language and framework (our formulation is in the language and framework of plural logic), but this does not make mereology$_{theo}$ *itself* a kind of logic. We have seen in Chapter 3 that, according to mereological monism (mereology$_{phi}$), CEM (mereology$_{theo}$) is a highly general doctrine and can, as a result, be called "formal," if *formality* is simply construed as a gradable form of generality and topic-neutrality. By contrast, if the formality of a theory is given by the fact that the truth of its principles is warranted by their form, then nobody thinks that this holds for CEM. Even for the most bigoted mereological monist, such as myself, predicates such as *P* should be interpreted in a specific way (that is, as expressing parthood) in order to obtain a model for mereology. Nobody thinks that *P* and other mereological predicates should be semantically treated as logical constants (while this happens for example for the identity predicate =, when it is added to the language of first-order logic).

Logicality might be confused with analyticity, but it is not the same thing. While the analytic/synthetic distinction is controversial in itself, prototypical cases of analytic truths such as "no bachelor is married" are obviously false for many interpretations of their nonlogical vocabulary. Obviously one could argue that logical principles too are analytic, but there is a huge difference between the alleged analyticity of "no bachelor is married" and the alleged analyticity of logical principles: the truth of sentences of the first kind depends on specific interpretations of nonlogical terms; the truth of sentences of the second kind depends on the *fixed* meaning of logical vocabulary (connectives, quantifiers, identity).

In any case, nobody thinks that CEM *in its full strength* consists of analytical truths. At most, some scholars think that a limited core of weak mereological principles in CEM is constitutive for the meaning of the term "part" (and thus could be considered analytic, because these principles would be true in virtue of the meaning of the mereological lexicon in them): this is sometimes held for Transitivity, or for Weak Supplementation.[2]

This contention is doubtful: from the perspective adopted in this book, the meaning of "part" plays no special role in assessing these principles; what we do in mereology$_{dis}$ is select and analyze the literal uses of parthood terms, with a special focus on spatial uses; after that, we assess whether there are counterexamples to the resulting principles, that is whether there are parts of parts that are not parts (in the case of Transitivity), or whether there are instances of proper parthood in which the whole does not have any part disjoint from the proper part (in the case of Weak Supplementation).

In some cases, the temptation arises to say that, without these principles, "parthood" and "proper parthood" would lose their expected meanings. However, this is not the aim of our enterprise; language has the important, heuristic function of helping to identify and demarcate the relations we want to study. But, after this phase, our purpose is to ascertain how these relations work, and the question of whether a certain principle is implicit in the alleged semantic content of certain predicates is of no real importance from this perspective.

In any case, there is no reason to think that *stronger* principles like Extensionalism, or Strong Supplementation, or Unrestricted Composition are *analytic*. Thus, CEM is not analytic, and mereological monists should not claim (and, as far as I know, do not claim) that CEM—the highly general theory of parthood and cognate relation—is analytic; on its part, analyticity is not logicality. As a result, mereology—in any of the three ways of meaning the word "mereology"—is far from logical. Thus, also even if plural logic fails to be logic, this is no reason not to use it in mereology$_{dis}$.

Even if mereology is not logic, it could be desirable to formulate it in a purely logical language. One could argue that the complexity of a theory depends on the number and formal features of the nonlogical predicates it includes.[3] Plural logic countenances a specific predicate (<) and distinguishes—for many predicates—two kinds of argument places: those which should be occupied by plural terms, and those which should be occupied by singular terms. If plural logic is logic, then this complexity is in no way specific to CEM, and should not be countenanced when we assess the complexity of CEM. Thus, if plural logic were logic, the nonlogical content of CEM could coincide with the *mereological* content of CEM, and this could be desirable from an analytic viewpoint.

The claim that plural logic is logic heavily depends on the way in which logicality is construed. Plural logic could qualify as logic in the sense that, in contrast with mereology itself, the truth of its principles seems to depend only on the form of its principles. Principles (such as the principle that no plurality is empty, or the comprehension principles) simply characterize the links between different kinds of variables, and between language and the admitted values of plural variables.

There are many other ways of construing logicality,[4] and I do not purport here to determine whether plural logic is logic under other points of view: for example, whether plural logic is *ontologically innocent*, or whether the fact that a plural expression can take many elements of the domain as its value entails a hidden ontological commitment to sets, under the deceptively diminutive sobriquet of *pluralities*. However, it is important to note that the risk of an implicit commitment to sets/pluralities is one to which any many-one operation in which the many are in a variable number is exposed. Mereological Fusion *is* such an operation: the input of Fusion are many things, considered *collectively*.

Thus, CEM is not logic, and it is not intrinsically problematic to express it within a framework (such as plural logic) whose logicality is dubious. Nonetheless, while not compulsory, it could be desirable to express CEM in a purely logical framework. However, the main sense in which plural logic risks failing to be logical concerns its alleged, implicit ontological commitment to pluralities, but this risk is implicit in *any* way of expressing a many-one relation or operation in which the number of the many (in our case, the number of the fused entities) is not fixed.

## 10.4 The alternatives to plural quantification: Sets

We have seen that the risk of an implicit commitment to pluralities characterizes mereological Fusion in itself. Perhaps, it characterizes plural quantification too (this should be determined within the debate on the logicality of plural logic); but, if this is the case, this is a *confirmation* that plural logic is the perfect tool for formulating CEM. This outcome finds some confirmation when plural quantification is compared to the alternative ways in which CEM can be and has been formulated.

The most obvious alternative is quantification over sets. Goodman himself, in spite of his rejection of sets as non-hyperextensional entities, defines Fusion as an operation from sets to individuals. Our above definition of mereological Fusion as a relation would be transformed as follows ($Y$ is a variable for sets, $\in$ is set-theoretical membership):

$$\forall x \forall Y (x\Sigma Y \equiv_{def} \forall z(z \in Y \rightarrow zPx) \land \forall z(zPx \rightarrow \exists w(w \in Y \land z \circ w)))$$

(Fusion–Set-theoretic Definition)

In a sense, there is no great difference between quantifying plurally over fused entities and quantifying over a set of fused entities. The only concern might be that—due to the need to avoid the set-theoretic paradoxes—for some choice of entities there is no set that includes them exactly. According to the most standard axiomatic set theories, there is no set whose elements are all the sets and nothing else, and no set whose elements are all the sets that are not members of themselves. But there is no real reason to fuse all the sets or all the Russell-paradoxical sets, thus the above set-theoretical definition of Fusion would not loose any significant generality.

Plural logic—from its origins in the works of George Boolos—was specifically motivated by the need to avoid sets. The shunning of sets is often motivated by ontological qualms: sets would be mysterious entities, which a traditional nominalist such as Goodman cannot stomach, for example because the distinction between a singleton *{x}* and its only element *x* is mysterious to him. But, for the kind of mereological monism we expound and motivate in this book, it is not clear that the ontological commitment to sets is to be avoided. After all, in Chapter 8, we have conceded that abstract entities are a difficult testbed for Extensionalism, insofar as nothing forecloses the possibility of stipulating entities that violate it. This puts sets *out* of the expected domain of application of mereological monism, and there would be nothing strange in resorting to some abstract entities such as sets—quite familiar and so useful in many other fields—in formulating CEM.

Thus, ontological concerns about sets are not a good reason to prefer plural quantification over sets.[5] Again, the commitment to some kinds of pluralities comes from the pivotal occurrence in CEM of a many-one operation whose number of inputs is variable. However, it would be wrong to infer from this that it is immaterial whether to resort to plural quantification or to quantification over sets in formulating CEM.

A good reason to prefer plural quantification over sets is that it would be a *categorical mistake* to involve sets. In the above set-theoretic definition of Fusion, we end up *literally* fusing a set: the relational predicate of Fusion is flanked by two singular referential expressions, which refer respectively to a set and a whole. Thus, the relation/operation expressed by the predicate would connect these referents. But the relation/operation that mereology aims to study is one that goes from the parts to the whole. The set of the parts is simply foreign to this context.

Categorical mistakes play an important role in the motivations for plural reference and quantification in general. Already Boolos remarked that "it is haywire to think that when you have some Cheerios, you are eating a *set*."[6] Plural expressions in natural language refer to *entities*, without any apparent mediation of abstract entities such as sets. The plural expressions, by themselves, do not "unify" these things into a further thing (a set) "representing" them.[7] What is "unifying" in a sentence like "I eat Cheerios" is that Cheerios (*many* Cheerios) occupy a single argument place of a predicate, in this case "eat."

Boolos's case of "I eat Cheerios" is perhaps not really a compelling example, because it is not clear that the predication over Cheerios is collective, and not distributive: after all, if I eat some Cheerios, I also eat each of them singularly, and the various actions of eating each of them are simply coordinated in space and time. It is true that it would be a categorical mistake to involve sets in the relation of eating. But perhaps, ideally, I could avoid *both* plural reference *and* sets in this case, because I could analyze "I eat Cheerios" in a long, quite unpractical conjunction of sentences about me and each of the Cheerios: "I eat Cheerios" would be a merely convenient abbreviation of this conjunction.

"I eat Cheerios" seems to be a *distributive* predication about Cheerios. In other cases, such as in the aforementioned sentence "the besiegers surrounded the building," it seems wrong to analyze them in terms of individual predications: the sentence does not imply that each besieger *individually* surrounded that building.

The occurrence of the term for the parts in a claim of mereological Fusion is more similar to that of "the besiegers" in "the besiegers surrounded the building," than to that of "Cheerios" in "I eat Cheerios." A claim of the sort "*t* is the fusion of *uu*" (such as "the chair is the fusion of four legs, a seat and a back") is *collectively about uu*: the chair is not a fusion of the back only, or of any other of the mentioned parts singularly. Thus, it is a case in which it is indispensable to find a way to talk about many things (the fused things), but in which it would be a categorical mistake to involve a set.

It is possible to insist that the set is merely a *representative* of a plurality, and that it is a mere expedient needed to fill a single argument place with many things; at a deep level, what is fused are the elements of the set, and not the set itself. However, it is not clear why an exception should be made to the general rule according to which a relation expressed by a predicate relates the entities denoted by the referential expressions that occupy the argument places of the predicate. If not out of a general hostility toward plural reference and quantification, there is no reason to adopt a kind of semantic revisionism according to which the denotation of the referential expressions is not what is involved in the relation/ operation of Fusion (namely, the parts), but a representative of them (a set). Thus, the reason to prefer plural quantification over sets in formulating CEM is that only plural quantification correctly identifies the real input of Fusion: the fused entities.

## 10.5 The alternatives to plural quantification: Schemas

Another quite popular alternative to plural quantification in the definition of Fusion, and in axioms such as Unrestricted Composition, is to involve a formula that is satisfied by all the fused entities and them alone. Given the legs, the seat, and the back of my chair, there would be an open formula $\varphi$ satisfied by those things and by nothing else.

For example, Varzi defines Fusion as follows:[8]

$$x \Sigma \phi y \equiv_{def} \forall y (\phi y \rightarrow y P x) \wedge \forall z (z P x \rightarrow \exists y (\phi y \wedge z \circ y)) \qquad \text{(Fusion–Varzi's Definition)}$$

This definition says that $x$ is the sum of those things that satisfy $\varphi$, on the usual conditions: each entity that satisfies $\varphi$ is part of $x$, and everything that is part of $x$ overlaps with at least one of the entities that satisfy $\varphi$.

The occurrence of $\varphi y$ on the left side of the definition requires some syntactic and semantic clarifications.[9] It is an open formula that occupies an argument place of the Fusion predicate. But usually open formulas do not occur in such a syntactic position, and it is not clear what they denote (and thus, in the specific case in question, what the input of a fusion is). It is meant by those who define Fusion in this way as a sort of plural referential expressions built from an open formula (a sort of *plural definite description*).[10]

In the formulation of Uniqueness of Composition and Unrestricted Composition, in order to express what we expressed in the version with plural quantification, we need to make sure that *something* satisfies $\varphi$. While the nonexistence of an empty plurality is warranted by a plural logic principle, here nothing warrants that $\varphi$ is simply unsatisfiable. For this reason, Uniqueness of Composition and Unrestricted Composition will need a restricting condition, which makes sure that $\varphi$ is satisfied:

$$\exists x(\phi x) \rightarrow \forall y(y\Sigma\phi x \rightarrow \forall z(z\Sigma\phi x \rightarrow z = y))$$

(Uniqueness of Composition–Schematic)

$$\exists x(\phi x) \rightarrow \exists y(y\Sigma\phi x)$$     (Unrestricted Composition–Schematic)

By replacing $\varphi$ in these *schemas* with any formula of the language, we would obtain an axiom of CEM.

Two technical concerns can be raised about the resulting formalization of CEM. The first is negligible, while the other unveils the real, philosophical problem that makes the axiomatization of CEM in plural logic preferable. A *first*, negligible technical concern is that, when Uniqueness of Composition or Unrestricted Composition are formulated schematically, CEM is not finitely axiomatizable: if our language includes an infinite number of formulas $\varphi$, each of them will give rise to an instance of Uniqueness of Composition and Unrestricted Composition. However, plural logic is not finitely axiomatizable either, thus the only difference is that, in these schematic versions of the principles, the nonfinite axiomatisability is simply moved from the underlying logic and brought to evidence.

A *second* technical worry is that the schema has as many instances as the formulas in our language. However, the language of first-order logic in which CEM would be expressed has only denumerably many formulas. However, as

Varzi writes, "for most purposes this limitation is negligible, as normally we are only interested in those sets of objects that we are able to specify."[11] It is actually enough to have in the language a name for each fused entity. In this case, we can introduce a formula that is satisfied only by what is identical to one among certain entities (thereby simulating what < expresses in plural logic). Given that "Tom" is the name of Tom, "Dick" is the name of Dick, and "Harry" is the name of Harry, the following predicate $\psi$, if defined as follows, will be satisfied by Tom, Dick, Harry and nothing else:

$$\forall x(\psi x \equiv_{def} x = Tom \lor x = Dick \lor x = Harry)$$

Given $\psi$, we could easily assert that Tom, Dick, and Harry have a unique fusion. What we obtain is *de facto* a way of speaking about Tom, Dick, and Harry and of presenting them as the input of the Fusion operation. This happens through the mediation of a rather artificial—yet successful—description.

One could say that the same happens in plural logic, insofar as plural logic is usually expected to include a comprehension principle, according to which, given a nonempty formula $\varphi$, there are some things such that each of them satisfies $\varphi$. The principle could be expressed—*in a schematic form*—in the following way:

$$\exists x(\phi x) \rightarrow \exists yy \forall x(x \prec yy \leftrightarrow \phi x)$$

The similarities between the various ways of defining mereological sums and formulating the principles of CEM about sums are not surprising: after all, nothing suggests that they differ in their adequacy, or even less that they make CEM a substantially different theory. The motivations for choosing one or the other have to do with philosophical perspicuity. From this viewpoint, the main reason why the formulation of CEM in plural logic seems preferable to me to the schematic formulation concerns the *division of labor* between the core of general purpose, logical expressive tools through which mereology$_{theo}$ (CEM) is expressed, and the controversial content of mereology$_{theo}$ (concerning parthood and cognate relations).

The schematic formulation and the formulation in plural logic differ in the ways in which they construe the connection between formulas and pluralities of entities satisfying these formulas. According to plural logic, this problem belongs to the logical core of general purpose expressive tools. The schematic formulation instead brings this aspect into play *within* CEM: since Uniqueness of Composition and Unrestricted Composition are expressed schematically through formulas, the problem of the correspondence between formulas and pluralities of entities that satisfy them ends up influencing *directly* the axiomatization of CEM—since the axioms are the instances of the schema in which a specific formula replaces $\varphi$, the exact list of axioms *depends* on the linguistic resources at disposal.

By contrast, this aspect should not belong to the contents of CEM at all. Mereological Fusion is far from being the only kind of collective predication. For example, in the description of human actions—such as in the above example of the besiegers surrounding the building, or in the case of some people forming a political party, or writing a book together—it is extremely important to attribute an action to many subjects, without thereby attributing that action to each of them. Thus, the need to regulate plural reference and quantification, and in particular the nexus with the linguistic resources at disposal, is a *general need*, that has no exclusive link with mereology.

Thus, general plural logic is the *right place where to regulate this aspect*, in particular through a schematic principle of comprehension. The exclusion of *empty pluralities* too is apt to be achieved at this level: it is not a peculiarity of CEM to exclude that a relation of Fusion in some cases connects *no entity* with a fusion. It is a general fact about collective predications that they are about one or more entities, and not about *zero* entities: thus, the restriction to satisfiable formulas in (Uniqueness of Composition—Schematic Version) and (Unrestricted Composition—Schematic Version) is simply out of place; the rejection of empty pluralities belongs to plural logic.

The supporter of the schematic formulations might counter that the formulation of CEM in plural logic *conceals* some problematic presuppositions, such as the linguistic limitations. However, it is *a virtue* to conceal these problems in CEM, because they concern collective predications in general, and should not be exposed in any single theory including collective predications.

More in general, the formulas which should replace $\varphi$ in the schematic formulations do not really play any role in mereology at all. In assessing Uniqueness of Composition and Unrestricted Composition, we do not reflect about the formulas that the fused entities satisfy exclusively. In many cases—that is, in all those cases in which no reasonably natural predicate is satisfied exclusively by the fused entities—the formula will be artificial, like $\psi$ in the above-mentioned example with Tom, Dick, and Harry.

Thus, the schematic version of the definition of Fusion brings into mereology$_{theo}$ problems that do not belong to mereology$_{theo}$. Moreover, there is no reason to prefer this version to the one in plural logic, except a *general aversion* to plural quantification (quite independent of mereological problems).

This is not the place for dispelling such an aversion, but perhaps the importance and pervasiveness of the relation of Fusion is in itself a good enough reason to think that we need an expressive tool for collective predication, without the intermediation of sets, and without any direct involvement of identifying formulas.

# 11

# The Definition of Fusion

## 11.1 What a fusion should be

I have justified my preference for formulations of the definition of Fusion, and of the related mereological principles, in plural logic in Chapter 10. We can now go back to analyzing the specific content of the definition of Fusion:

$$\forall x \forall yy (x\Sigma yy \equiv_{def} \forall z(z \prec yy \to zPx) \wedge \forall z(zPx \to \exists w(w \prec yy \wedge z \circ w)))$$

(Fusion—Definition)

In the *definiens*, there is a binary conjunction of individually necessary and jointly sufficient conditions which *y* must satisfy in order to qualify as a fusion of *xx*. The first conjunct ensures that every fused entity is itself part of the fusion. The second conjunct requires that whatever is part of the fusion has a part in common (i.e., overlaps) with one of the fused entities.

(Fusion—Definition) is neither simple nor immediately perspicuous. However, a recent, important paper by Paul Hovda[1] has shown that it is the most suitable formulation, when you adopt an axiomatization of CEM *from above*. In other words, this is an apt definition for the formulation of Uniqueness of Composition and Unrestricted Composition, which—together with Transitivity—constitute an adequate formalization of CEM, delivering as theorems all the other principles discussed in this book (such as Reflexivity, Antisymmetry of *P*, Weak and Strong Supplementation).

Other, seemingly more perspicuous definitions of Fusion are actually unfit for this task; nonetheless, when the axioms resorting to these more perspicuous formulations are conjoined with *other* mereological principles, then you obtain other axiomatizations of CEM of equal strength. Since these different axiomatizations of CEM ultimately prove the same theorems, and since our purpose in this book is to discuss and defend the metaphysical contents of CEM from a philosophical perspective, I will limit my analysis (in particular in

Section 11.2) to only another, quite attractive and plausible definition of Fusion, and show how it differs from (Fusion—Definition).

However, it is interesting to ask beforehand *what expectations* a definition of Fusion should satisfy. When we analyze these expectations, we discover that the prima facie abstract and intimidating (Fusion—Definition) satisfies them quite nicely, also in comparison with the (prima facie more attractive) alternative definition we are going to discuss. In order to illustrate these expectations, it is useful to consider a prototypical, spatial scenario. Let us take the example of a chair again. Insofar as it is extended, the chair is partially located in many places: it is a bit where its back is, a bit where its seat is, and a bit where each leg is. The chair on the one hand and its parts collectively, on the other, have something in common: the parts are collectively located where the chair is. It does not matter whether I am considering *disjoint* parts or not. I can also *cover* the chair with overlapping parts: the body of the chair (composed of the back and of the seat), the back, the seat, and the legs; or even the chair itself, and the four legs. The parts in each of these lists are collectively located where the chair is.

There are many different lists of things that are collectively located where the chair is. There is no spatial region such that the chair is partially in that region, and in one of these lists nothing is partially there. Nor is there any spatial region such that something in one of the lists is partially in that spatial region, while the chair is not partially in that spatial region.

Now, forget about space: mereology *is not* the theory of spatial parthood, both because it is meant to be applied also to other instances of parthood and because a proper treatment of space requires subtleties that mereology does not offer. Still, the same idea seems to be at work. Suppose that you wanted to assess whether a particular is the mereological fusion of the properties it instantiates. What you should expect is that there is nothing in the individual that is not in at least one of the properties; and that the properties are such that they collectively *cover* whatever the individual is.

The picture just drawn has some metaphorical elements. It is not clear what we mean by locutions such as "cover" or "whatever the individual is." But the purpose of mereology is precisely to clarify these slippery concepts. (Fusion—Definition) manages to qualify a fusion as something that includes whatever is collectively in the fused entities and nothing else.

$$\forall x \forall yy (x \Sigma yy \equiv_{def} \forall z(z \prec yy \rightarrow zPx) \wedge \forall z(zPx \rightarrow \exists w(w \prec yy \wedge z \circ w)))$$

(Fusion—Definition)

The first conjunct of (Fusion—Definition) ensures that every fused entity is part of the fusion. It is clear why this is a necessary condition for something to be a fusion: if a fused entity were not part of the fusion, then it would somehow be outside it. But it is not a sufficient condition, and this is why the *definiens* must include a second conjunct. It is not sufficient because many other things "bigger" than the chair have its back, seat, and legs as parts. Given Transitivity (an axiom of CEM), whatever has the entire chair as part, has the parts of the chair as its parts as well. And the chair is part of the furniture of the room in which it is, of the furniture of the building, and of many other very inclusive objects.

We need to exclude objects that are *too big*. The second conjunct of (Fusion—Definition) achieves this result: it requires that nothing is part of the fusion unless it overlaps with at least one of the fused entities. Suppose that, by contrast, something is part of the fusion, but does not overlap with any of the fused entities. Then this part of the fusion would be something that is nowhere to be found in the fused entities.

It is noteworthy that we cannot obtain the same result by requiring that the fusion has no part that is not *a part* of one of the fused entities, because the fusion must include entities that are a bit in one of the fused entity and a bit in another. In the example of the chair, consider again the *body* of the chair, made of the back and of the seat, but not of the legs. Now, the chair includes the body as a part; and should count as the fusion of the back, of the seat, and of the four legs. But the body *is not* part of any of these fused entities. Thus, a patently legitimate case of Fusion would be ruled out by the following, undesirable definition of Fusion:

$$\forall x \forall yy(x\Sigma yy \equiv_{def} \forall z(zPx \rightarrow \exists w(w \prec yy \land zPw))$$

The chair would not be the fusion because it would include a part that is not part of any of the fused entities. These additional parts can be obtained by *fusing* some of the fused entities, or some parts of the fused entities. In any case, they are never *disjoint* from all the fused entities. And this is exactly what (Fusion—Definition) soundly rules out in its second conjunct.

## 11.2 Minimal upper bounds and fusions

If other principles of CEM were assumed as axioms, there would be other ways of precisely satisfying the expectation that a fusion includes the fused entities and nothing extraneous to them. But these other definitions are not suitable for an axiomatization of CEM in which Transitivity, Uniqueness of Composition, and Unrestricted Composition are the only axioms. This is the reason why we employ (Fusion—Definition). After all, in spite of its prima facie complexity, it proved to be quite faithful to our *desiderata*.

Nonetheless, it is interesting to take a quick look at an alternative definition. It characterizes a fusion as what, in the chains of parthood relations, is the first common thing you find when going up from the fused entities: you can imagine parthood relations as a tree (Hasse diagrams picture them precisely in this way), and the fusion is the first node you reach no matter from which of the fused entities you set out.[2] This means that the fusion would be part of anything of which *all* the fused entities are parts.

This intuitive characterization corresponds to the algebraic notion of *minimal upper bound*. Indeed, we can define the *Minimal Upper Bound* (MUB) relation in mereology as follows:

$$\forall x \forall yy(x MUByy \equiv_{def} \forall z(z \prec yy \to zPx) \wedge \forall z(\forall w(w \prec yy \to wPz) \to xPz))$$

(Minimal Upper Bound—Definition)

Not every Minimal Upper Bound is a mereological fusion. It can happen that one or more things have a Minimal Upper Bound which includes also something completely extraneous to them. Consider the following Hasse diagram, in which $b$ and $c$[3] have $a$ as their Minimal Upper Bound, in spite of the fact that $a$ includes also $d$, which is completely extraneous to $b$ and $c$.

However, there is something *deviant* in this diagram, and it is difficult to find a metaphysically plausible scenario in which a Minimal Upper Bound of some things is not their fusion. Consider the seat and the back of my chair. Obviously, the chair *is not* their fusion, because it also includes the legs. *Nor* is the chair their Minimal Upper Bound. The above mentioned *body* of the chair is their Minimal Upper Bound: it is the first thing you meet when you go upward along the parthood relations within the chair.

A case in which a Minimal Upper Bound of some things is not their fusion is a case in which, for some reason, *something is missing* in the chains of parthood relations. If what we have called the *body* of the chair did not exist, and no proper part of the chair were to include both the seat and the back and nothing else, then the chair itself would be the Minimal Upper Bound of the seat and the back, but would not be their fusion. In this scenario, the chair would be with respect to the seat and the back what *a* is in the above Hasse diagram with respect to *b* and *c*.

However, this scenario is hardly realistic. Why should the body of the chair (as well as all the intermediate partial objects *between* the body and the chair in the chain of parthood relations) not exist? It seems that Minimal Upper Bounds and fusions diverge only in models of mereology (such as the one pictured in the Hasse diagram above, or the case in which a chair has a seat and a back, but no body) in which there are some metaphysically inexplicable omissions.

Now, if you have CEM in full strength, however it is axiomatized, you can rule out these deviant scenarios, and show that any Minimal Upper Bound is a fusion and vice versa.[4] In particular, the following principle—a theorem of CEM, dubbed Filtration—is needed:

$$\forall x \forall y \forall zz((xPy \land yMUBzz) \to \exists w(w \prec zz \land x \circ w)) \qquad \text{(Filtration)}$$

Filtration warrants that a Minimal Upper Bound has no part that does not overlap with at least one of the things of which it is the Minimal Upper Bound: exactly what a Minimal Upper Bound of some things needs in order to be their fusion as well. The above Hasse diagram violates Filtration, insofar as *a* is the Minimal Upper Bound of *b* and *c*, but has also *d* as a part, in spite of the fact that *d* does not overlap with *b* and *c*.

In the next chapters, we will focus only on (Fusion—Definition), and try to understand what reasons can be adduced for and against Unrestricted Composition, according to which given some entities (however chosen), there is their fusion.

12

# Allegedly Counterintuitive Entities

## 12.1 These fusions do not exist

In the debate about Unrestricted Composition, the resort to intuitions is extraordinarily widespread. Intuitions are a very controversial topic in contemporary metaphilosophy[1]: some philosophers attribute an evidential value to them (whereby intuiting that $p$ would provide some kind of prima facie justification for $p$), others a purely motivational value (whereby intuiting that $p$ would be simply a motivation for trying to argue in favor of $p$, by providing non-intuitive evidence for $p$), and others still reject the idea that intuitions might play any role whatsoever in serious philosophy.

Any of these positions can be combined with different contentions about what intuition is. For example, intuition can be a strictly individual mental state or event, or be connected to an objective feature of its content: in this latter case, $p$ is said to be *intuitive*, in the sense that $p$ has a disposition to be intuited, quite independently of how often and in which circumstances this disposition is manifested.

When Unrestricted Composition is at stake, a very common claim is that Unrestricted Composition is a *counterintuitive* principle, because it forces us to accept the existence of lots of entities which instead, according to some *intuitions*, would not exist. The role of $p$ in this debate is played by some negative existential statements, concerning mereological fusions. Consider the following examples:

(a) The fusion of the chair and of the Statue of Liberty does not exist.
(b) The fusion of the White House and of the Colossus of Rhodes does not exist.
(c) The fusion of David Cameron and of one of his counterparts in another possible world does not exist.
(d) The fusion of David Cameron and of the number 2 does not exist.

None of these sentences stands in *direct* contradiction to the principle of Unrestricted Composition. Indeed, the principle says that, for *any things* (plural quantification), there is their mereological fusion, but does not say *which things there are*. Thus, the principle is not in charge of establishing whether the chair and the Statue of Liberty, the counterparts of Cameron and the number 2 exist, but only makes a general and *conditional* claim: if the entities to be fused exist, then their fusion exists.

This means that there is an easy and—from our perspective—quite uninteresting way of defending Unrestricted Composition from the allegedly intuitive claims (a)–(d) (however their intuitiveness is meant): one could agree that the sums at stake do not exist, because in each case one or both the allegedly fused entities do not exist either. The plausibility of this attitude varies from case to case. Some of the entities involved are object of hoary ontological controversies. In particular, in (c), the existence of counterparts of Cameron depends on the existence of counterparts, and in general on the existence of entities in other possible worlds, and indirectly on the existence of possible worlds themselves. In (d), the existence of the number 2 seems to depend on the general existence of natural numbers.

However, while ontological controversies are particularly acute in these cases, in the other cases too, for broad philosophical reasons, you could doubt the existence of the entities to be fused. For example, according to some philosophers (the so-called *presentists*), only *present* entities exist, and thus the Colossus of Rhodes does not exist.

In some cases, however, the reasons to doubt the existence of the entities to be fused are not independent of the debate about Unrestricted Composition, but presuppose that Unrestricted Composition is false. Peter van Inwagen argues that composition happens only in those cases in which a life is involved.[2] According to him, among the entities in (a)–(d), only David Cameron exists. According to so-called *nihilists*, such as Theodore Sider,[3] composition *never* happens, except in the limit case in which mereological atoms are the fusions of themselves. As a result, *none* of the entities to be fused in (a)–(d) exist (at least if—as it seems—they are not atoms).

## 12.2 Negative existential intuitions

It is useful to put aside the controversies about the existence of the entities to be fused. Let us grant that they exist and ask why intuitions—according to some philosophers—support (a)–(d), thereby clashing with Unrestricted Composition. In this section I will try to voice and analyze these intuitions, while in Section 12.3 I will suggest that it is contentious to assess their exact content and—even more— to translate them into a viable *alternative* to Unrestricted Composition.

The negative existential (a) ("the fusion of the chair and of the Statue of Liberty does not exist") is about the fusion of two categorically homogeneous entities, which we usually classify as artifacts. The reason to doubt that their fusion exists is that, if it existed, it would be a *spatially discontinuous* and seemingly *causally inefficient* entity. Given (Fusion—Definition), the fusion would include the chair and the Statue of Liberty as parts, and would be such that all its parts overlap either with the chair or with the Statue of Liberty. From a spatial point of view, the resulting fusion would be partially where the chair is (in my room), and partially where the Statue of Liberty is. Moreover, both the chair and the Statue of Liberty are involved in some causal chains: they have been produced in a certain way; the Statue of Liberty slightly deviates the wind that hits it; the chair intercepts my body when I let myself fall onto it. Is the fusion involved in some *further* causal process? One can argue that it is not.

Case (b) ("the fusion of the White House and of the Colossus of Rhodes does not exist") also involves two categorically homogeneous entities, again two artifacts. However, the difference with (a) is that these entities could be thought to have existed at different times. The Colossus of Rhodes was destroyed by an earthquake in the year 226 B.C., and the White House was completed 2026 years later, in A.D. 1800. Thus, there is an additional reason (in comparison to the reasons for case (a)) to doubt the existence of their fusion: the fusion is a temporally disconnected entity that would cease to exist at a certain point and would resume existing later.

While (a) involves a *spatially* disconnected fusion and (b) a *temporally* disconnected fusion, the disconnection in (c) ("the fusion of David Cameron and of one of his counterparts in another possible world does not exist") is *modal*. The fused entities would inhabit different possible worlds. Suppose that counterpart theory is integrated with Lewis's modal realism, according to which possible worlds and the individuals inhabiting them (construed as parts of possible worlds) exist in the same exact sense in which our world and their parts exist. Then, the fusion in (c) would still be categorically homogeneous (it would be the fusion of two people, if we assume that the involved counterpart of Cameron is a person), but would raise further concerns: it would not be simply spatially sparse, but such that its parts are mutually not at any distance in space and time—indeed, according to modal realism, possible worlds are closed under relations of spatiotemporal distance, and this means that if two things are in different worlds, then they *are not* reciprocally very far in space-time, but lack reciprocal spatiotemporal relations on the whole. Moreover, also their lack of causal efficiency would be more radical, and—so to say—a matter of principle, since it would be grounded on the general fact that possible worlds are also closed under causal relations, so that inter-world causality is foreclosed.

Finally, in modal realism, possible individuals are parts of possible worlds. But the fusion at stake would not be part of any single possible world. Some of its parts would be part of the possible world of which Cameron is part (that is, of the actual world). Some others would be part of the different possible world of which Cameron's involved counterpart is part. Some others (such as the fusion of Cameron's left arm and the nose of his counterpart) would not be part of any world. Thus, the fusion in question would not be a *possible individual*. But "possible individual" could be deemed synonymous with "possible existent"; thus, the fusion would not be a possible existent, and *a fortiori* would not be an actual existent: the conclusion that the fusion does not exist (as (c) claims) would thus be easily reached.

In (d) ("the fusion of David Cameron and of the number 2 does not exist"), the terms of the operation of Fusion—that are also parts of the fusion, in the light of the first conjunct of (Fusion—Definition)—would be categorically heterogeneous, from the viewpoint of the distinction between concrete and abstract entities. Given any plausible way of drawing the abstract/concrete divide, Cameron and the number 2 fall on opposite sides of the distinction, that is, Cameron is concrete, and 2 is abstract: for example, persons are involved in causal processes, while numbers are not; persons have a location in space-time, numbers lack such a location.

It would be hard to classify the fusion at stake as concrete or abstract: it would be a hybrid thing. However, one could argue that the abstract/concrete divide is exhaustive. Given a thing whatsoever, either it is concrete or abstract: either it participates in causal processes or it does not; either it is located in space-time or it is not. Insofar as the fusion in (d) seems to fall short both of being abstract and of being concrete, one could conclude that (d) simply does not exist.

## 12.3 A variety of intuitions

In Chapter 13 we will see how the defender of Unrestricted Composition can react to these lines of thought, and finally *translate* some of them into an *argument* that is, surprisingly, in favor of Unrestricted Composition. But, before this, it is important to ask to what extent and in what sense (a)–(d) are intuitive. There are important differences among them.

In some cases, we are not given a proper reason to believe in negative existential statements. In cases such as (a) ("the fusion of the chair and of the Statue of Liberty does not exist") and (b) ("the fusion of the White House and of the Colossus of Rhodes does not exist") in particular, the denier of Unrestricted Composition aims to argue that spatially sparse and temporally sparse entities are unacceptable ontological commitments, and does so in the light of general principles that merely express the claim that those things do not exist.

In some other cases, however, an intermediate step is introduced. For example, there are some appeals to the principle that nothing is noncausally efficient; and since the fusions are considered causally inefficient, it is inferred that they do not exist. However, it is not exactly clear what motivates the principle that only causally efficient things exist. After all, it is a very contentious principle (sometimes dubbed the *Eleatic Principle*) that would also forbid the existence of number 2 involved (in the role of fused entity) in (d).[4] It seems as though an *evidential* use of intuition is made in support of the general principle that only causally efficient things exist, also when it is not made *directly* in support of the negative existential statement.

Thus, in cases (a) and (b), the appeals to intuition seem to be really brute: also when a general principle is involved, this general principle is simply motivated by the same intuitions that motivate the specific negative existential intuition.

(c) and (d) are significantly different from (a) and (b). In the case of (c) ("the fusion of David Cameron and of one of his counterparts in another possible world does not exist"), we lack arguably any intuition about counterparts, quite independently of the evidential or nonevidential value of intuitions. Counterpart theory is a philosophically motivated logical framework for paraphrasing modal claims into standard quantified claims. The reasons adduced *against* inter-world fusions make appeal to the way in which counterpart theory and modal realism are built: this apparatus forbids us to consider inter-world individuals possible. Also in the case of (d) ("the fusion of David Cameron and of the number 2 does not exist"), we have probably no intuition, and the reasoning is built upon the alleged exhaustiveness and exclusiveness of the abstract/concrete divide.

Some critics of Unrestricted Composition are explicit in assigning decisive value to intuitions in support of (a) and (b). For example, Daniel Korman thinks that (a) and (b) are true counterexamples to the principle, and that they falsify it.[5] Their justification would lie in intuition, and Korman refers to Juri Bengson's theory of intuition as a quasi-perceptual, truth-conducive intellectual mental state or event.[6] One could attempt to counter Korman's viewpoint from a general, methodological perspective, but intuition is a complicated methodological issue that cannot adequately be discussed in this book.

What we will try to show in Chapter 13—following the so-called Lewis-Sider argument for Unrestricted Composition—is that these intuitions cannot be translated into an alternative to Unrestricted Composition, and that they can be respected *without* denying Unrestricted Composition. In Chapter 14 we will also see that, in articulating some of these intuitions, some metaontological assumptions about the nature of existence play an important role.

13

# The Argument from Vagueness

## 13.1 Quine, Williams, and the argument from vagueness

The most powerful, as well as the most criticized, argument in favor of Unrestricted Composition has been formulated by Lewis in a few pages of his book *On the Plurality of Worlds*.[1] The reason why this argument appears for the first time in Lewis's masterpiece on modal realism is connected with (c) ("the fusion of David Cameron and of one of his counterparts in another possible world does not exist"). According to Lewis, the argument for Unrestricted Composition is so powerful that it forces modal realism to admit trans-world individuals of all sorts (not only the relatively sober one considered in (c)), in spite of the fact that these trans-world individuals do not play any explanatory role in modal realism and counterpart theory.

Trans-world individuals (that is, individuals with parts in different possible worlds) are not counterparts of anything. Due to a principle of counterpart theory, every counterpart is part of a world.[2] The reason why Lewis admits trans-world individuals such as the fusion of Cameron and one of his counterparts is that, according to him, the argument we are about to expound is a compelling one: thus modal realism should make room for trans-world individuals, in spite of their being hardly useful and highly problematic.

The argument was made explicit by Lewis for the first time in 1986, and was later substantially improved by Sider. However, it was partially implicit in some considerations previously advanced in favor of Unrestricted Composition by other mereological monists, and these forerunners' simple formulations are actually quite useful for appreciating the gist of the argument.

Nelson Goodman, in "A World of Individuals," presents Fusion as a "generating relation" that goes from some things (the entities to be fused) to a single thing (their fusion). As we know, Goodman cared a lot about the comparison with sets. Unrestricted Composition too was motivated in his view by the need to put wholes on par with sets. In sets, given any individuals and/or sets whatsoever (no matter how sparse, categorically heterogeneous, or causally disconnected), there is—except in those cases that are ruled out by the need to avoid Russell-like paradoxes—another set whose elements are those very things. The calculus of individuals was expected to differ from set theory inasmuch as it identifies whatever is built from the same basic constituents, but also to *match the power* of set theory in other respects: therefore, Unrestricted Composition was needed.[3]

The idea was also that Fusion is a central notion of the calculus of individuals, and that it is a virtue of the calculus that this basic operation is always defined: it is a virtue that, if we take a denoting term and apply the operator "the fusion of" to it, we are warranted to obtain a denoting term. This was probably felt to contribute to the formal character of the calculus. Mereology$_{dis}$ should not deal at all with the complex net of intuitions and controversial, topic-specific theoretical assumptions that can lead us to assent to the negative existentials (a)–(d).

When you review the motivations in favor of (a)–(d) in Chapter 3, Section 3.2, it is quite evident that it could be risky to countenance them when assessing an axiom of the right theory of parthood: they have nothing to do with parthood and cognate relations at all, and embody controversial metaphysical theses on other subjects (such as the nonexistence of causally inefficient items, the meaning of the expression "possible individual," or the exhaustiveness of the abstract/concrete divide).

However, the need to have an always defined operation of Fusion and the nonformal character of the motivations against Unrestricted Composition are not, by themselves, compelling motivations in favor of Unrestricted Composition. It is easy for the opponent of Unrestricted Composition and of mereological monism in general to object that the need for an always defined operation and the formal character of mereology$_{dis}$ could simply *fall* together with Unrestricted Composition, as mutually entangled facets of mereological monism. The mereological monist cannot invoke these as reasons for endorsing Unrestricted Composition. Her opponent *is precisely arguing* that composition is restricted, that Fusion is not an always defined operation (if it is an operation at all), and that mereology$_{dis}$ *should not* be formal and topic-neutral, because the conditions for some things to compose another thing *are* topic-specific.

However, what matters is not that the criteria that would lead us to subscribe (a)–(d) are nonformal, but that they are not suitable to be translated into a clear-cut condition that limits the domain of what exists.

This theme already emerges in two short declarations by Quine and by Donald Williams (an important—but long disregarded—father of twentieth-century metaphysics, who applied mereology to his own theory of *tropes*). In 1981 Quine wrote:

> More objects are wanted, certainly, than just bodies and substances. We need all sorts of parts and portions of substances. For lack of a definable stopping place, the natural solution at this point is to admit as an object the material content of any portion of space-time, however irregular and discontinuous and heterogeneous. (Quine 1981, p. 11)

Quine is here talking exclusively of concrete entities, and—again within this limited domain—he is not saying that, given some entities however chosen, there is their mereological fusion. He is saying that in "any portion of space-time, however irregular and discontinuous and heterogeneous" there is an object. Thus, the domain is narrower than that of Unrestricted Composition, and the claim is about the presence of an object in space-time. These differences notwithstanding, it is interesting that the only reason provided by Quine in support of his thesis is the "lack of a definable stopping place."

Consider (a) ("the fusion of the chair and of the Statue of Liberty does not exist"), and suppose that I decide that the chair and the Statue of Liberty have no fusion, because they are too far apart in space. How could we translate "too far apart" into a condition under which the operation of Fusion is defined? On my desk there is a PhD dissertation, printed on unstapled sheets. Since I am in the process of reading it, it actually consists of two heaps of sheets: one with the sheets I have already read, and another with the sheets still to be read. Within each heap, the sheets are very close, one on top of another. By contrast, the two heaps are at a certain distance from one another, about 7 centimeters. Is there any reason to think that both the sheets already read and those yet to be read have a fusion, while the two heaps (or—equivalently—all the sheets) do not? Is there a *threshold* of distance within which there is a fusion, and beyond which there is no fusion? It would seem outrageously arbitrary to fix such a threshold.

You might feel that the chair and the Statue of Liberty are *definitely* too far apart, while the sheets read are *definitely* close enough to one another. You might even insist on a definite outcome about the two heaps of sheets of the same dissertation, and say for example: some sheets have a fusion if and only if they are such that we can go from any of the sheets to any other through a chain of sheets that are *in touch*.

The exact content of these criteria will be difficult to establish (for example, it is not easy to explain what "being in touch" means[4]), and it is apparent that these criteria are far from formal and inter-categorical: a bikini is admitted as a fusion of its two parts, in spite of the fact that its parts are spatially disconnected. It seems that entities such as bikinis—or tea sets—are such that their parts are *expected* to be spatially disconnected: if the two parts of a bikini were welded, that would not be strictly speaking a bikini any more; and if the cups, teaspoons, sugar bowl, and so on, were all glued together, this would produce a very anomalous tea set.

In cases such as (a), it is difficult to identify a "definable stopping place" (in Quine's words), and even if one insists and finds it, it seems that the imposed conditions are so specific to *kinds* of objects that they actually *do not concern* fusions at all, but rather the fact of belonging to those specific kinds. The bottom and the top constitute a *bikini* on the necessary constitution of *not being* welded. Some sheets constitute a *heap of sheets* if and only if they touch one another.

We could even consider the same entities to be fused, and obtain different outcomes. Thus the sheets on my desk *do seem to compose* an unstapled copy of a PhD dissertation. And the copy of the PhD dissertation seems to be their fusion (it includes the sheets as parts, and does not overlap with anything that does not overlap with at least one of the sheets). Thus, there exists the fusion of the sheets, and our tendency to deny that they have a fusion can be viewed as the tendency to deny that they form a heap of sheets; as a form of restrictivism about heaps of sheets—and not about fusions; and there is nothing strange in the fact that the conditions for something to be a heap of sheets are not formal, but specific to heaps of sheets.

This approach also makes sense of the absence of "a definable stopping place." The lack of a definite threshold between what counts as a heap of sheets and what does not is not surprising at all: the concept of heap is a prototypical example of a *vague* concept. We have clear cases of heaps (including *a lot* of sheets) and clear cases of non-heaps (including *very few* sheets), but there is no threshold (no exact number of sheets) within which there is no heap and beyond which there is. It is sensible to argue that the number of sheets is not the only factor in being a heap of sheets: the spatial proximity between the sheets also comes into play. From this viewpoint, there are clear cases of heaps (in which the sheets are glued together, or perfectly stacked) and clear cases of non-heaps (in which the sheets are separated by other objects), but there is no *threshold of proximity* (no maximal distance, no pseudo-scientific concept of continuity) within which there is no heap and beyond which there is.

Vagueness is a very complex philosophical and logical issue. But—whatever theory of vagueness you adopt—it seems that there is nothing strange in the fact that, when you spell out the conditions for something to fall under a vague concept, these conditions too are vague. If they were not vague, if they imposed a threshold beyond which something falls under the concept and below which it does not (say, in the case of the heap of sheets: 100 sheets), then the conditions would not provide a sound, conservative analysis of the vague concept. By contrast, they would provide a specific *precisification* of the vague concept.

According to *supervaluationism* (one of the most popular semantic treatments of vagueness[5]), any vague concept can be made precise (precisified) in several ways: in the case of the concept of *heap of sheets* one could suggest different thresholds; but *none* of these precisifications constitutes a correct analysis of the concept. By contrast, a correct analysis should have as many possible precisifications as the vague concept analyzed.

In all cases in which we have the temptation to say that composition is restricted according to certain criteria, this temptation can be *reinterpreted* and *satisfied* by saying that these criteria actually concern the application of certain concepts; and that, in cases of disparate fusions, no contentful concept can be applied, and *a fortiori* no criteria of application for these concepts.

Unrestricted Composition does not say that something falls under a certain concept. It says that something (the fusion) exists on the condition that some things (the fused entities) exist. Fusion is a relation: but *to be a fusion of something* is not a contentful concept. It is coextensional with existence: everything is the fusion of itself; thus, whatever exists is a fusion of something, namely of itself (and, trivially, whatever is a fusion exists).

The notion of existence that is often presupposed in the debate about Unrestricted Composition is such that existence is univocal, is adequately expressed by the so-called particular or *existential* quantifier of first-order logic, and is not a contentful or discriminating concept. It is the so-called Quinean concept of existence, strictly connected to Kant's and Moore's thesis that existence is not a predicate or a property—a thesis upheld by Quine throughout his philosophical career, and further refined and made explicit by Peter Van Inwagen in several works.[6] Lewis—the creator of the vagueness argument we are going to discuss—was strictly faithful to Quinean orthodoxy about existence.

When existence is thus conceived, existence is not a concept, is not primarily expressed by a predicate, and can hardly be regarded as a bearer of vagueness: the claim that a fusion exists can be expressed (and is primarily expressed) without any predicate, and thus without anything to which vagueness is typically attributed.

Together with Quine, the other forerunner of the Lewis-Sider argument for Unrestricted Composition is Donald Williams. In 1959, many years before the Quine's text quoted above, Williams discussed his adoption of Goodman's calculus of individuals—which was at the time a rather novel and controversial apparatus—to his own theory of tropes. In this context, Williams resorts to the concept of vagueness in the discussion of Unrestricted Composition.

Williams remarks that it is very common, in particular among neo-Aristotelian philosophers, "to distinguish 'real things' or 'wholes,' like an atom, an axe, a cabbage, a man, from 'mere sums': the former are solid, they contrast with the milieu, they hang together while they move, and so forth." However, these conditions are not suitable for restricting the domain of fusions, that—at least if mereological monism is admitted—is also the domain of unrestricted quantifiers, that is, the domain of what exists or there is according to Quinean metaontology. And the reason for this is that "the idea is vague."[7]

Consider solidity, for example: we can build a so-called *soritic* series of things $t_k$ where $k$ varies from 0 to n, such that, for each $k$, $t_{k+1}$ is more solid than $t_k$. But there is no value $k$ such that from that point of the series onward $t_k$ is solid. Thus, if solidity were used as a criterion for existence (or for being a fusion), existence itself would be vague. But since existence is not vague, solidity and similar features should not be used as a criterion of existence.

## 13.2 Lewis's version of the argument

Lewis's version of the argument in *On the Plurality of Worlds*, while standing in ideal continuity with Quine's and Williams's versions, makes various points clearer, and in particular stresses a semantic aspect: nothing in the sentence that expresses the existence of a fusion is vague. By contrast, the conditions under which we would want to restrict composition are vague: this means that these conditions *cannot* be satisfied.

In Quine's and Williams's simple versions, this semantical aspect was not made explicit. According to Quine, there are actually no general, "definable" restricting conditions. According to Williams, the restricting conditions are vague, and vague conditions cannot restrict "formal" features, such as existing or being a fusion. Against Quine and Williams, the restrictionist could object that restricting conditions can be defined in a case by case way, and it is simply a prejudice that no vague condition can restrict existence. Many restrictionists nowadays hold that existence is vague, and can therefore be restricted by vague conditions.

Lewis writes:

> We are happy enough with mereological sums of things that contrast with their surroundings more than they do with one another; and that are adjacent, stick together, and act jointly. We are more reluctant to affirm the existence of mereological sums of things that are disparate and scattered and go their separate ways. A typical problem case is a fleet: the ships contrast with their surroundings more than with one another, they act jointly, but they are not adjacent nor do they stick together. (Lewis 1986b, p. 211)

The criteria according to which we would tend to restrict composition are different, and are in some cases in mutual conflict: a fleet seems to contrast with what surrounds it, but is made of spatially sparse parts (the ships). In most cases, the ships of a fleet move in the same direction (they "act jointly"), but this is not always the case: it happens that some ships of a fleet leave for an expedition, while other ships of the same fleet stay moored in the harbor.

One can also imagine a soritic series of intermediate conditions, or of more radical forms of separation among the ships. Again, it seems that vague conditions are involved, and that they are conditions for the fusion of the ships to be a fleet (i.e., to fall under the concept *fleet*), but not condition for there to be a fusion of the ships. In the soritic series at stake, we have various fusions that gradually (and without a precise threshold) count more and more as a fleet. It is the concept of *fleet* that is vague, and the fusions are *the domain* of what is gradually more and more of a fleet in the soritic series.

Nonetheless, one could insist that composition *is* restricted. What we intuit—the restrictionist insists—is not only that a bunch of distant and uncoordinated ships are not a fleet, but also that they do not compose anything. If intuition is a personal mental state or event, it is irrelevant that I—for example—do not share this intuition. My own intuition is that a bunch of distant and uncoordinated ships does not compose a fleet, but composes something that does not deserve a specific sortal predicate in natural language, at least not one more specific than "bunch of ships." However, the restrictionist has a different intuition, and the clash between my intuitions and hers risks ending up in a dialectical stalemate.

However, at this point, Lewis objects to the restrictionist that the vague conditions at play—no matter whether and to what extent they are supported by intuition—*cannot* restrict composition because composition is expressed in a part of language in which nothing is vague. Lewis writes:

> The trouble with restricted composition is as follows. It is a vague matter whether a given class satisfies our intuitive desiderata for composition. Each desideratum taken by itself is vague, and we get still more vagueness by trading them off each against each other. [...] But if composition obeys a vague restriction, then it must be sometimes a vague matter whether composition takes place or not. And that is impossible. (Lewis 1986b, p. 212)

When I claim that some things have a fusion (given our definition of Fusion, which is quite similar to the definition that Lewis later adopted in *Parts of Classes*), I am claiming that there is something such that the fused entities are its parts and that each of its parts overlaps with at least one of the fused entities. The language I am employing includes logical language (quantifiers, truth-functional connectives, the predicate < of plural logic, parentheses) and the mereological language: the relational constants for parthood (*P*) and for Overlap (°). But, as we know, ° is introduced by a definition in terms of parthood, and, when all the definitions are resolved, the only nonlogical predicate is *P*. Thus, in order to satisfy our "intuitive" motivations for restricting composition, vagueness should concern the claim that a certain fusion exists. This requires that either parthood or logical language is vague.

The idea is that, given a vague condition for composition, vagueness could not fail to be inherited by the claim that the fusion exists. A restriction on composition would take the following schematic form, in which φ expresses the vague, restricting condition, and Σ could be analyzed in terms of *P* and logical language through the definitions of Fusion and Overlap:

$$\forall xx(\phi xx \leftrightarrow \exists y(y\Sigma xx)) \qquad \text{(Restricted Composition)}$$

But, if φ is vague and (Restricted Composition) holds, the right side of the biconditional in (Restricted Composition) cannot fail to be vague. Moreover, within the right side of the biconditional in (Restricted Composition), at least one subsentential expression should be vague too, because vagueness does not concern sentences only.[8] The fact that a sentence is vague (that it has several precisifications, or that it has an intermediate degree of truth, according to the semantic analysis of vagueness that is adopted) depends on the vagueness of something in its vocabulary. The most obvious bearers of vagueness at the subsentential level are predicates. Once the definitions are resolved, the only predicates at stake in (Restricted Composition) are P and the plural-logical predicate <. Could any of these two predicates be vague?

# 13.3 What cannot be vague

<, in plural logic, is closely connected to *plural identity*. It is actually used in the standard definition of plural identity, according to which some things *xx* are identical to some things *yy* if and only if anything that is one of (<) *xx* is also one of *yy* and vice versa.[9] However, identity is not vague: there are powerful and refined arguments against vague identity in the literature.[10] For our limited purposes, it is enough to observe that identity—at least in its standard characterization—is that relation that anything has with itself and with nothing else. What could be vague in identity? If identity is not vague, < cannot be vague either.

What about *P*? *P* is a constitutive piece of a theory of parthood that, while being highly general according to mereological monism, fails to be logical. Thus—one could argue—there is nothing wrong in thinking that parthood is vague. Consider a cloud: it seems to lack definite boundaries. One could think that, in the peripheral area of the cloud, there are some water molecules that are borderline cases of parts of the cloud.

However, there is at least one quite convincing alternative that accounts for cloud-like scenarios, without making parthood vague. In the case of the cloud, one could follow Lewis and claim that there are actually many objects (that are plausible candidates for the role of reference of "the cloud"), each of which has a definite domain of parts. Vagueness would not concern parthood, but the reference of the expression "the cloud."

This alternative is obviously preferable to vague parthood, if you have adopted a standard conception of identity *together with* another pivotal piece of mereological monism, namely Extensionalism. If *P* is vague, then *PP* is vague. Extensionalism claims that nonatomic things are identical if and only if they have the same proper parts: thus identity would inherit the vagueness of *PP*.

In any case, it is not necessary to *presuppose* mereological principles, and exclude in this way that parthood is affected by vagueness. The point is that if composition is restricted by *vague* conditions, then it is indeterminate what exists. As we have already seen, since everything is a fusion of itself, the domain of what exists coincides with the domain of what is the fusion of something.

In the Quinean tradition, existence is adequately expressed by the existential quantifier of first-order logic, but in order to obtain a syntactically well-formed existence claim, we need to factor in at least one predicate. The most obvious choice is the identity predicate, insofar as identity is in turn closely connected to existence: identity is the relation that anything has with itself and nothing else; this means that the extension of the identity relation will include all and only those ordered couples, each of which includes two times whatever exists. Thus, to claim that Fusion is limited by a vague condition is to say that *existence* is limited by a vague condition, and that there is something vague in some claims of this sort (where *a* would be a constant referring to a fusion, the existence of which is vague):

$$\exists x (x = a)$$

We have already excluded the hypothesis that identity is vague (which—given the tight connection between identity and existence—is already a way to exclude that existence is vague). The underlying idea behind the vagueness argument for Unrestricted Composition is that Fusion is a "generating relation" (a label already introduced by Goodman for Fusion and for the operation that associates the basic elements of a set to the set itself): it is an existential claim. By contrast, the intuitions that militate against Unrestricted Composition involve the idea that some vague conditions should restrict composition; but vague conditions cannot restrict existence, because existence is not vague.

Why cannot existence be vague? An important reason to rule out the possibility that existence is vague has been provided by Sider.[11] This additional reason may be required by those who do not share some of the general philosophical assumptions underlying Lewis's version of the argument (as illustrated above). For example, it might seem that the non-vagueness of parthood *depends* on mereological monism, and should not be presupposed when arguing in favor of one of its claims; or that the non-vagueness of logical language (including the quantifier ) is simply assumed as an aspect of the overall adoption of a Quinean metaontology, in turn deeply entrenched within mereological monism due to a combination of historical and substantial reasons.

Sider *directly* defends the idea that it cannot be indeterminate which fusions exist, by connecting the existence of fusions to numbers: if it were vague whether certain things have a fusion, it would be vague whether these things exist, and then it would be vague *how many* things exist. But numerical sentences cannot be vague. As Sider claims, "mereological terms are *not* needed to express numerical sentences" (p. 127). Thus, any residual doubt about the vagueness of the mereological lexicon is irrelevant.

There is a rather close link between numerical ascriptions and existential claims. The claim that "there are exactly three things" is usually paraphrased in first-order logic in the following way (and thus in terms of identity, quantifiers, and connectives, without any residue of nonlogical language):

$$\exists x \exists y \exists z (x \neq y \wedge y \neq z \wedge x \neq z \wedge \forall w (w = x \vee w = y \vee w = z))$$

*Unanalyzed* cardinality ascriptions add a level at which vagueness is more clearly unacceptable. What could be vague in the English sentence "there are exactly three things"? What—if, for example, supervaluationism is adopted—could be precisified in different ways? Numbers are an unlikely candidate for vagueness. Vagueness would be inherited from the restricting conditions up to the cardinality ascriptions. Thus, if vagueness is unacceptable at the level of cardinality ascriptions, it is unacceptable already at the level of the restrictions on composition.

## 13.4 The Lewis-Sider argument versus intuitions

We can now compare the *alleged counterexamples* to Unrestricted Composition (a)–(d) with the Lewis-Sider argument *for* Unrestricted Composition. It is important to scrutinize the differences among the four cases.

(a) The fusion of the chair and of the Statue of Liberty does not exist.
(b) The fusion of the White House and of the Colossus of Rhodes does not exist.
(c) The fusion of David Cameron and of one of his counterparts in another possible world does not exist.
(d) The fusion of David Cameron and of the number 2 does not exist.

The difference between (a) and (b) is quite negligible: (a) denies the existence of a spatially disconnected fusion; (b) of a temporally disconnected fusion. Spatially and temporally disconnected fusions will tend to be devoid of causal power, will fail to act jointly, and will not move in coordinated ways. But all these features—as well as the underlying spatial and temporal disconnectedness—will come in degrees and allow for soritic series of gradually closer, more integrated, and more coordinated entities. To draw a sharp boundary in these series would be arbitrary, and would simply not respect the expected criteria. In order to respect these criteria, it should be vague when composition happens, what exists, and how many things there are. The Lewis-Sider argument shows that how many things there are and what exists cannot be vague, and hence that there is no way to limit composition in the way which (a) and (b) would suggest.

On the other hand, (c) (involving a fusion whose inputs inhabit different possible worlds) and (d) (involving a fusion whose terms are one abstract and the other concrete) are significantly different. The difference lies in the fact that the two distinctions are arguably exempt from vagueness. Assume Lewis's modal realism. Given two entities whatsoever,[12] either they inhabit the same world, or they inhabit different worlds.

Also in the case of (d) the abstract/concrete divide seems to be sharp and exempt of vagueness. We have already seen that it can be understood in several ways, but this means at most that terms such as "concrete" or "abstract" are *ambiguous*, not that they are vague.

Thus, while we have good reasons in support of (c) and (d), it seems that these reasons can be satisfied without incurring in any form of vagueness: the restrictionist can argue that, definitely, no inter-world fusion and no hybrid abstract/concrete fusion exists. The Lewis-Sider argument—as we have presented it—cannot be directly used against these *sharp* limitations of compositions.

Both Lewis and Sider were aware of this limitation. More exactly, Lewis discusses a case such as (c), and Sider explicitly excludes a case such as (d) from the targets of his argument. In a long parenthetical comment, Lewis writes:

> (To be sure, a ban against trans-world composition would not itself be a vague restriction, so it would not fall victim to the argument just given. But taken by itself it would be unmotivated. To motivate it, we have to subsume it under a broader restriction. Which can't be done, because a well-motivated broader restriction *would* be vague.) (Lewis 1986b, p. 213)

The idea is that modal realism is (or was, when Lewis was writing) a new theory: Lewis is presenting it in *On the Plurality of Worlds*. In this context, he considers whether composition happens when the entities to be fused inhabit different worlds. The exclusion of inter-world individuals would actually *benefit* modal realism. Given the acceptance of Unrestricted Composition, Lewis is forced to admit inter-world individuals as *impossible individuals*. In his system, to be a possible individual is to be part of a possible world. Inter-world individuals are not parts of possible worlds and so are—by definition—impossible. Impossible individuals cannot be counterparts, and, as was later pointed out,[13] it is quite difficult to establish what it means for them to have a property possibly or necessarily. According to Lewis, we simply exclude them usually from our domains of quantification. They do not serve any explanatory purpose. The only reason to accept them is given by the fact that *other* restrictions to composition are unacceptable inasmuch as they are vague; and thus it would be unacceptable to restrict composition only in this case, without a legitimating precedent at our disposal.

Lewis's argument against a *definite* restriction of composition and the resulting ban on inter-world individuals are not very compelling. First of all, it is not clear why we should have a precedent, a "broader restriction," as Lewis writes in the passage above. Since in this case we have a definite criterion for rejecting inter-world individuals, it is not clear why it does matter that we lack a definite criterion *elsewhere*. Moreover, cases such as (d) might seem to offer the precedent expected by Lewis: a ban on mixed fusions of abstract and concrete entities is exempt from any kind of vagueness.

However, Lewis would not have admitted such a precedent. In *Parts of Classes*, Lewis admits also fusions of individuals and classes (and thus, of prototypical cases of concrete and abstract entities respectively): "I am committed to all manner of unheard-of things: trout-turkeys, fusions of individuals and classes, all the world's styrofoam, and many, many more" (Lewis 1991, p. 80). In spite of the heterogeneity of these fusions, it seems that for Lewis the commitment to all of them is justified by the general argument for Unrestricted Composition, which he had already set forth in *On the Plurality of Worlds*, and reformulates in *Parts of Classes*.

Vagueness seems to be absent both for inter-world fusion and abstract-concrete fusions, and it is tempting to conclude that the Lewis-Sider argument should not be applied to these cases; that—*pace* Lewis—the abstract/concrete divide is clear and important enough to justify a specific and nonarbitrary restriction of composition; and, finally, that, once this limitation is admitted, other sharp, non-vague limitations could be accepted, as in the case of inter-world fusions for example (in this case, we should always remember that they matter only if we admit the existence of entities in other possible worlds: Unrestricted Composition *does not* dictate the existence of fusions of *nonexistent* things).

Sider, who presents his own version of the argument in *Four-Dimensionalism*, and so within a treatment of the persistence of concrete entities in time, explicitly restricts his attention to concrete entities[14]—no matter how sparse in space and time—for which the desirable restrictions on composition are arguably vague.

## 13.5 Unrestricted Composition and formal mereology

It is worth examining Lewis's formulation of the argument for Unrestricted Composition in *Parts of Classes*, because it offers an interesting hint about the general idea that underlies the argument. This general idea militates against *any* restriction of composition, quite independently of the vagueness or definiteness of the restricting conditions we are inclined to impose on composition. Moreover, it makes explicit the connection between the Lewis-Sider argument and Quinean metaontology, to which we will return in Chapter 14 (by asking what would happen if we adopted a *different* metaontology).

Lewis writes:

> Existence is not some special distinction that befalls some of the things. Existence just *means* being one of the things there are, nothing else. The fuzzy line between less queer and more queer fusions cannot possibly coincide with the sharp edge where existence gives out and nothing lies beyond. (Lewis 1991, p. 81)

In this book, we are presenting mereology$_{dis}$ as an area of metaphysics that concerns the formal features of the parthood relation and the conditions of identity and existence for wholes, and *mereological monism* (mereology$_{phi}$) as the philosophical thesis that CEM tells the complete truth *about these subjects*. According to the standard Quinean conception, identity and existence are topic-neutral concepts, and are expressed in logical language (through the specific "logical" predicate "=", to be added to first-order logic, and through the existential quantifier, respectively). No condition should be satisfied in order to exist or to be self-identical (the domain of what exists coincides with the domain of what is self-identical).

No substantial, categorical distinction between entities has any bearing on *existence*. Unrestricted Composition is the piece of CEM that is about existence: it provides existence conditions for wholes. These conditions should not lead us out of the field of topic-neutral concepts, such as existence and identity. Thus, the only condition we are allowed to impose concerns the *existence* of the fused entities.

Specific, substantial conditions should not concern existence. The fact that in many cases—such as those motivating the restriction at which (a) ("the fusion of the chair and of the Statue of Liberty does not exist") and (b) ("the fusion of the White House and of the Colossus of Rhodes does not exist") aim— these conditions are vague is simply a symptom of the fact that no condition should be imposed at all. Vagueness can only concern conditions (and the predicates which express these conditions), while existence has—so to say—no condition.

What is at stake here is the *neutrality* of mereology. Mereology is not logic (for the reasons I have explained in Chapter 10, Section 10.3), but a metaphysical doctrine. Nonetheless, mereology is deeply connected to logical notions, such as those of existence and identity. Existence "is not some special distinction," and should not be limited by specific conditions that depend on controversial, substantial, metaphysics-laden distinctions, such as spatially compact versus spatially sparse, or temporally continuous versus temporally discontinuous, or abstract versus concrete, or intra-world versus inter-world.

In the case of the first two distinctions, their inadequacy to limit existence is made clear by their vagueness or fuzziness ("the fuzzy line between less queer and more queer fusions"), while the latter two distinctions are exempt from vagueness. Nonetheless, they are contentful and depend on categorical distinctions; they impose a "special distinction that befalls some of the things."

It should be admitted that there is a difference between the Lewis-Sider argument and this general stance underlying it (and which only Lewis makes explicit). The argument shows that the expected vague limitations on composition cannot be accomplished, because nothing can be vague in what concerns the existence of fusions. The general stance is not an argument: it is the staunch conviction, rooted in Quinean metaontology, that existence *should not* be limited by category-specific conditions.

This conviction is strictly connected to the idea that mereology$_{dis}$ is *only about* formal features of parthood and identity and existence conditions for wholes, and should not be mixed with theories about spatial and temporal continuity, causal efficacy, possible and impossible individuals, or abstract/concrete distinctions.

If you disagree with this conviction, the Lewis-Sider argument for Unrestricted Composition is still there, but it is powerless against counterexamples such as (c) and (d). These cases could still be treated piecemeal. (c) ("the fusion of David Cameron and of one of his counterparts in another possible world does not exist") depends very clearly on controversial doctrines about modality (such as modal realism), and could be avoided if these doctrines are rejected.

(d) ("the fusion of David Cameron and of the number 2 does not exist") involves an abstract entity (the number 2) and could, as a consequence, be compared with the conclusions we reached in our discussion of Extensionalism in Chapter 8. There we showed that the strategies to defend Extensionalism are more successful in the case of concrete entities than in that of abstract entities, and that this could legitimize a restriction of the degree of generality of mereological monism: perhaps, CEM tells the complete truth about the identity conditions of concrete entities *only*. From this viewpoint, the limitation of Unrestricted Composition to concrete entities (the admission that there is no fusion when *some* of the entities to be fused are abstract) could confirm that mereological monism should limit its ambitions to the realm of concrete entities.

The kind of formality to which mereology aspires is—as we have argued in Chapter 3—gradable, and the limitation to concrete entities leaves mereological monism still with a large domain of application. Moreover—as we have already noted in Chapter 8—this limitation could be explained by the fact that abstract entities are the object of *stipulations*, and that there is nothing surprising in the fact that stipulative entities can violate Unrestricted Composition (as much as they can violate Extensionalism): it is enough to stipulate that they violate it.

## 13.6 What about intuitions?

Let us recap the results of our analysis: the Lewis-Sider vagueness argument works primarily in cases such as (a) and (b). In cases such as (c) and (d) it needs to be supported by a general characterization of mereology$_{dis}$ as a formal discipline, deeply associated with formal notions such as those of existence and identity. The mereological monist in me is more than happy to embrace this characterization of mereology$_{dis}$, but arguably it is not fair to presuppose this characterization when arguing in favor of Unrestricted Composition, a pivotal thesis of mereological monism itself. Those who do not endorse this characterization of mereology$_{dis}$ may prefer to accept that certain kinds of fusions (such as hybrid abstract/concrete fusions and inter-world fusions) do not exist. In the especially important case (d) ("the fusion of David Cameron and of the number 2 does not exist"), the limitation coheres with the idea that mereological monism in general should limit its ambitions of generality to concrete entities.

What about the intuitions in support of (a)–(d)? We have seen that they are much more vivid in the case of (a) and (b) (spatially and temporally disconnected fusions), and these cases are more directly affected by the powerful Lewis-Sider argument. With regard to these intuitions, we have not yet established whether they are *evidential intuitions* or *motivating intuitions*. According to Korman's recent defense of a restrictionist approach to composition—according to which only so-called *ordinary objects* exist—intuitions have an evidential role: the counterexamples to Unrestricted Composition *would show* that Unrestricted Composition is false.[15]

The evidential value of the intuitions in support of (a) and (b) can be doubted, quite independently of the general, arduous problem of whether intuitions can have any evidential value or not.[16] The problem is that those intuitions that support (a) and (b) are too *unspecific* to be taken as evidence, quite independently of any specific stance about the evidential roles of intuitions in philosophy or elsewhere. It is not clear at all what "existence" the fusions at stake would lack. Indeed, the *motivations* brought forward in support of (a) and (b) suggest that there is a tight connection between the features that the fusions would lack, and the kind of existence that they would lack. The same would actually hold in the case of (c) and (d), if (c) and (d) were supported by intuitions at all (which—as we have seen—is doubtful).

(a)–(d) are reasons against Unrestricted Composition *only if* it is assumed that existent things have causal powers, are spatially or temporally continuous, inhabit a single world, and are either totally abstract or totally concrete. But this *presupposes* a connection between existence and these features. It is far from clear that (a)–(d) in themselves militate against Unrestricted Composition, because Unrestricted Composition claims that fusions exist in the sense of existence expressed by the existential quantifier: Unrestricted Composition *does not say* that fusions have causal powers, are spatially or temporally continuous, and so on.

(a)–(d) do not easily translate into arguments against Unrestricted Composition because it is not clear that they really are counterexamples to the kind of generalized existential statement that Unrestricted Composition is. And so, Lewis is right in treating them not as counterexamples, but as *unsatisfiable motivations* for restricting composition. They are undetermined hints, in which it is not clear which notion of existence is at stake. They are not enough to obtain counterexamples to Unrestricted Composition. Nonetheless, they are enough to be *motivated* to assess if it is plausible to confront them with a restriction of composition, that is, with a restriction of existence in the Quinean sense. Given the Lewis-Sider argument, it turns out that—at least when the restricting condition is vague, as happens in the realm of concrete entities—these motivations cannot be satisfied.

# Unrestricted Composition and Metaontology

## 14.1 Unrestricted Composition, Meinongian existence, Williamson's concreteness

Unrestricted Composition is about existence. It warrants that Fusion is an always defined operation: if the entities to be fused exist, then their fusion exists. What does this say *about fusions*? Nothing, except that they exist. It does not require them to play any explanatory role, participate in causal links, or play any role in an exhaustive description of the world. We have seen that inter-world fusions—in reference to which Lewis formulates the first mature version of the argument, after Quine's and Williams's early sketches—are more of a problem than an asset for modal realism. This seems to hold also in other cases. Unrestricted Composition delivers heterogeneous and redundant entities that are never to be mentioned outside of philosophy: within the concrete domain (in cases such as (a) and (b), Chapter 12, Section 12.1), the heterogeneity, redundancy, irrelevance come in degrees, and can generate soritic series. Nonetheless, in the high ranks of the soritic series, we get entities that are definitely *useless*.

These useless entities would exist, but fail to instantiate any interesting, *autonomous* properties. They would inherit the properties of their parts. As Lewis writes, "the trout-turkey in no way defies description. It is neither fish nor fowl, but it is nothing else: it is part fish and part fowl. [...] Its character is exhausted by the character and relations of its parts" (Lewis 1991, p. 80). But this means that every significant property is already instantiated by the parts of these fusions.

Now, one could be tempted to ask: why should we care at all about this kind of existence? In serious metaphysics, we should only care about what exists in a *thicker* sense. Contemporary metaontology offers a great variety of alternatives to Quinean orthodoxy,[1] in which various thicker notions of existence play a role.

Many kinds of Meinongians think that the existential quantifier (which it would be less misleading to call *particular quantifier*) does not express existence, which would be expressed by a genuine, discriminating predicate. The discriminating property expressed by this predicate can be meant in several ways. For example, Francesco Berto thinks that to exist is to have causal powers.[2]

Timothy Williamson thinks that existence is an abused notion, and that it is better to get rid of the label "existence" in philosophy, and to replace it with two notions. One is the notion of "being something," or "being identical to something," and is adequately expressed by the existential quantifier (it corresponds to *Quinean* existence). The other notion is concreteness.[3]

Kit Fine, and other philosophers who assign prominence to the notion of grounding,[4] are ready to concede that existence is expressed by the existential quantifier, but thinks that existence should not be the central concern of ontology: ontology should instead focus on what is *real* or *fundamental*. Reality comes in degrees, defined by the grounding relation: what grounds is more real than what it grounds. Fundamentality is the attribute of what is at the beginning of the chains of grounding: what grounds other things, but is in turn ungrounded.

What impact could these alternative metaontologies have on Unrestricted Composition? Unrestricted Composition is usually formulated and has been defended by Lewis in the context of Quinean metaontology. Metaontology *matters*: given a certain metaontology, the significance of Unrestricted Composition could change, and we could have at our disposal a richer or poorer stock of notions to express distinctions among the domain of admitted fusions.

What surely does not change from one metaontology to another is the literal content of Unrestricted Composition:

$$\forall xx \exists y (y \Sigma xx) \qquad \text{(Unrestricted Composition)}$$

Unrestricted Composition states that, for every things, *something* in the domain of the existential quantifier is their fusion. For the Quineans, this means that the fusion exists. For the Meinongians, it does not mean this. Some Meinongians (such as Terence Parsons[5]) think that the particular quantifier corresponds to the natural language quantifier "there is." Some more recent Meinongians (the so-called *noneists*[6]) think that no ontological feature is expressed by the particular quantifier.

Some of these debates can be interpreted as disagreements about which *terms* should be used to designate what is in the domain of unrestricted quantifiers:

for these terms the traditional label *transcendentals* is sometimes used.[7] While these disagreements may be pragmatically important (insofar as it is important to use a perspicuous and unambiguous terminology in philosophy), they have no direct bearing on the question of what is in the domain of unrestricted quantifiers.

Meinongians enjoy the advantage of having a specific predicate (*exist*) for the fusions that really matter. They could accept Unrestricted Fusion, and still subscribe to (a)–(d), and deny the existence of many "undesirable" fusions. Since "existence" is a predicate for them, the Lewis-Sider argument cannot be applied to their notion of existence: there is nothing strange in the fact that a predicate irreducible to a logical notion is *vague* (predicates are the standard-bearers of vagueness). Nonetheless, the argument *can* be developed in support of the principle as it is, except for the fact that the principle does not speak of the existence of fusions, but rather of their being in the domain of the unrestricted quantifier.

One can see the advantage of reserving the word "existence" for the restricted, vaguely delimited domain. However, the restricting conditions at play in (a)–(d) are highly heterogeneous: spatial continuity, temporal continuity, causal efficacy, and so on do not seem to characterize any single concept, such as Meinongian "existence." Moreover, we have seen that Berto construes existence specifically as causal efficacy. As a consequence, the restrictions that would be *motivated* by the intuitions in support of (a)–(d) would not always identify the domain of what exists in Berto's understanding of existence.

Similar considerations concern Williamson's repudiation of *existence* in favor of *being something* and *concreteness*. Clearly, Unrestricted Composition, if conjoined with Williamson's metaontology, concerns *being something*: it affirms that, given any entities whatsoever, their fusion is something—that it is identical to something. As in the Meinongian case, the intuitions underlying (a)–(d) could be instead referred to the *other* notion, concreteness. Concreteness can be meant as being in space-time, or as having causal efficacy.[8] Also in these cases, the variety of motivations supporting (a)–(d) do not seem to identify any unitary notion of existence as concreteness.

## 14.2 Fine's metaontology

In the above cases of non-Quinean metaontology, the only difference that concerns Unrestricted Composition is that both the Meinongians and Williamson have at their disposal a notion (existence for the Meinongians, concreteness for

Williamson) whose extension does not correspond to the unrestricted domain of quantification. This notion can be used to interpret (a)–(d). However, nothing changes in the arguments in support of Unrestricted Composition. The domain of fusions is still the domain of unrestricted quantification, in spite of the fact that the latter domain is now distinguished from the narrower domain of existents or of concrete entities.

Fine's metaontology—and in general the kind of anti-Quinean metaontology that is often adopted by grounding theorists—might seem to be better equipped to look at Unrestricted Composition in a way significantly different from the Quinean one. Grounding is a kind of order, and, as such, is well equipped to characterize degrees of distinction. Moreover, the explanatory hierarchies defined by the grounding relation are not univocal: grounding is a relation, and no common feature (such as existence or concreteness) is expected to be shared by every fundamental entity, or to be instantiated to a higher degree by what grounds than by what is grounded.

Thus, the grounding theorist can admit that all the fusions exist, but insist that their roles in the explanatory hierarchies is extremely different. She can explain the negative existential judgments such as (a)–(d) in terms of *degrees of reality*: the heterogeneous fusions at stake would have a low degree of reality, in spite of existing and being in the range of our quantifiers.

However, an element of complication is Fine's *opposition to unrestricted quantification*. According to him, no quantifier is *absolutely unrestricted*, and the domain of our quantifiers can be indefinitely expanded by postulations.[9] The clearest case of these expansions would be the passage from the quantification over natural numbers to the quantification over relative numbers, and then over rational numbers, over real numbers, and so on: these expansions would not consist in the discovery of previously existing but unknown numbers, but in a sort of *creative postulation*.

This means that, from Fine's viewpoint, also the admission of new fusions could be a sort of expansion by postulation. In one of the discussions of his *expansionist* or *postulationist* metaontology, Fine concedes something very similar to Unrestricted Composition. He claims that, even if at present we have no need to quantify over a given strange and heterogeneous fusion, this need could arise at a future time, for unforeseeable reasons. He compares this situation to what happens in the case of numbers.

Fine takes a car-bouquet as an example. It is a temporally extended entity that is initially a car and later becomes a bouquet of flowers: given some assumptions about the ontology of time that cannot be discussed here, the existence of this entity would be imposed to us by Unrestricted Composition. Fine thinks that at present the car-bouquet is not in the domain of our quantifiers, but that the domain could be expanded to include it:

> We may imagine that some future religious sect holds the view that cars are endowed with souls who migrate to a neighboring bouquet of flowers after a gestation period of nine months (stranger religious views have been held). The putative bodies of these souls are called "car-bouquets" and, although everyone is willing to recognize the existence of car-bouquets, there is considerable disagreement over whether they have souls. Again, we may explain why it is correct for us to deny the existence of car-bouquets and yet also correct for the future generations to affirm their existence by appeal to a difference in what each of us has introduced into the ontology. (Fine 2007, p. 165)

As we have seen in Part Two, Fine himself is a mereological pluralist: in his *Towards a Theory of Part*, the existence conditions for wholes are—together with identity conditions and the connected principles of obliteration—an aspect of a pluralist approach to parthood; thus, we should expect that various theories of parthood differ in restricting, or nonrestricting composition.[10] However, quite independently of his mereological pluralism, Fine's peculiar non-Quinean metaontology leads him to adopt a sort of Unrestricted Composition *at the meta-level*: given some entities (no matter how disparate), *we can always expand our domains of quantification* and include them.

It is also interesting that this claim of indefinite expandability of the domain to new fusions is conceded by Fine, precisely because there is no precise (i.e., exempt from vagueness) and principled (i.e., nonarbitrary) criterion for limiting it.

> [...] there appears to be no precise and principled line of division between those objects—such as cars and bouquets of flowers—whose existence we are ordinarily inclined to accept and those objects—such as "car-bouquets"—whose existence we are ordinarily inclined to reject. It therefore appears that there can be no theory that is internally satisfactory in providing a precise and principled basis for determining what exists and yet also externally satisfactory in being consonant with what we ordinarily take to exist. (Fine 2007, pp. 162–163)

Thus, the very impossibility of satisfying vague and arbitrary conditions of restriction drives Fine to concede unrestricted expansions of the domain to include fusions. If you want to reject mereological monism, it seems that the combination of Fine's pluralism with his own postulationism in metaontology is a promising (but at present largely unexplored) alternative, one that is surprisingly consonant with mereological monism at a deeper level (insofar as—for example—it replaces Unrestricted Composition with unrestricted expandability). When you add to that picture a theory of grounding, you have also a tool to differentiate between various fusions you quantify over in terms of degrees of reality.

However, Fine's position depends on various controversial assumptions, most notably the rejection of unrestricted quantification, and the related idea that the domains of quantification are indefinitely expandable. After all, without unrestricted quantification, also the literal formulation of Unrestricted Composition has no settled, definitive meaning. However, it is not clear that there are any good arguments to reject unrestricted quantification. In the literature, there are also compelling *defenses* of unrestricted quantification (e.g., by Williamson[11]), and it is beyond the purpose of this book to settle such a general problem. If unrestricted quantification is admitted, the fusions cannot be *added* at a later point to the domains of quantification, when a certain need arises. In order to serve future needs, disparate fusions must be—so to say—*always there*, in the domain of unrestricted quantifiers: the evolving, heterogeneous, and *vague* conditions of inclusion cannot be satisfied by a continuous alteration of the domain itself.

According to the picture drawn by the backers of Unrestricted Composition, all the fusions are in the unrestricted domain of quantification. The vague and revisable limitations on what matters for us are interpreted as limitations on what is relevant, or spatially continuous, or intra-world: for all these limitations, simple or complex predicative expressions are available, and these predicates will be in most cases vague.

It seems that Unrestricted Composition can handle car-bouquets with relative ease: they exist even if they do not matter; if and when they matter, our stock of predicates can be adjusted to the need to qualify them. Fine's metaontology could be independently motivated, and in this case it would offer an interesting alternative to mereological monism, in which Unrestricted Composition would be replaced by a metaprinciple of indefinite expandability of the domain of fusions. However, as far as mereology$_{\text{dis}}$ is concerned, the need not to exclude by vague criteria car-bouquets and similarly bizarre entities (which might become relevant in the future due to unforeseeable events) is perfectly served by Unrestricted Composition and mereological monism: the car-bouquet is a fusion, whose existence (expressed by the existential/particular quantifier of first-order logic) is warranted by the existence of the car and of the bouquet of flowers (the fused entities).

## 14.3 Unrestricted Composition and the narrow understanding of mereology

There are some solid arguments in support of Unrestricted Composition, in particular when no abstract/concrete hybrid fusion is involved. Nonetheless, many philosophers reject Unrestricted Composition, and try to resist the Lewis-Sider argument with various strategies. Some claim that existence is vague;[12] others that composition is restricted in a definite and *brutal* way, rather than by vague, explicit criteria, and hence that the argument from vagueness cannot apply;[13] other philosophers still—the so-called mereological nihilists—argue that there is another way of avoiding vague and arbitrary limitations of the domain of what exists, namely by claiming that composition never occurs, that no things have a fusion (except in the limiting case in which a mereological atom is the fusion of itself).[14]

In this book we cannot discuss any of these alternatives, partly due to space constraints and partly because the motivations and the articulation of these stances do not belong to mereology$_{dis}$ according to the narrow understanding of it. For example, the idea that existence is vague, in spite of the fact that seemingly no expression is vague in existential statements and in the related numerical sentences, must be supported by a full-fledged theory of vagueness. The idea that composition happens *brutally* and primitively in some cases and not in others requires a method for discriminating admissible and nonadmissible primitives in metaphysics. Mereological nihilism requires a massive strategy of reconciliation with our referential and cognitive practices, which seem to involve lots of complex entities with parts, and perhaps no mereological atom at all. The mere remark that these alternatives require seemingly expensive assumptions outside narrow mereology$_{dis}$ is obviously not a compelling reason to reject them: perhaps these assumptions are legitimate and independently motivated.

To my mind, the Lewis-Sider argument and its ideological gist are completely convincing, and the intuitive counterexamples (even when they are actually *intuitive*) do not really concern the Quinean kind of existence expressed by existential/particular quantifiers. To exist or to be in the domain of an unrestricted quantifier is not to be important, to instantiate some kind of distinguished feature, or to instantiate a predicate; it is to be in the domain of what can instantiate predicates. The chair-statue (as much as Lewis's trout-turkey, and Fine's more complex car-bouquet) could *become* relevant, and begin to fall under certain sortal predicates.

It is not difficult to carry out a quick *mental experiment* in which this happens. Consider a deviant sect, somewhat similar to the one considered by Fine in the passage quoted in Section 14.2, but keen on fusions of a different kind. This other sect claims that each artifact in the world is deeply connected to another artifact somewhere in the world: these couples of artifacts are in a close relation of *artifact-twinness*.

The sect is convinced that, in order to properly and efficiently use an artifact, it is important for us to be aware of its twin, and consider in our mind the two artifact-twins as a single thing. Suppose also that the chair and the Statue of Liberty are, according to the sect, artifact-twins. When we use the chair, in order to sit on it properly and efficiently, we should consider in our mind the chair-Statue of Liberty (the fusion of the artifact-twins).

Fine would say that in this case the domain of quantification is expanded, while the defender of Unrestricted Composition claims that the chair-statue existed beforehand: what the sect has done is not bring something new into existence (indeed, no physical change happened in the vicinity of the chair and of the statue), but endow it with a new role.

Mereology$_{dis}$, according to the mereological monist, should not deal at all with the kind of change that happens when the sect develops a certain belief about the chair and the statue. The kind of arbitrary, plausibly vague, hardly definable process that consists in becoming relevant (or in becoming unitary or cohesive) should not be investigated by a discipline that is so strongly caught up with *logical* notions such as identity or existence. Unrestricted Composition allows mereology$_{dis}$ to stay clear of these problems, and this might be taken to be the ultimate reason why mereological monism endorses it.

# Appendix: Mereological Monism, without Composition as Identity

## 15.1 Ontological innocence?

In this book, we have analyzed mereological monism. However, there are some things we have never said, but that are often said when mereological monism is discussed. Namely, we have never said that:

(a) a fusion is nothing over and above the fused entities;
(b) a fusion is not a further ontological commitment over the fused entities;
(c) a fusion and the fused entities are the same portion of reality;
(d) a fusion is identical to the fused entities;
(e) CEM is ontologically innocent.

By contrast, in Part Three and in particular in Chapter 14, we have underlined that there is a strong connection between the viewpoint of mereological monism on Unrestricted Composition and Quinean metaontology. According to Quinean metaontology, existence is adequately expressed by the existential/particular quantifier of first-order logic. This means that according to Unrestricted Composition, given some things, *there is* their fusion; or, equivalently, that their fusion *exists*. Thus, CEM, as a theory, *is ontologically committed* to the existence of a fusion for any choice of entities, if ontological commitment is meant in a Quinean sense. As we know, it is not committed to the idea that fusions exist in a thicker sense, have causal powers, exist in space-time, are concrete, are fundamental, and so on; however, it is committed to their belonging to the domain of the unrestricted quantifiers, and this is what ontological commitment consists in from a Quinean point of view.

Nothing in CEM suggests that this ontological commitment is identical to the fused entities, and hence that it is not a further ontological commitment with respect to them. Nothing suggests that fusion is an exclusively reflexive relation that does not bring us anything new.

Nelson Goodman classified fusion as a "generating relation."[1] A generating relation leads us from some things (the fused entities) to *another* thing that it is generated by them. Goodman was well aware that there are liminal cases in which the fusion is identical to the fused entities, namely when there is only one fused entity; and that there are other cases in which the fusion is identical to one of the fused entities, namely those in which all the fused entities are parts of one of them. In these liminal cases, the fusion is one of the fused entities, and as a result is not a further ontological commitment. Nothing is generated by the generating relation in these cases. However, these liminal cases are precisely liminal; they are the least interesting cases of fusion. In every other application of the Fusion operation, there is a *new, further* ontological commitment, *contra* (b): in order for the existential statement about the fusion to be true, something different from the parts has to be included in the domain of quantification.

No endorsement of theses such as (a)–(e) is to be found in Goodman, Quine, or other mereological monists of their generation. In those days, it was clearer than today that mereological monism and nominalism are closely connected (Goodman and Quine were among the staunchest champions of nominalism as well). Nominalists assign great importance to ontological economy. Nonetheless, mereological monism was not thought to be a tool of ontological economy in the sense characterized by (a)–(e). Mereological monism was quite rightly *only* associated with nominalism about structure.

Nominalism about structure actually delivers *a kind of ontological economy*: given some entities, mereological Fusion delivers only one whole, while, for example, an infinite number of sets can be obtained. Goodman's principle that there is no difference that is not a difference in content—in spite of the shortcomings we discussed in Sections 5.5 and 5.6—captures the kind of ontological economy at which mereological monism aims—in particular, through Uniqueness of Composition and Extensionalism. This ontological economy consists in not having more than one whole with the same proper parts (Extensionalism), or more than one fusion from the same fused entities (Uniqueness of Composition). It does not consist in the whole or the fusion being nothing over and above the parts or the fused entities.

Nonetheless, many more recent mereological monists—such as Lewis—have committed themselves to some among (a)–(e). In some cases, they have attributed to the resulting philosophical contention—dubbed Composition as Identity by Lewis himself—a sort of unifying or grounding function for mereological monism. Their idea seems to be that, given Composition as

Identity, mereological monism becomes much more reasonable than it would otherwise be; or even that some principles of CEM can be inferred from claims such as (a)–(e).

In Section 15.2 I analyze (a)–(e), their mutual connections, and their role as facets of the philosophical contention dubbed Composition as Identity. In the Section 15.3 I try to explain why many philosophers think that mereological monism is unified or grounded by (a)–(e) (or by some of them), and argue that the connection between mereological monism and Composition as Identity is actually weak. Finally, in Section 15.4 I suggest that mereological monists should actually stay clear of Composition as Identity, because Composition as Identity extends the expected explanatory duties of mereology$_{dis}$, in sharp contrast to the way in which mereological monists construe mereology$_{dis}$.

With this analysis I aim to show not that (a)–(e) are false (even though I am personally convinced that they are[2]), but rather that they are extraneous to mereological monism. It is coherent and advisable to adopt the philosophical stance defended in this book without thereby subscribing to any of those claims.

## 15.2 Is the whole nothing over and above its parts?

The debate on Composition as Identity hinges upon the claims (a)–(e). (a)–(e) are not an indivisible package of claims: some philosophers endorse only some of them, while rejecting others.

(a) ("a fusion is nothing over and above the fused entities") can be taken as the common core of the sometimes shaky intuitions at stake in the debate on Composition as Identity, mainly because it can be understood in several ways. What does it mean to be "nothing over and above"? This expression has sometimes been regarded as obscure and hardly intelligible.[3] However, it is perhaps simply ambiguous, and, once disambiguated, (a) turns out to express something intelligible after all, albeit highly controversial.

One can imagine at least three interpretations of "nothing over and above." In a *first sense*, it means that the fusion is identical to the fused entities, as much as the most important philosopher born in Oberlin is identical to David Lewis. There is no thing that David Lewis is identical to, and the most important philosopher born in Oberlin is not identical to, because they are mutually identical. The same would hold for—say—Benelux on the one hand, and the Netherlands, Belgium, and Luxembourg on the other.

This leads to (d), which is the most obvious formulation of the principle of Composition as Identity. It also delivers (b) and (e): if a thing $x$ is identical to a thing $y$, then $x$ is not a further ontological commitment with respect to $y$, and does not make any theory or any sentence committed to $x$ ontologically more guilty or burdened than it already was for being committed to $y$.

The idea behind this reasoning is that Fusion works exactly as identity and, as a consequence, delivers the same kind of ontological innocence. Identity is a rather well-known relation, characterized by some principles. Most importantly, it obeys the Indiscernibility of Identicals. If Tully is identical to Cicero, then they instantiate exactly the same properties and relations. Thus, the expectation is that a fusion and the fused entities instantiate exactly the same properties and relations. And this, at least prima facie, seems false. Consider Benelux, the fusion of the Netherlands, Belgium and Luxembourg: it is a single multinational entity, and it has Belgium as a proper part. By contrast, the Netherlands, Belgium, and Luxembourg are three nations and none of them has Belgium as a proper part.

Nonetheless, a huge literature in defense of Composition as Identity, by philosophers such as Einar Bøhn, Aaron Cotnoir, Paul Hovda, and Megan Wallace,[4] tries to defend the idea that a fusion and the fused entities are—against all appearances—indiscernible. In order to accomplish this result, they follow various routes, such as relativizing the properties and relations that seem to make a whole discernible from its parts to a *concept*, a *viewpoint*, or a *way of counting*.

A *second interpretation*—one not discussed in the literature, yet quite credible as an interpretation of what "nothing over and above" means in general—is *even more directly* connected to indiscernibility. The quantification in "nothing" could be a second-order quantification. This kind of quantification would be similar to that expressed by "something" in "London is something that Cockington Forge is not: namely, a metropolis." In this reading, (a) would mean that the fusion has no feature that its parts lack. Also in this case, a kind of semantic revisionism is needed in order to dispel the impression that—for example—the fusion is one, while the parts are many.

Thus, also this second interpretation is committed to an indiscernibility claim. The so-called weak or moderate forms of Composition as Identity, endorsed by Lewis, Sider, and Bricker,[5] admit that a whole is not indiscernible from its parts. They are moderate because they accept that composition is not governed by the same principles that govern identity, and in particular that composition fails to respect the Indiscernibility of Identicals. Moderate Composition as Identity renounces (d), and only claims that composition is analogous to identity, but is not, strictly speaking, identity. Alternatively, the champions of Moderate

Composition as Identity could claim that composition is an identity relation, but that this identity is of a kind that does not obey the Indiscernibility of Identicals. In both cases, they admit that the fusion *is* discernible from the fused entities. As Lewis writes: "What's true of the many is not exactly what's true of the one. After all they are many while it is one."[6]

While these moderate forms of Composition as Identity are not committed to the claim that a fusion is indiscernible from the fused entities, they nonetheless need to *replace* indiscernibility in some way. The claim that fusion is analogous to identity, but does not respect the Indiscernibility of Identicals, is exposed to the charge of cheating. As Sider writes, any defender of Composition as Identity who claims that Indiscernibility does not hold for composition "would arouse the suspicion that their use of 'is identical to' does not really express identity."[7] In order to avoid this charge, weak Composition as Identity needs to show that the whole and its parts, while not strictly speaking indiscernible, enjoy a kind of intimacy analogous to indiscernibility.

In order to make composition significantly analogous to identity, the champion of Composition as Identity needs to replace indiscernibility with a milder kind of dependence between the features of a whole and those of its parts. This leads some defenders of Composition as Identity to introduce *portions of reality*, and to subscribe to claim (c), that is, a fusion and the fused entities are the same portion of reality. While the notion of portion of reality is never really clarified, the idea is that in reality a fusion and the fused entities play the same role in a way. When I ask what there is in Benelux, I can reply in various ways: I can say that there is Benelux; or that there are the Netherlands, Belgium, and Luxembourg; or that there are the molecules constituting Benelux. Each of these replies is exhaustive: given a list of entities that *cover* Benelux, it would be redundant to add something else to that list. This is because each of these answers would cover the same portion of reality, whatever a portion of reality might be.

Thus, the portion of reality would be the bearer of the substantial features that are common to the fusion and to the fused entities, while other, more superficial and less objective features could vary between things that are the same portion of reality. Lewis, according to whom Indiscernibility *does not* hold for composition, writes: "the many and the one are the same portion of Reality and the character of that portion is given once and for all whether we take it as many or take it as one."[8] He then adds: "It does matter how you slice it [the portion of reality], not to the character of what's described, of course, but to the form of the description."

Thus, even when you deny that Indiscernibility holds for composition, you still end up connecting in some way the important features of the fusion (its "character," as Lewis writes) to the analogously important features of the fused entities. How this works might be a mystery,[9] but—if the analogy between composition and identity has any content—it seems unavoidable that the features of the whole and the features of the parts are strictly connected, either by Indiscernibility or in a weaker—but nonetheless contentious—way.

This could happen also in the *third* interpretation of (a). The champion of this last interpretation is free to reject the other four claims (b)–(e). Expressions such as "over and above" can be interpreted in a way that does not amount to *identity* or *indiscernibility* between its terms, but rather to *metaphysical grounding*.[10] The nature of grounding and of its *relata* has become the subject of a lively and increasingly complex debate over the last decades, but, for the sake of relative simplicity, let us simply assume that grounding relates facts.[11] The idea would be that $x$ is nothing over and above $y$ if and only if some facts concerning $y$ explain (in a metaphysical sense) or ground at least the most important facts concerning $x$. In our case (in which the place of $y$ would be taken by a plurality of parts $yy$), the fact that the parts exist or that the parts have certain features would explain or ground the fact that the whole exists or that it has certain features.

It makes sense to interpret the claim that the whole is nothing over and above its parts in terms of *grounding*, because grounding is expected to be an exhaustive kind of explanation, without any residuum: thus the idea would be that, given $y$, no further explanation is needed for $x$.

An important difference between this interpretation and the other two is that the relation at play is not symmetric. Identity is obviously symmetric, as is indiscernibility. Grounding is generally thought to be *asymmetric*;[12] insofar as it is a kind of *explanation*, it cannot go both ways, because no real, noncircular explanation is expected to go both ways.

This interpretation of "nothing over and above" can involve the features of the whole and of the parts, if the facts that ground and are grounded concern these features; if—in the example of the chair—the solidity of the chair is grounded in the way in which the back, the seat and the legs are chemically composed and glued together. Grounding is expected to be a *hyperintensional* notion, and to warrant a necessary connection between its terms: this means that, in this hypothetical instance of grounding, the fact that the parts of the chair have certain features would *necessitate* the fact that the chair has certain features.

By contrast, if the facts involved concern only the *existence* of the whole and of the parts, then the idea would be that the existence of the parts *explains* the existence of the whole. The existence of the parts would therefore also necessitate the existence of the whole. No other features of parts and whole would be involved in this case.

At this point, it is clear that, according to the way in which the ambiguous claim (a) is interpreted, the relatively clearer claims (b)–(e) will or will not follow. However, in all cases, you end up endorsing philosophical claims that do not belong to mereology$_{dis}$ in its narrow sense: they are neither claims about the formal features of parthood relations nor claims about the conditions of identity and existence of complex entities. In most interpretations, what is at stake are the *features* of parts and whole, and their mutual link.

In spite of the fact that the philosophical gist of Composition as Identity does not belong to mereology$_{dis}$, all the philosophical claims (a)–(e) are often discussed in the contemporary literature about mereology. David Lewis has explicitly defended Composition as Identity in his manifesto of mereological monism in *Parts of Classes*, albeit in the moderate variety.[13] Kathrin Koslicki, in her book *The Structure of Objects*, devotes an entire chapter to criticizing Composition as Identity,[14] because she aims to criticize mereological monism and feels that Composition as Identity is a central aspect of mereological monism. But why does she feel so, if claims (a)–(e)—which represent various facets of Composition as Identity—are not about mereology$_{dis}$?

## 15.3 From Composition as Identity to mereological monism?

Let me try to explain why Composition as Identity has been often seen as an aspect of mereological monism, by assessing whether it is possible to argue in favor of Composition as Identity on the basis of mereological monism, or whether it is possible to argue in favor of mereological monism on the basis of Composition as Identity.

There is no convincing argumentative route from mereological monism to Composition as Identity. There are many varieties of Composition as Identity, and subtle differences among (a)–(e). For the sake of simplicity, let us focus on a single thesis, namely (d)—the most obvious and literal formulation of Composition as Identity—according to which a fusion is identical to the fused entities.

If you insist on finding a connection between (d) and mereological monism, this connection will probably involve nominalism about structure. As we have seen in Part Two, mereological monism denies any role to structure in the identity conditions for complex entities. As a consequence—one might be tempted to argue—why should a fusion be *different* from the fused entities?

Structure cannot account for this difference, so the mereological monist should concede that there is no difference at all, but identity.

This line of argument is misleading. First of all, Extensionalism and Uniqueness of Composition simply affirm that structure cannot mark a difference between different wholes with the same parts. They do not say anything about the difference between the parts and the whole, between the fused entities and the fusion.

Fusion in CEM is an operation that connects—in its most interesting instances—many things to one thing. Fusion *presupposes and determines* several *differences* between its inputs and its output: the inputs are many, the output is one; the output is a fusion of the inputs, while the inputs are not the fusion of themselves; in many cases the output has all the inputs as proper parts, and in many of these cases the inputs do not have all of themselves as proper parts.

However, the difference between the fusion and the fused entities could also consist in something else. There could be many other *differences* between fused entities and fusion, about which CEM is completely silent. As far as mereological monism is concerned, a whole could instantiate emergent properties, which are not only different from the properties and inter-relations of the parts, but also modally and explanatorily independent of them.

As we have seen in the previous section, Composition as Identity—according to most ways of construing it—is committed to a kind of dependence between the features of the whole and those of its parts; this kind of dependence will be absolute indiscernibility, or partial indiscernibility, or modal dependence, or grounding, according to the variety of Composition as Identity adopted. This arguably leads to an incompatibility between Composition as Identity and emergent properties.[15] However, this incompatibility is only an outcome of Composition as Identity, and not of mereological monism. As a consequence, mereological monists may argue that a fusion is *made different* not only by the fact that the fusion is obtained from the parts through a many-one operation, but also by many other kinds of features that are simply not investigated by mereology$_{dis}$, and about which the mereological monist is proudly neutral and silent.

Thus, there is no argumentative route from mereological monism to Composition as Identity. The argumentative route in the opposite direction, from Composition as Identity to mereological monism, is only slightly more convincing.

It is true that Composition as Identity entails Uniqueness of Composition (and thus Extensionalism, which is a weaker consequence of Uniqueness of Composition, as we have seen in Chapter 6, Section 6.1). Consider the seat, the back, and the legs. Suppose that Uniqueness of Composition fails, and in particular that the seat, the back, and the legs have two different fusions, $f_1$ and $f_2$. However, given (d), *both* $f_1$ and $f_2$ are identical to the seat, the back, and the legs. But identity is transitive; thus, $f_1$ *is* identical to $f_2$. Assuming Composition as Identity, we have reduced the failure of Uniqueness of Composition to a contradiction. Thus, Uniqueness of Composition follows from Composition as Identity.

The route from Composition as Identity to Unrestricted Composition is much more arduous, and has been convincingly criticized by Kris McDaniel and Ross Cameron.[16] One could say something along the lines of this: if Cicero and Tully are identical and Cicero exists, then Tully cannot fail to exist. Fair enough: but we are presupposing that Cicero and Tully are identical. This presupposition is legitimate in the case of Cicero and Tully. However, when this reasoning is exported to composition, the corresponding presupposition *is not* supported by Composition as Identity.

Composition as Identity warrants that *if* the Netherlands, Belgium, and Luxembourg compose Benelux, *then* the Netherlands, Belgium, and Luxembourg are identical to Benelux. But it *does not warrant* the antecedent of this conditional; that is, it does not warrant that the Netherlands, Belgium, and Luxembourg compose Benelux. In the specific case of Benelux, it might seem obvious that there is composition (although mereological nihilists would disagree). By contrast, consider a controversial fusion of spatially sparse entities, such as Pisa's Leaning Tower and Agra's Taj Mahal. The restrictionist of composition simply denies that they compose anything, that their fusion *exists*. Thus, the restrictionist can endorse (d), and still consistently deny that the Leaning Tower and the Taj Mahal are identical to their fusion, because according to her the Leaning Tower and the Taj Mahal have no fusion at all.

Only the conjunction of Unrestricted Composition and Composition as Identity warrants that the Leaning Tower and the Taj Mahal are identical to their fusion. But then the reasoning *presupposes* Unrestricted Composition, and is not a way of arguing for Unrestricted Composition on the basis of Composition as Identity.

No other interesting principle of CEM is entailed by Composition as Identity. Thus, also the route from Composition as Identity to mereological monism merely consists in the fact that Composition as Identity entails Uniqueness of Composition and Extensionalism. But Uniqueness of Composition and Extensionalism are very reasonable principles in themselves, for which—as we have seen in Part Two—it is actually very hard to find a counterexample, at least in the domain of concrete entities.

Composition as Identity is a comparatively much more controversial doctrine, which may be defended—if at all—by adopting venturous and underexplored semantic tools. As a result, the mereological monist should not endorse Composition as Identity *because* Composition as Identity entails Uniqueness of Composition and Extensionalism. It is wiser to directly defend Uniqueness of Composition and Extensionalism.

## 15.4 Why mereological monists should stay clear of Composition as Identity

To recap: the reason why Composition as Identity is often mentioned in the debates about mereological monism is that there are some *seeming* connections between them. These connections, once analyzed, boil down to the modestly interesting fact that Composition as Identity entails Uniqueness of Composition and Extensionalism.

Thus, there is no good reason why mereological monists should endorse Composition as Identity. While in the previous section we have focused on (d), the same seems to hold also for the other claims (a), (b), (c), and (e) in the ideological vicinity of Composition as Identity.

No principle of mereological monism entails Composition as Identity. On the other hand, no principle of mereological monism entails that Composition as Identity is false. Nonetheless, there are good reasons for mereological monists *not* to endorse Composition as Identity *qua* mereological monists.

Composition as Identity is committed to some controversial theses that do not belong to mereology$_{dis}$ at all. Due to the extension of the Indiscernibility of Identicals to composition or to the controversial denial of emergent properties we have discussed in Section 15.2, Composition as Identity is a thesis *mainly* about the properties of wholes and the properties and interrelations of parts. Identity is constitutively connected to the sharing of features: to say that some things are identical *is* to rule out that they have different—or at least autonomous—features.

Identity without any kind of indiscernibility is simply not identity at all. Mereological monism does not entail any kind of indiscernibility between a fusion and the fused entities, and in general any claim about substantial features of whole and parts. Thus, mereological monism has simply no significant tie with Composition as Identity. Any confusion between mereological monism and Composition as Identity conflicts with the programmatic restriction of mereological monism to a narrow understanding of mereology$_{dis}$, and is a potential source of discredit for mereological monism.

# Notes

## Introduction

1  Some confusions may arise between philosophical mereology and mereology$_{phi}$. It is useful to restate the distinction. I always use "philosophical mereology" as equivalent to general mereology$_{dis}$: a philosophical discipline that studies the relation of parthood and other cognate relations. By contrast, I use "mereology$_{phi}$" to designate a specific philosophical thesis, namely the thesis (also dubbed "mereological monism") that classical mereology is the general and exhaustive theory of parthood and composition.

2  Fine (1994), p. 138.

3  Lewis (1991), pp. 72–87.

4  Simons (1987).

5  Varzi (2016). The first edition of the entry was published in 2003.

6  Koslicki (2008), Sattig (2015). Some collective books about related topics also include a similarly succinct presentation of mereology$_{theo}$, for example, Cotnoir and Baxter (2014), Calosi and Graziani (2014), Kleinschmidt (2014).

7  Eberle (1970).

8  Lewis (1991), p. 75. This unfortunate characterization of mereology by Lewis is criticized in Bennett (2015).

9  The very status of logic as a neutral tool that can be applied to any kind of reasoning, without being an autonomous subject of controversy, is highly dubious, but this topic falls outside the scope of our present inquiry.

10  See Chapter 3 for a discussion of a kind of formality/generality that comes in degrees.

11  Lewis (1991), p. 82.

12  Bøhn (2014), Cotnoir (2013a), and Wallace (2011b), among others.

13  Many recent, important papers on Composition as Identity are collected in Cotnoir and Baxter (2014).

## Chapter 1

1  The expression "mereological harmony" is employed in a similar (but more refined) sense in Uzquiano (2011).

2  According to Yablo (1998), the difficulty of drawing a sharp line between literal and metaphorical claims is a widespread methodological issue in ontology, which

becomes especially acute in the case of existential claims. As Yablo makes clear, some metaphorical claims (the so-called *dead metaphors*) are nonetheless about reality. In the lexical area of mereology, "the neck of the bottle is part of the bottle" includes a metaphor, but is nonetheless about spatial, prototypical parthood in reality. In many of these cases, it seems that the metaphorical component does not directly concern the term "part" or other mereological lexicon, but the referential terms for parts and wholes (in this case, the metaphorical referential expression is "the neck of the bottle").

3   The application of mereological concepts to words, sentences, and other linguistic items will be discussed in Chapter 8, Section 8.4.

# Chapter 2

1   Lewis (1991).

2   Lewis does not mention an explicit polemical target, namely a philosopher according to whom the elements of a set are parts of it. This claim was later defended by Fine (2010). Lewis (1986a) argues in a similar way against Armstrong's and Forrest's *structural universals*; Lewis (1998) argues against Armstrong's *states of affairs*.

3   The most famous is Donald Williams: see Williams (1953). Paul (2002) is a contemporary defense of the claim that *universal* properties are parts of individuals. In our example, we make no claim to be adequately representing any specific, viable theory of properties.

4   Both the seminal joint work with Leonard (Goodman and Leonard 1940) and the more mature version of it in Goodman (1951, ch. II) can be considered presentations of CEM *from above* in the sense explained in the text.

5   Simons (1987), ch. 2. Both Moltmann (1997) and Casati and Varzi (1999) identify *from below* a sort of minimal mereology, whose contents allegedly reflect the meaning of part terms in natural languages.

# Chapter 3

1   We will later see (in particular in Chapter 4, Section 4.3) that it is useful to distinguish between *parthood* and *proper parthood*, but that this distinction does not amount to any substantial kind of dualism.

2   The notion of topic-neutrality was originally developed by Gilbert Ryle. See, for example, Ryle (1954), p. 116.

3   A refined analysis of the different senses in which logic can be said to be formal is MacFarlane (2000). At least two of the three senses of formality I distinguish in this section (namely, the first and the second) are discussed by MacFarlane. See also MacFarlane (2002), Beall and Restall (2006), Dutilh Novaes (2011).

4   Smith (2003).
5   While it is evident that generality can come in degrees, "topic-neutrality" could seem like a feature that either holds or not. I do not aim to oppose this lexical intuition about "topic-neutral." I simply stipulate that topic-neutrality, as it is understood in this book, is instantiated at a high degree by a theory that holds true for a lot of various entities. A highly topic-neutral theory is neutral between these various entities; the theory holds true no matter which *among these entities* are our *topic*.
6   See, for example, Van Inwagen (1998, 2014).

# Chapter 4

1   Rescher (1955).
2   Varzi (2006).
3   Fine (2010), p. 560.
4   The definitions of mereological predicates are meant in this book as linguistic definitions (and not as metalinguistic definition). That is, they enrich the language of a theory (in this case, the theory is CEM) with a new predicate, which is satisfied at the conditions indicated on the right side of the definition. They belong to the object language. The variables flanking the defined predicate are explicitly universally quantified. This is done for the mere sake of linguistic economy (no need to use metavariables) and uniformity with the axioms. There would be nothing wrong in replacing them with metalinguistic definitions. See Simons (1987), p. 21 e p. 46, for some (also historical) remarks on linguistic and metalinguistic definitions in mereology.
5   See, for example, Schaffer (2009) and Sider (2011), ch. 1.
6   Every asymmetric relation is trivially antisymmetric, insofar as no couple of entities in an asymmetric relation satisfies the antecedent of Antisymmetry.
7   See Gilmore (2014) for an introduction, and Kleinschmidt (2014) for a collection of essays on mereology and location.
8   In the literature it is possible to find a number of potential counterexamples to Locke's thesis. See in particular Fine (2000) and Spolaore (2012). These counterexamples are not directly connected to mereological problems, and we will not discuss them.
9   This position in the debate on material constitution was originally set forth in Thomson (1998). In Chapter 9 we will discuss how it was further developed by Cotnoir (2010).
10   Among the deniers of Locke's thesis, Koslicki (2008) chooses this option.
11   See, for example, Varzi (2000) and Varzi (2014).
12   A different stipulation is sometimes made in the literature about the meaning of "composition" (for example, in Van Inwagen (1995) and Varzi (2014)), according to

which composition is an operation that has only nonoverlapping things as inputs. In our reconstruction of mereological monism, this operation does not play any role. The choice to make "Fusion" and "Composition" coreferential also highlights the fact that, in CEM, there is a *single* operation that goes from many things to one thing.

13   Also the two principles of CEM could be dubbed Uniqueness of Fusion and Unrestricted Fusion, respectively.

# Chapter 5

1   See Gruszczyński and Varzi (2015) for a different picture of the twentieth-century origins of mereology, in which the Leśniewski's tradition is opposed to Husserl's tradition—which construes mereology$_{dis}$ in a very broad sense—and Goodman's contribution is given much less importance.

2   See Burgess (2015) for a balance on Lewis's project from the perspective of contemporary set theory.

3   Varzi (2016), § 1.

4   It is worth noting that Goodman has also rather non-spatial cases in mind, such as the relation between a property and an individual instantiating it. This was the main application of the *calculus of individuals* in Goodman (1951).

5   Goodman (1956).

6   The verb "to build" is here used in a metaphorical sense: neither Goodman nor anyone else in the debate thinks that it corresponds to an action of building performed by a subject.

7   In some axiomatic set theories, the Singleton Axiom warrants that this operation is always defined.

8   This relation is the transitive closure of set-theoretic membership. Given a relation *R,* its *transitive closure S* is the smallest transitive relation of which *R* is a subrelation. The "bottom ends" (the ultimate elements, in the case of sets) are such that they are in the relation *S* with the sets, but nothing is in the relation *S* with them.

9   See Shiver (2015) about the problem of defining atomism and universal decomposability in atoms.

10   This is warranted by the so-called Axiom of Foundation, according to which every non-empty set is disjoint from one of its elements.

11   See, in particular, the *third* kind of formality discussed in Chapter 3, Section 3.1.

12   See, Arnztenius (2008) for an overview of the scientific topics for which the hypothesis of gunk is relevant. See also Zimmermann (1996) for the relation between gunk and naïve physics.

13   In Borghini and Lando (2016), I have argued that Humean supervenience and mereological monism are actually mutually incompatible.

14  Lewis (1994) argues that there is an a priori and necessary core in HS, according to which "'how things are' is fully given by the fundamental, perfectly natural, properties and relations that those things instantiate." But the identification of fundamental relations with spatiotemporal ones and the thesis that fundamental properties are instantiated by "points" or "point-sized occupants of points" are characterized as "yet another speculative addition to the thesis that truth supervenes on being," restricted to possible worlds "like ours" (p. 474).

15  Maudlin (2007) (in particular Ch. 2). See also Hüttemann (2004).

16  This shortcoming is also discussed in Oliver (1993).

17  Fine (2010), in particular §§ V–VI.

18  For an in-depth discussion of the relation between facts and Extensionalism, see Betti (2015) (in particular Ch. 2). Betti invokes mereological Extensionalism within an argument against the existence of facts.

19  At least if the relation is not conceived in a very peculiar way. According to Betti and Wieland (2008), the so-called *relata-specific relations* can play the role of truth makers. The relation at stake in our example would be specific to Marseille and Paris, in the sense that, if the relation exists, then Marseille and Paris exist too and are connected by that relation.

# Chapter 6

1  Varzi (2008) distinguished different, nonequivalent ways of expressing mereological Extensionalism and their mutual relations (see in particular pp. 108–111).

2  The formulation in terms of parts *tout court* could be analyzed in the same way as well. Also in this case, the right-to-left direction is trivial.

3  By contrast, various kinds of revisionists about identity may be tempted to reject the Indiscernibility of Identicals. This happens with so-called relative identity (see, for example, the classic Geach 1967) and with other kinds of pluralism about identity (see Baxter 1988, 1989, 1999).

4  See, for example, Armstrong (1997), p. 122. See Bennett (2015), pp. 251-252 for some interesting remarks about the interaction between Lewis and Armstrong on this topic.

# Chapter 7

1  See, for example, Varzi (2001b).

2  The typical follower of this line of attack to Extensionalism adopts a theory of ontological vagueness, such as that of Tye (1990) or Korman (2015), ch. 9.

However, for the sake of relative simplicity, here we will refrain from focusing on a specific stance.

3 A classical argument against ontological vagueness builds upon the impossibility of vague identity (see Evans (1978)), but the link between ontological vagueness and vague identity has been criticized by Noonan (2008) and Paganini (2011).

4 In the theory of indeterminate identity, the converse of the Indiscernibility of Identicals is sometimes differentiated from the Indiscernibility of Identicals, and the former is rejected, while the latter is accepted (see Parsons 2000, pp. 38–39). This distinction requires a form of logical revisionism and will not be discussed in the present book. The theory of indeterminate identity is also connected with the admission of fuzzy objects, which we have seen in Section 7.1 to be in tension with mereological monism.

5 This aspect of counterpart theory is more clearly expressed in the mature version of Lewis (1986b) than in the original version of Lewis (1968). It is also expressed quite clearly in the postscript C—"Vagueness and Variety of Counterpart Relations"—added in Lewis (1983), pp. 42–43 to the reissue of Lewis (1968).

6 See Schnieder (2006). See also Varzi (2002).

7 Baxter (1988) makes the first step: objects can instantiate and fail to instantiate one and the same properties, and be discernible from themselves. Baxter explicitly rejects—in a number of works and with a plurality of motivations—the Indiscernibility of Identicals. According to him, Professor Sambunjak is identical to Petra the chamois, but discernible from her. See also Baxter (1989). While, due to space constraints, I cannot discuss Baxter's approach in this book, it should be noted that it is compatible with Extensionalism.

8 Schnieder's example presupposes that it is true that the dog at stake is a cur, in spite of the fact that it is impolite to call it so. Otherwise, the negation could be understood as a standard, truth-functional negation. For a more refined analysis of analogous examples, see Predelli (2013), § 5.8 and § 8.3.

9 Varzi (2008). See also Varzi (2000).

10 Varzi (2008), pp. 121–122.

11 See in particular Laycock (2006) and McKay (2016).

12 A kind of dualism is explicitly applied to the relation of an artifact with its matter/ stuff in McKay (2015). It is noteworthy that McKay feels the need to formulate a specific mereology for stuff. As a consequence, his overall approach does not conform to mereological monism. The ensuing kind of dualism can also be compared with Thomas Sattig's quasi-hylomorphism, as it is expounded in Sattig (2015).

13 Thomson (1998) and Cotnoir (2010).

14 See Hawley (2015) for a general introduction to perdurantism.

15 Two important readings on this problem are Gilmore (2009) and Giaretta and Spolaore (2012).

16 If quantification over indices is deemed logically deviant, one could prefer to turn PP into a three-place predicate, where the additional argument place would be for times. See Giaretta and Spolaore (2012) for an assessment of the two options.

# Chapter 8

1 Cotnoir (2013b), pp. 842–843, n. 6 claims that "non-classical mereology is a bit of a misnomer," since it might wrongly suggest that the deviance from classicalness concerns logic. However, the same remark could be made about the classical versus nonclassical distinction in mechanics or economics: also in these cases, the classicalness from which some approaches deviate does not need to involve logic.

2 For a thorough, critical analysis of structured facts, see again the first part of Betti (2015). Several reasons to doubt that structured propositions (and in general mind-independent propositions) exist are discussed in Iacona (2002).

3 For a contemporary defense of adverbialism, see Kriegel (2008).

4 An anti-extensionalist mereology countenancing *slots* has been sketched out in Bennett (2013). See also Chapter 9, Section 9.2.

5 As a side remark, it should be noted that facts and propositions are mutually entangled in notorious ways. As a result, given identity conditions for facts and propositions in which the order and repetition of constituents is accounted for, it is upon those who think that both structured facts and Russellian propositions exist to provide a way to distinguish—for example—the fact that Paris is west of Berlin from the (true) proposition that Paris is west of Berlin. Otherwise, it is also possible to identify facts and true propositions.

6 Lewis (1991), p. 78.

7 It is controversial that an expression of the form "the same P" can really express qualitative identity. See, for example, McGinn (2000), ch. 1.

8 Goodman and Quine (1947), Goodman (1968), and Sellars (1963).

9 Kaplan (1990). See also Hawthorne and Lepore (2011) and Sainsbury (2015).

10 Varzi (2008), p. 128.

11 This set-theoretical codification of ordered *n*-tuples is usually attributed to Felix Hausdorff.

12 This codification of order is inspired by the so-called Wiener–Kuratowski definition of ordered couples.

13 See the classical Benacerraf (1965).

14 Also the stronger claim that what is abstract is necessarily abstract is—as far as I know—undisputed. The stronger claim that what is concrete is necessarily concrete is rejected—for reasons independent of the present discussion—by Williamson (see, for example, Williamson 2013, pp. 7–8).

15  Wittgenstein (1961), 1.1. See Lando (2007) for a discussion of the application of mereological tools to Wittgenstein's metaphysics.
16  See, for example, Hossack (2007).
17  The idea that facts contain particular and universals has been widely criticized for a variety of reasons, and various alternatives have been discussed, for example, in Fine (1982), Lowe (1998), and Vallicella (2002).

# Chapter 9

1  This example is first mentioned in Sanford (1993).
2  The example has been introduced in Gilmore (2007) from the perspective of the relations between mereology and space, and in Effingham and Robson (2007) from the perspective of the philosophy of time. The simplified exposition presented here can be found in Cotnoir (2010), p. 841.
3  For a general introduction to the philosophical controversies concerning the possibility of time travels, see, for example, Smith (2013).
4  Bennett (2013).
5  Fine (1999), Johnston (2006), and Koslicki (2008), among others.
6  See, for example, Simons (1987), p. 28.
7  See Smith (2009) for an analysis and defense of nonclassical mereologies in which Weak Supplementation is dropped.
8  The first exposition of this proposal is in Cotnoir (2010), where it is presented as a reaction to Varzi's defense of mereology in Varzi (2008). See also Cotnoir (2015).
9  Cotnoir (2010), p. 401.
10  Ibid., p. 402. See also Simons (1987), p. 117.
11  See Forrest (2012) for an overview of the debate on the Identity of Indiscernibles.
12  In the debate about the principle of Identity of Indiscernibles, the risk of indefinite multiplication of colocated entities is considered by Della Rocca (2005) as a reason to endorse the principle itself.

# Chapter 10

1  For a short introduction to plural logic and the controversies surrounding it, see Linnebo (2014). For a more in-depth study, see Oliver and Smiley (2013).
2  On Weak Supplementation, see, for example, Simons (1987), p. 116.
3  This idea of simplicity is roughly inspired by Goodman's *calculus of simplicity* (Goodman (1951), ch. III).

4   See Linnebo (2014), § 3 for a distinction of the various ways in which the expected logicality of plural quantification could be meant.

5   If, however, the ontological commitment to sets is deemed intrinsically undesirable, then it is important to interpret plural quantification in a way that avoids any implicit commitment to set-like pluralities. See Carrara and Martino (2009) for an interesting attempt in this direction, and for the application of it to CEM.

6   Boolos (1984), pp. 448–449.

7   However, in defense of the idea that sets have—in the semantics of plural expressions—the role of unique representatives of many things, see Black (1971) and Simons (1982).

8   Varzi (2016), § 4.3.

9   While the other definitions in this book are all meant as linguistic definitions (see Chapter 4, n. 4), Varzi's definition of Fusion should be meant as a metalinguistic definition: the left side and the right side of the definition are metalinguistic names of the same formula in the object-language. Thus, the problem that a formula is not usually allowed to occupy the argument place of a predicate can raise legitimate philosophical concerns (which I discuss in the next pages), but does not jeopardize the syntactic well-formedness of the definition. Metavariables should be introduced, but I skip over this complication. It is expected that $z$ and $x$ do not occur free in $\varphi$.

10  See Oliver and Smiley (2013), ch. 8, for a discussion of plural definite descriptions.

11  Varzi (2016), § 4.3.

# Chapter 11

1   Hovda (2009).

2   Ibid., p. 63, for a more in-depth discussion.

3   Also $c$ and $d$, $b$ and $c$, and each of $b$, $c$, and $d$ individually have $a$ as their Minimal Upper Bound in the scenario pictured by the above diagram.

4   See again Hovda (2009), pp. 65–66, for the proofs.

# Chapter 12

1   See Gendler (2010) for an overview.

2   Van Inwagen (1995).

3   Sider (2013).

4   Armstrong (1978), p. 5 and Field (1989), p. 62 are two classical defenses of the Eleatic Principle. See Oddie (1982) for an analysis of different versions of it.

5   Korman (2015), ch. 4.

6   Bengson (2015).

# Chapter 13

1   Lewis (1986b), pp. 211–213.

2   See postulate P3, Lewis (1968), p. 114.

3   In Goodman and Leonard (1940), the equivalent of Unrestricted Composition is the first axiom I.1 (p. 48).

4   On this topic, see, for example, Zimmermann (1996).

5   See, for example, Fine (1975) and Lewis (1982) for two (significantly different) forms of supervaluationism about vagueness.

6   Quine (1948) and Van Inwagen (1998, 2014).

7   Williams (1959), p. 219.

8   *Pace* Korman (2015), ch. 9. According to Korman, the indeterminacy at play in composition restrictions does not depend—in some cases—on any semantic feature of subsentential expressions. As a consequence, indeterminacy is a non-compositional semantic feature of sentences.

9   See, for example, Yi (2005), p. 487 and Yi (2006), p. 243.

10  The debate on vague identity hinges upon the short argument presented by Evans (1978).

11  Sider (2001), § 4.9.

12  For the sake of simplicity, we exclude here from the inputs of Fusion inter-world entities (entities that have themselves parts in different worlds). Their existence is imposed to modal realism by Unrestricted Composition itself.

13  See Varzi (2001a). Inter-world individuals are, by contrast, explicitly defended by the so-called doctrine of five-dimensionalism, according to which individuals have modal parts, analogous to the temporal parts postulated by many four-dimensionalists. See Graham (2015) for a recent defense of this thesis.

14  See, for example, Sider (2001), p. 127.

15  Korman (2015). See also Korman (2010).

16  See Williamson (2007), ch. 7 for the most influential rejection of evidential uses of intuition.

# Chapter 14

1   See Berto and Plebani (2015) for an introduction to contemporary metaontology (in particular chs. 7–8).

2    Berto (2013), ch. 4.

3    Williamson (2013), ch. 1.

4    See Fine (2001) and Fine (2012). The metaontology of Schaffer (2009) is, from our limited viewpoint, in agreement with Fine's metaontology. By contrast, Audi (2012) sketches a theory of grounding that is compatible with a Quinean metaontology.

5    Parsons (1980).

6    See, for example, Priest (2005).

7    See Lando and Spolaore (2014) for the distinction between transcendental disagreement and ontological disagreement. David Lewis sometimes uses the expression "blanket term" for transcendentals (see, for example, Lewis (1986b), p. 100).

8    Williamson (2013) (p. 6, n. 6) chooses to remain neutral on the correct characterization of concreteness.

9    See Fine (2006). Fine (2005) applies postulationism to the philosophy of mathematics.

10   Fine (2010) is not explicit about existence conditions for various kinds of wholes. In other words, nothing plays for existence conditions the role played in Fine's framework by the principles of obliteration I have discussed in Chapter 5, Section 5.7. This is perhaps due to the fact that Fine (2010) is merely sketching a future pluralistic theory of parthood.

11   Williamson (2006).

12   Koslicki (2008) and Korman (2015).

13   Markosian (1998).

14   Sider (2013). While their stances differ in many important respects that we cannot analyze here, also Unger (1979), Van Inwagen (1995), Merricks (2001), and Rosen and Dorr (2002) can be classified as nihilists or quasi-nihilists.

# Appendix

1    See Goodman (1951), § II.3, Goodman (1956), p. 17, and Goodman (1958).

2    For some objections to some important formulations of Composition as Identity, see Carrara and Lando (2016).

3    Van Inwagen (1994), pp. 210–211. See also Van Inwagen (2006), n. 1.

4    Bøhn (2014), Cotnoir (2013a), and Wallace (2011b). For an introduction to the general debate on Composition as Identity, see Cotnoir (2014) or Wallace (2011a).

5    Lewis (1991), pp. 81–87, Sider (2007), and Bricker (2015).

6    Lewis (1991), p. 87.

7    Sider (2007), p. 59.

8    Lewis (1991), p. 87.

9   In Borghini and Lando (2016) we have shown that the connection between the features of the whole and the features of its parts—as it is envisaged by the moderate forms of Composition as Identity—is a peculiar kind of supervenience. See also McDaniel (2008) and Calosi (2016).

10  See Cameron (2014) for a much more in-depth interpretation of Composition as Identity in terms of grounding. See also Loss (2016).

11  This is, for example, the contention of Rosen (2010). For an introduction to metaphysical grounding, see Correia and Schnieder (2012) and Raven (2015).

12  Asymmetry is explicitly indicated as a pivotal feature of grounding in key texts such as Fine (2012), Rosen (2010), and Schaffer (2009). However, Rodríguez-Pereyra (2015) has proposed some counterexamples to the asymmetry of grounding.

13  There is some exegetical controversy about the kind of Composition as Identity that should be attributed to Lewis. See Bøhn (2011).

14  Koslicki (2008), Ch. III.

15  See Borghini and Lando (2016) for a detailed analysis of this incompatibility.

16  McDaniel (2010) and Cameron (2012). However, Harte (2002), Merricks (2001), and Bøhn (2014) defend the idea that Composition as Identity entails universalism.

# References

Armstrong, David. 1978. *A Theory of Universals. Universals and Scientific Realism Volume II*. Cambridge: Cambridge University Press.

Armstrong, David. 1989. *A Combinatorial Theory of Possibility*. Cambridge: Cambridge University Press.

Armstrong, David. 1997. *A World of States of Affairs*. Cambridge: Cambridge University Press.

Arnztenius, Frank. 2008. "Gunk, Topology, and Measure." In *Oxford Studies in Metaphysics: Volume 4*, edited by D. Zimmermann, 225–47. Oxford: Oxford University Press.

Audi, Paul. 2012. "A Clarification and Defense of the Notion of Grounding." In *Metaphysical Grounding*, edited by F. Correia and B. Schnieder, 101–21. Cambridge: Cambridge University Press.

Baxter, Donald. 1988. "Identity in the Loose and Popular Sense." *Mind* 97 (388): 575–82.

Baxter, Donald. 1989. "Identity through Time and the Discernibility of Identicals." *Analysis* 49 (3): 125–31.

Baxter, Donald. 1999. "The Discernibility of Identicals." *Journal of Philosophical Research* 24: 37–55.

Beall, J. C., and Gregory Restall. 2006. *Logical Pluralism*. Oxford: Oxford University Press.

Benacerraf, Paul. 1965. "What Numbers Could Not Be." *The Philosophical Review* 74 (1): 47–73.

Bengson, John. 2015. "The Intellectual Given." *Mind* 124 (495): 707–60.

Bennett, Karen. 2013. "Having a Part Twice Over." *Australasian Journal of Philosophy* 91 (1): 83–103.

Bennett, Karen. 2015. "'Perfectly Understood, Unproblematic, and Certain.'" In *A Companion to David Lewis*, edited by B. Loewer and J. Schaffer, 250–61. Chichester: Wiley Blackwell.

Berto, Francesco. 2013. *Existence as a Real Property*. Berlin: Springer.

Berto, Francesco, and Matteo Plebani. 2015. *Ontology and Metaontology*. London: Bloomsbury.

Betti, Arianna. 2015. *Against Facts*. Cambridge, MA: The MIT Press.

Betti, Arianna, and Jan Wieland. 2008. "Relata-Specific Relations: A Response to Vallicella." *Dialectica* 62 (4): 509–24.

Black, Max. 1971. "The Elusiveness of Sets." *The Review of Metaphysics* 24 (4): 614–36.

Bøhn, Einar. 2011. "Commentary on *Parts of Classes*." *Humana.Mente* 19: 151–8.

Bøhn, Einar. 2014. "Unrestricted Composition as Identity." In *Composition as Identity*, edited by A. Cotnoir and D. Baxter, 143–65. Oxford: Oxford University Press.

Boolos, George. 1984. "To Be Is to Be a Value of a Variable (or to Be Some Values of Some Variables)." *The Journal of Philosophy* 81 (8): 430–49.

Borghini, Andrea, and Giorgio Lando. 2016. "Humean Supervenience and Mereological Monism." *Synthese*, OnlineFirst, 1–21.

Bricker, Philip. 2015. "Composition as a Kind of Identity." *Inquiry* 59 (3): 264–94.

Burgess, John. 2015. "Lewis on Mereology and Set Theory." In *A Companion to David Lewis*, edited by B. Loewer and J. Schaffer, 459–70. Chichester: Wiley Blackwell.

Calosi, Claudio. 2016. "Composition, Identity, and Emergence." *Logic and Logical Philosophy* 25 (3): 429–43.

Calosi, Claudio, and Pierluigi Graziani (eds). 2014. *Mereology and the Sciences*. Berlin: Springer.

Cameron, Ross. 2012. "Composition as Identity Doesn't Settle the Special Composition Question." *Philosophy and Phenomenological Research* 84 (3): 531–54.

Cameron, Ross. 2014. "Parts Generate the Whole, but They Are Not Identical to It." In *Composition as Identity*, edited by A. Cotnoir and D. Baxter, 90–110. Oxford: Oxford University Press.

Carrara, Massimiliano, and Giorgio Lando. 2016. "Composition, Indiscernibility, Coreferentiality." *Erkenntnis* 81 (1): 119–42.

Carrara, Massimiliano, and Enrico Martino. 2009. "On the Ontological Commitment of Mereology." *The Review of Symbolic Logic* 2 (1): 164–74.

Casati, Roberto, and Achille Varzi. 1999. *Parts and Places*. Cambridge, MA: The MIT Press.

Correia, Fabrice, and Benjamin Schnieder. 2012. "Grounding: An Opinionated Introduction." In *Metaphysical Dependence: Grounding and Reduction*, edited by F. Correia and B. Schnieder, 1–36. Cambridge: Cambridge University Press.

Cotnoir, Aaron. 2010. "Antisymmetry and Non-Extensional Mereology." *The Philosophical Quarterly* 60 (239): 396–405.

Cotnoir, Aaron. 2013a. "Composition as General Identity." *Oxford Studies in Metaphysics: Volume 8*, edited by K. Bennett and D. Zimmermann, 295–322. Oxford: Oxford University Press.

Cotnoir, Aaron. 2013b. "Strange Parts: The Metaphysics of Non-Classical Mereology." *Philosophy Compass* 8/9: 834–45.

Cotnoir, Aaron. 2014. "Composition as Identity: Framing the Debate." In *Composition as Identity*, edited by A. Cotnoir and D. Baxter, 3–23. Oxford: Oxford University Press.

Cotnoir, Aaron. 2015. "Abelian Mereology." *Logic and Logical Philosophy* 24 (4): 429–47.

Cotnoir, Aaron, and Donald Baxter (eds). 2014. *Composition as Identity*. Oxford: Oxford University Press.

Della Rocca, Michael. 2005. "Two Spheres, Twenty Spheres, and the Identity of Indiscernibles." *Pacific Philosophical Quarterly* 86 (4): 480–92.

Dutilh Novaes, Catarina. 2011. "The Different Ways in Which Logic Is (Said to Be) Formal." *History and Philosophy of Logic* 32 (4): 303–32.

Eberle, Rolf. 1970. *Nominalistic Systems*. Dordrecht: Reidel.

Effingham, Nick, and Jon Robson. 2007. "A Mereological Challenge for Endurantism." *Australasian Journal of Philosophy* 85: 633–40.

Evans, Gareth. 1978. "Can There Be Vague Objects?" *Analysis* 38 (4): 208.

Field, Hartry. 1989. *Realism, Mathematics & Modality*. Oxford: Blackwell.

Fine, Kit. 1975. "Vagueness, Truth, and Logic." *Synthese* 30 (3/4): 265–300.

Fine, Kit. 1982. "First-Order Modal Theories III —Facts." *Synthese* 53 (1): 43–122.

Fine, Kit. 1994. "Compounds and Aggregates." *Noûs* 28 (2): 137–58.

Fine, Kit. 1999. "Things and Their Parts." *Midwest Studies in Philosophy* 23 (1): 61–74.

Fine, Kit. 2000. "A Counter-Example to Locke's Thesis." *The Monist* 83 (3): 357–61.

Fine, Kit. 2001. "The Question of Realism." *Philosophers' Imprint* 1 (1): 1–30.

Fine, Kit. 2005. "Our Knowledge of Mathematical Objects." In *Oxford Studies in Epistemology: Volume 1*, edited by T. Z. Gendler and J. Hawthorne, 89–110. Oxford: Oxford University Press.

Fine, Kit. 2006. "Relatively Unrestricted Quantification." In *Absolute Generality*, edited by A. Rayo and G. Uzquiano, 20–44. Oxford: Oxford University Press.

Fine, Kit. 2007. "Response to Kathrin Koslicki." *Dialectica* 61 (1): 161–6.

Fine, Kit. 2010. "Towards a Theory of Part." *The Journal of Philosophy* 107 (11): 559–89.

Fine, Kit. 2012. "Guide to Ground." In *Metaphysical Grounding*, edited by F. Correia and B. Schnieder, 37–80. Cambridge: Cambridge University Press.

Forrest, Peter. 2012. "The Identity of Indiscernibles." In *The Stanford Encyclopedia of Philosophy*, edited by E. Zalta, Winter 2012 (first edition 1996), http://plato.stanford.edu/archives/win2012/entries/identity-indiscernible/

Geach, Peter. 1967. "Identity." *The Review of Metaphysics* 21 (1): 3–12.

Gendler, Tamar Szabó. 2010. *Intuition, Imagination, and Philosophical Methodology*. Oxford: Oxford University Press.

Giaretta, Pierdaniele, and Giuseppe Spolaore. 2012. "A Mereology for the Change of Parts." In *Between Logic and Reality*, edited by N. Mičêvić, M. Trobok, and B. Zarnicć, 243–59. Dordrecht: Springer.

Gilmore, Cody. 2007. "Time Travel, Coinciding Objects, and Persistence." In *Oxford Studies in Metaphysics: Volume 3*, edited by D. Zimmermann, 177–98. Oxford: Oxford University Press.

Gilmore, Cody. 2009. "Why Parthood Might Be a Four-Place Relation, and How It Behaves if It Is." In *Unity and Time in Metaphysics*, edited by L. Honnefelder, E. Runggaldier and B. Schick, 83–133. Berlin: De Gruyter.

Gilmore, Cody. 2014. "Location and Mereology." In *The Stanford Encyclopedia of Philosophy*, edited by E. Zalta, Fall 2014 (first edition 2013), http://plato.stanford.edu/archives/fall2014/entries/location-mereology/

Goodman, Nelson. 1951. *The Structure of Appearance*. Cambridge, MA: Harvard University Press.

Goodman, Nelson. 1956. "A World of Individuals." In *The Problem of Universals: A Symposium*, edited by I. Bochensky, A. Church, and N. Goodman, 13–31. Notre Dame, IN: University of Notre Dame Press.

Goodman, Nelson. 1958. "On Relations That Generate." *Philosophical Studies* 9 (5): 65–66.

Goodman, Nelson. 1968. *Languages of Art: An Approach to a Theory of Symbols.* Indianapolis: Bobbs-Merrill.

Goodman, Nelson, and Henry Leonard. 1940. "The Calculus of Individuals and Its Uses." *The Journal of Symbolic Logic* 5 (2): 45–55.

Goodman, Nelson, and Willard Van Orman Quine. 1947. "Steps towards a Constructive Nominalism." *The Journal of Symbolic Logic* 12 (4): 105–22.

Graham, Andrew. 2015. "From Four to Five-Dimensionalism." *Ratio* XXVIII (1): 14–28.

Gruszczyński, Rafał, and Achille Varzi. 2015. "Mereology Then and Now." *Logic and Logical Philosophy* 24 (4): 409–27.

Harte, Verity. 2002. *Plato on Parts and Wholes.* Oxford: Oxford University Press.

Hawley, Katherine. 2015. "Temporal Parts." In *The Stanford Encyclopedia of Philosophy*, edited by E. N. Zalta, Winter 2015 (first edition 2004), http://plato.stanford.edu/archives/win2015/entries/temporal-parts/

Hawthorne, John, and Ernest Lepore. 2011. "On Words." *The Journal of Philosophy* 108 (9): 447–85.

Hossack, Keith. 2007. *The Metaphysics of Knowledge.* Oxford: Oxford University Press.

Hovda, Paul. 2009. "What Is Classical Mereology?" *Journal of Philosophical Logic* 38 (1): 55–82.

Hüttemann, Andreas. 2004. *What's Wrong with Microphysicalism?* London: Routledge.

Iacona, Andrea. 2002. *Propositions.* Genova: Name.

Johnston, Mark. 2006. "Hylomorphism." *The Journal of Philosophy* 103 (12): 652–98.

Kaplan, David. 1990. "Words." *Proceedings of the Aristotelian Society, Supplementary Volumes* 64: 93–119.

Kleinschmidt, Shieva (ed.). 2014. *Mereology & Location.* Oxford: Oxford University Press.

Korman, Daniel. 2010. "The Argument from Vagueness." *Philosophy Compass* 5 (10): 891–901.

Korman, Daniel. 2015. *Objects. Nothing Out of the Ordinary.* Oxford: Oxford University Press.

Koslicki, Kathrin. 2008. *The Structure of Objects.* Oxford: Oxford University Press.

Kriegel, Uriah. 2008. "The Dispensability of (Merely) Intentional Objects." *Philosophical Studies* 141 (1): 79–95.

Lando, Giorgio. 2007. "Tractarian Ontology: Mereology or Set Theory?" *Forum Philosophicum* 12 (2): 24–39.

Lando, Giorgio, and Giuseppe Spolaore. 2014. "Transcendental Disagreement." *The Monist* 97 (4): 597–620.

Laycock, Henry. 2006. *Words without Objects.* Oxford: Oxford University Press.

Lewis, David. 1968. "Counterpart Theory and Quantified Modal Logic." *The Journal of Philosophy* 65 (5): 113–26.

Lewis, David. 1982. "Logic for Equivocators." *Noûs* 16 (3): 431–41.

Lewis, David. 1983. *Philosophical Papers. Volume I.* New York: Oxford University Press.

Lewis, David. 1986a. "Against Structural Universals." *Australasian Journal of Philosophy* 64 (1): 25–46.

Lewis, David. 1986b. *On the Plurality of Worlds.* Oxford: Blackwell.

Lewis, David. 1986c. *Philosophical Papers. Volume II.* New York: Oxford University Press.

Lewis, David. 1991. *Parts of Classes.* Oxford: Blackwell.

Lewis, David. 1992. "Critical Notice of D. Armstrong, *A Combinatorial Theory of Possibility*." *Australasian Journal of Philosophy* 70 (2): 211–24.

Lewis, David. 1993. "Many, but Almost One." In *Ontology, Causality, and Mind: Essays on the Philosophy of D.M. Armstrong*, edited by J. Bacon and L. Reinhardt, 23–38. Cambridge: Cambridge University Press.

Lewis, David. 1994. "Humean Supervenience Debugged." *Mind* 103 (412): 473–90.

Lewis, David. 1998. "The Truthmakers." *Times Literary Supplement* 4948: 30.

Linnebo, Øystein. 2014. "Plural Quantification." In *The Stanford Encyclopedia of Philosophy*, edited by E. Zalta, Fall 2014 (first edition 2004), http://plato.stanford. edu/archives/fall2014/entries/plural-quant/

Loss, Roberto. 2016. "Parts Ground the Whole and Are Identical to It." *Australasian Journal of Philosophy* 94 (3): 489–98.

Lowe, Jonathan. 1998. *The Possibility of Metaphysics.* Oxford: Clarendon.

MacFarlane, John. 2000. "What Does It Mean to Say That Logic Is Formal?" PhD thesis, Pittsburgh: University of Pittsburgh.

MacFarlane, John. 2002. "Frege, Kant, and the Logic in Logicism." *The Philosophical Review* 111: 25–65.

Markosian, Ned. 1998. "Brutal Composition." *Philosophical Studies* 92 (3): 211–49.

Maudlin, Tim. 2007. *The Metaphysics within Physics.* New York: Oxford University Press.

McDaniel, Kris. 2008. "Against Composition as Identity." *Analysis* 68 (2): 128–33.

McDaniel, Kris. 2010. "Composition as Identity Does Not Entail Universalism." *Erkenntnis* 73 (1): 97–100.

McGinn, Colin. 2000. *Logical Properties.* Oxford: Oxford University Press.

McKay, Thomas. 2015. "Stuff and Coincidence." *Philosophical Studies* 172 (11): 3081–100.

McKay, Thomas. 2016. "Mass and Plural." In *Plurality and Unity. Logic, Philosophy, and Linguistics*, edited by A. Arapinis, M. Carrara, and F. Moltmann, 171–93. Oxford: Oxford University Press.

Merricks, Trenton. 2001. *Objects and Persons.* Oxford: Oxford University Press.

Moltmann, Friederike. 1997. *Parts and Wholes in Semantics.* New York: Oxford University Press.

Noonan, Harold. 2008. "Are There Vague Objects?" *Analysis* 64 (2): 131–4.

Oddie, Graham. 1982. "Armstrong on the Eleatic Principle and Abstract Entities." *Philosophical Studies* 41: 285–95.

Oliver, Alex. 1993. "Classes and Goodman's Nominalism." *Proceedings of the Aristotelian Society* 93: 179–91.

Oliver, Alex, and Timothy Smiley. 2013. *Plural Logic*. Oxford: Oxford University Press.

Paganini, Elisa. 2011. "Vague Objects without Ontically Indeterminate Identity." *Erkenntnis* 74 (3): 351–62.

Parsons, Terence. 1980. *Nonexistent Objects*. New Haven: Yale University Press.

Parsons, Terence. 2000. *Indeterminate Identity: Metaphysics and Semantics*. Oxford: Oxford University Press.

Paul, Laurie. 2002. "Logical Parts." *Noûs* 36 (4): 578–96.

Predelli, Stefano. 2013. *Meaning without Truth*. Oxford: Oxford University Press.

Priest, Graham. 2005. *Towards Non-Being*. New York: Oxford University Press.

Quine, Willard Van Orman. 1948. "On What There Is." *The Review of Metaphysics* 2 (5): 21–38.

Quine, Willard Van Orman. 1981. *Theories and Things*. Harvard: Harvard University Press.

Raven, Michael. 2015. "Ground." *Philosophy Compass* 10 (5): 322–33.

Rescher, Nicholas. 1955. "Axioms for the Part Relation." *Philosophical Studies* 6 (1): 8–11.

Rodríguez-Pereyra, Gonzalo. 2015. "Grounding Is Not a Strict Order." *Journal of the American Philosophical Association* 1 (3): 517–34.

Rosen, Gideon. 2010. "Metaphysical Dependence: Grounding and Reduction." In *Modality: Metaphysics, Logic, and Epistemology*, edited by B. Hale and A. Hoffmann, 109–36. Oxford: Oxford University Press.

Rosen, Gideon, and Cyan Dorr. 2002. "Composition as a Fiction." In *The Blackwell Guide to Metaphysics*, edited by R. Gale, 151–74. Oxford: Blackwell.

Ryle, Gilbert. 1954. *Dilemmas*. Cambridge: Cambridge University Press.

Sainsbury, Mark. 2015. "The Same Name.", *Erkenntnis* 80 (2): 195–214.

Sanford, David. 1993. "The Problem of the Many, Many Composition Questions." *Noûs* 27 (2): 19–28.

Sattig, Thomas. 2015. *The Double Lives of Objects*. Oxford: Oxford University Press.

Schaffer, Jonathan. 2009. "On What Grounds What." In *Metametaphysics*, edited by D. Chalmers, D. Manley and R. Wasserman, 347–83. Oxford: Oxford University Press.

Schnieder, Benjamin. 2006. "By Leibniz's Law: Remarks on a Fallacy." *The Philosophical Quarterly* 56 (222): 39–54.

Sellars, Wilfrid. 1963. "Abstract Entities." *The Review of Metaphysics* 16 (4): 627–71.

Shiver, Anthony. 2015. "How Do You Say 'Everything Is Ultimately Composed of Atoms'?" *Philosophical Studies* 172 (3): 607–614.

Sider, Theodore. 2001. *Four-Dimensionalism*. Oxford: Oxford University Press.

Sider, Theodore. 2007. "Parthood." *The Philosophical Review* 116 (1): 115–97.

Sider, Theodore. 2011. *Writing the Book of the World*. Oxford: Oxford University Press.

Sider, Theodore. 2013. "Against Parthood." In *Oxford Studies in Metaphysics: Volume 8*, edited by K. Bennett and D. Zimmermann, 237–93. Oxford: Oxford University Press.

Simons, Peter. 1982. "Plural Reference and Set Theory." In *Parts and Moments: Studies in Logic and Formal Ontology*, edited by B. Smith, 199–260. Munich: Philosophia.

Simons, Peter. 1987. *Parts*. Oxford: Oxford University Press.

Smith, Barry. 2003. "Ontology." In *Blackwell's Guide to the Philosophy of Computing and Information*, edited by L. Floridi, 155–66. Oxford: Blackwell.

Smith, David. 2009. "Mereology without Weak Supplementation." *Australasian Journal of Philosophy* 87: 505–11.

Smith, Nicholas J. J. 2013. "Time Travel." In *The Stanford Encyclopedia of Philosophy*, edited by E. Zalta, Spring 2016, http://plato.stanford.edu/archives/spr2016/entries/time-travel/

Spolaore, Giuseppe. 2012. "Not Just a Coincidence. Conditional Counter-Examples to Locke's Thesis." *Thought* 1 (2): 108–15.

Thomson, Judith. 1998. "The Statue and Its Clay." *Noûs* 32 (2): 149–73.

Tye, Michael. 1990. "Vague Objects." *Mind* 99 (396): 535–57.

Unger, Peter. 1979. "There Are No Ordinary Objects." *Synthese* 41 (2): 117–54.

Uzquiano, Gabriel. 2011. "Mereological Harmony." In *Oxford Studies in Metaphysics: Volume 6*, edited by K. Bennett and D. Zimmermann, 199–224. Oxford: Oxford University Press.

Vallicella, William. 2002. "Three Conceptions of States of Affairs." *Noûs* 34 (2): 237–59.

Van Inwagen, Peter. 1994. "Composition as Identity." *Philosophical Perspectives* 8: 207–20.

Van Inwagen, Peter. 1995. *Material Beings*. Ithaca, NY: Cornell University Press.

Van Inwagen, Peter. 1998. "Meta-Ontology." *Erkenntnis* 48 (2): 233–50.

Van Inwagen, Peter. 2006. "Can Mereological Sums Change Their Parts?" *The Journal of Philosophy* 103 (12): 614–30.

Van Inwagen, Peter. 2014. *Existence*. Cambridge: Cambridge University Press.

Varzi, Achille. 2000. "Mereological Commitments." *Dialectica* 54 (4): 283–305.

Varzi, Achille. 2001a. "Parts, Counterparts, and Modal Occurrents." *Travaux de Logique* 14 (1): 151–71.

Varzi, Achille. 2001b. "Vagueness in Geography." *Philosophy & Geography* 4 (1): 49–65.

Varzi, Achille. 2002. "Words and Objects." In *Individuals, Essence, and Identity: Themes of Analytic Metaphysics*, edited by A. Bottani, M. Carrara, and P. Giaretta, 49–75. Dordrecht: Kluwer.

Varzi, Achille. 2006. "A Note on the Transitivity of Parthood." *Applied Ontology* 1 (2): 141–6.

Varzi, Achille. 2008. "The Extensionality of Parthood and Composition." *The Philosophical Quarterly* 58 (230): 108–33.

Varzi, Achille. 2014. "Counting and Countenancing." In *Composition as Identity*, edited by A. Cotnoir and D. Baxter, 47–69. Oxford: Oxford University Press.

Varzi, Achille. 2016. "Mereology." In *The Stanford Encyclopedia of Philosophy*, edited by
    E. Zalta, Spring 2016 (first edition 2003), http://plato.stanford.edu/archives/spr2016/
    entries/mereology/

Wallace, Megan. 2011a. "Composition as Identity: Part 1." *Philosophy Compass* 6 (11):
    804–16.

Wallace, Megan. 2011b. "Composition as Identity: Part 2." *Philosophy Compass* 6 (11):
    817–27.

Williams, Donald. 1953. "On the Elements of Being: I." *The Review of Metaphysics* 7 (1):
    3–18.

Williams, Donald. 1959. "Mind as a Matter of Fact." *The Review of Metaphysics* 16 (4):
    203–25.

Williamson, Timothy. 1994. *Vagueness*. London: Routledge.

Williamson, Timothy. 2006. "Absolute Identity and Absolute Quantification." In
    *Absolute Generality*, edited by A. Rayo and G. Uzquiano, 369–89. Oxford: Oxford
    University Press.

Williamson, Timothy. 2007. *The Philosophy of Philosophy*. Oxford: Blackwell.

Williamson, Timothy. 2013. *Modal Logic as Metaphysics*. Oxford: Oxford University
    Press.

Wittgenstein, Ludwig. 1961. *Tractatus Logico-Philosophicus*. London: Routledge &
    Kegan Paul.

Yablo, Stephen. 1998. "Does Ontology Rest on a Mistake?" *Proceedings of the
    Aristotelian Society, Supplementary Volume* 72: 229–61.

Yi, Byeong-Uk. 2005. "The Logic and Meaning of Plurals. Part I." *Journal of
    Philosophical Logic* 34 (5–6): 459–506.

Yi, Byeong-Uk. 2006. "The Logic and Meaning of Plurals. Part II." *Journal of
    Philosophical Logic* 35 (3): 239–88.

Zimmermann, Dean. 1996. "Could Extended Objects Be Made Out of Simple Parts? An
    Argument for Atomless 'Gunk." *Philosophy and Phenomenological Research* 56 (1):
    1–29.

# Index